POWERS AND SUBMISSIONS

Challenges in Contemporary Theology

Series Editors: Gareth Jones and Lewis Ayres
Canterbury Christ Church University College, UK and Emory University, US

Challenges in Contemporary Theology is a series aimed at producing clear orientations in, and research on, areas of 'challenge' in contemporary theology. These carefully co-ordinated books engage traditional theological concerns with mainstreams in modern thought and culture that challenge those concerns. The 'challenges' implied are to be understood in two senses: those presented by society to contemporary theology, and those posed by theology to society.

Published

POWERS AND SUBMISSIONS

Spirituality, Philosophy and Gender

Sarah Coakley

Blackwell
Publishing

BLACKWELL PUBLISHING
350 Main Street, Malden, MA 02148-5020, USA
9600 Garsington Road, Oxford OX4 2DQ, UK
550 Swanston Street, Carlton, Victoria 3053, Australia

First published 2002 by Blackwell Publishing Ltd

2   2006

Library of Congress Cataloging-in-Publication Data

Coakley, Sarah, 1951–
    Powers and submissions : spirituality, philosophy, and gender / Sarah
Coakley.
        p.cm. — (Challenges in contemporary theology)
    Includes bibliographical references and index.
    ISBN 0-631-20735-X (alk. paper) — ISBN 0-631-20736-8 (pbk. : alk. paper)
    1. Feminist theology. I. Title. II. Series.
    BV5083.M37   1998

    BT83.55 C63 2002
    230'.082—dc21

                                                    2001043964

ISBN-13: 978-0-631-20735-1 (alk. paper) — ISBN-13: 978-0-631-20736-8 (pbk. : alk.
paper)

A catalogue record for this title is available from the British Library.

Set in 10.5 on 12.5 pt MBembo
by Kolam Information Services Pvt Ltd, Pondicherry, India
Printed and bound in the United Kingdom
by TJ International, Padstow, Cornwall

The publisher's policy is to use permanent paper from mills that operate a
sustainable forestry policy, and which has been manufactured from pulp
processed using acid-free and elementary chlorine-free practices. Furthermore,
the publisher ensures that the text paper and cover board used have met
acceptable environmental accreditation standards.

For further information on
Blackwell Publishing, visit our website:
www.blackwellpublishing.com

For Edith and Agnes Etheldreda,
the future feminists

Contents

ACKNOWLEDGEMENTS

With the exception of the 'Prologue', all the essays in this volume have appeared in other settings, and have been included here with light revisions. Where the copyright lies with the earlier publisher, I am grateful for permission to reproduce the material. The details of publication are as follows:

'*Kenōsis* and Subversion: On the Repression of "Vulnerability" in Christian Feminist Writing', in Daphne Hampson (ed.), *Swallowing A Fishbone? Feminist Theologians Debate Christianity* (London, SPCK, 1996), 82–111.

'Traditions of Spiritual Guidance: Dom John Chapman OSB (1865–1933) on the Meaning of "Contemplation"', as 'Traditions of Spiritual Guidance: Dom John Chapman OSB (1865–1933)', in *The Way* 30 (1990), 243–57.

'Creaturehood Before God: Male and Female', in *Theology* 93 (1990), 343–53.

'Visions of the Self in Late Medieval Christianity: Some Cross-Disciplinary Reflections', in Michael McGhee (ed.), *Philosophy, Religion, and the Spiritual Life: Royal Institute of Philosophy Supplement* (Cambridge, Cambridge University Press, 1992), 89–103. © 1992 Royal Institute of Philosophy.

'Gender and Knowledge in Modern Western Philosophy: The "Man of Reason" and the "Feminine" "Other" in Enlightenment and Romantic Thought', in E. Schüssler Fiorenza and A. Carr (eds.), *The Special Nature of Women: Concilium* 1991/6 (London, SCM Press, 1991), 75–83. © Concilium, Nijmegen, The Netherlands.

'Analytic Philosophy of Religion in Feminist Perspective: Some Questions', as 'Feminism', in Charles Taliaferro and Philip Quinn (eds.), *A Companion to Philosophy of Religion* (Oxford, Blackwell, 1997), 601–6.

' "Persons" in the "Social" Doctrine of the Trinity: Current Analytic Discussion and "Cappadocian" Theology', as ' "Persons" in the "Social" Doctrine of the Trinity: A Critique of Current Analytic Discussion', in Stephen T. Davis, Daniel Kendall, SJ and Gerald O'Collins, SJ (eds.), *The Trinity: An Interdisciplinary Symposium on the Doctrine of the Trinity* (Oxford, Oxford University Press, 1999, by permission of Oxford University Press), 123–44.

'The Resurrection and the "Spiritual Senses": On Wittgenstein, Epistemology and the Risen Christ', as 'The Resurrection: The Grammar of "Raised" ', in D. Z. Phillips et al. (eds.), *Biblical Concepts and Our World* (London, St Martin's Press, forthcoming).

'The Eschatological Body: Gender, Transformation and God', in *Modern Theology* 16 (2000), 61–73.

The publishers apologize for any errors or omissions in the above list and would be grateful to be notified of any corrections that should be incorporated in the next edition or reprint of this book.

PREFACE

The idea for this book first arose on my arrival at Harvard from Oxford: my new American students encountered difficulty finding my articles in somewhat obscure (and usually English) publications. Gradually the idea took shape for a volume of *Gesammelte Schriften*. I am grateful to Alison Mudditt, Alex Wright, and Joanna Pyke at Blackwell for seeing the book through to publication and for guiding me in my choice of texts.

One of the interesting things in reviewing one's own essays – often written under pressure and for particular events and deadlines – is that only retrospectively does one see the constellation of themes that has dominated one's thought for a number of years. In my case, this constellation was centred on the profound paradox of an inalienable surrender ('submission') to God that – as I argue – must remain the secret ground of even feminist 'empowerment'. Elsewhere I have termed this 'the paradox of power and vulnerability'. Such a paradox may be surprising to some, whereas to others it will be outrightly offensive: disappointingly conventional, a sign of feminist 'false consciousness', or an apolitical retreat into introspective piety. I devote the 'Prologue' to explaining why I believe it is none of these things, and indeed how an analysis of the act of 'contemplation' may cause us to rethink the standard binary of 'power' and 'submission' altogether.

It is customary to thank one's friends, teachers and interlocutors in the preface to a book such as this. My debts are numerous; in some cases I have recorded my thanks to critics and respondents at the end of particular essays. The influence of other colleagues and mentors is infused more subtly and generally throughout these pages: Maurice Wiles, Andrew Louth, Rowan Williams, Mary Douglas, Fergus Kerr, OP, Daphne Hampson, John Milbank, Caroline Bynum, Brian Daley, SJ, Elisabeth Schüssler Fiorenza, Francis Schüssler Fiorenza, David Hall, Nicholas Constas, Richard

Swinburne, Hilary Putnam and Nicholas Wolterstorff. Since the members of this particular 'cloud of witnesses' would be unlikely to agree on even one item of theological controversy, they must nonetheless believe me when I say that I have learned from them all, with enormous gratitude and respect.

Without the generous support of the Lilly Foundation, which funded a sabbatical year for 2000–1, I doubt whether this book would even now be ready for the publishers. To Dorothy Bass and Craig Dykstra at Lilly: *gratias ago vobis*. Two Harvard research assistants, Heather Curtis and Todd Billings, have given cheerful assistance with practical and bibliographical matters. Finally, John Privett, SJ afforded me the luxury of a hiding place in Faber House, Cambridge, MA, during the last stages of the editorial work: this was an invaluable asset, reminding me again of the significance of silence.

S. C.
Cambridge, MA
St David, 2001

PROLOGUE: POWERS AND SUBMISSIONS

In the 'liberal' and affluent West, 'power' is undeniably in vogue, not only with those who debate its meaning;[1] 'submission' most emphatically is not – unless perhaps as a titillating form of sexual bondage.[2]

This state of affairs may give even the secular cultural critic some pause for thought. The Enlightenment demand for an empowered human 'autonomy', despite all the intellectual criticism it has accrued in recent philosophical debate,[3] has in practice barely been softened by postmodernity's more nebulous quest for the state of 'agency',[4] and its implicit adulation of infinite consumer choice. In neither case – that of 'autonomy' or 'agency' – is any concomitant form of human 'submission' an obvious asset; if there is such surrender, it is seemingly at the *cost* of 'freedom' (so understood), a delimitation of options, a clamp on the desire for delicious risk-taking

[1] See, for instance, S. R. Clegg, *Power, Rule and Domination* (London, 1975), esp. Ch. 1 ('The Problem of Definition'); S. Lukes (ed.), *Power* (New York, 1986); M. Kelly (ed.), *Critique and Power: Recasting the Foucalt/Habermas Debate* (Cambridge, MA, 1994); and the lucid little encyclopedia article, 'Power' (M. Philp), in A. and J. Kuper (eds.), *The Social Science Encyclopaedia* (London, 1985), 635–9.

[2] See the illuminating discussion, from a feminist perspective, of Pauline Réage's sadomasochistic *Story of O*, in J. Benjamin, *The Bonds of Love* (New York, 1990), Ch. 2.

[3] See, for instance, for current feminist debate on this Enlightenment heritage: L. J. Nicholson (ed.), *Feminism/Postmodernism* (New York, 1990); S. Benhabib, *Situating the Self* (New York, 1992); S. Benhabib, J. Butler, D. Cornell and N. Fraser, *Feminist Contentions* (New York, 1995).

[4] For an influential discussion of the difference between modern 'autonomy' and postmodern 'agency', considered from an anthropological and post-colonial perspective, see T. Asad, *Genealogies of Religion* (Baltimore, MD, 1993), 1–24.

possibilities. As Mary Douglas has shown us, in the culture of individualism, 'risk' can replace a dedicated commitment to a larger societal whole.[5]

Yet this perceptible cultural resistance to 'submission' is quite at odds with the lessons of a sophisticated philosophical discussion – reaching back to Hegel's Master/Slave parable – of how the subjugated 'other' can nonetheless strangely have the edge on the Master's position of 'power' – if his 'power', that is, alienates him finally from himself.[6] The notable demise of socialism in the West has, it seems, tended to occlude – at least in the debates of public politics – the wisdom that this parable enshrined, however elusively and ambiguously.[7] Nonetheless it is this same conundrum – that of the problem of the recognition of the 'other', and of the profound personal and political dangers of failure in this task – that has so greatly exercised academic continental philosophy in recent decades, especially in the wake of the Holocaust.[8] The issue of 'alterity' has been at the heart of post-Kantian ethics in our new age of pluralism (and dangerous neo-Nazism) in Europe; and emergent post-colonial theory has, more recently, contributed its insights about the 'hybrid' self that has to negotiate a plethora of traditions and authorities.[9] To this (already complicated) debate secular feminist theory has added its distinctive voice, reminding 'malestream' philosophy of the specifically *gendered* nature of much political marginalization and subordination, and of the insidious entanglement of gender with race, class and other factors of discrimination in the hierarchy of oppressions.[10]

---

[5] For a recent analysis of this theme in Mary Douglas's work, see R. Fardon, *Mary Douglas: An Intellectual Biography* (London, 1999); and in Douglas's own voluminous work on the theme of 'risk', see, *inter alia*, with Aaron Wildavsky, *Risk and Culture* (Berkeley, CA, 1982); *Risk Acceptability According to the Social Sciences* (London, 1986); *Risk and Blame* (London, 1992).

[6] G. W. F. Hegel, *The Phenomenology of Mind* ([1]1807; New York, 1967), 'Lordship and Bondage', 229–40.

[7] For an astute and critical analysis of the demise of socialist thought in the *milieu* of postmodernity, see T. Eagleton, *The Illusions of Postmodernism* (Oxford, 1996).

[8] See most famously E. Lévinas, *Totality and Infinity* ([1]1961; Pittsburgh, PA, 1969), esp. 'Ethics and the Face', 194–219.

[9] See, for instance, H. K. Bhabha, *The Location of Culture* (New York, 1994); R. J. C. Young, *Colonial Desire: Hybridity in Theory, Culture and Race* (New York, 1995); P. Werbner and T. Modood (eds.), *Debating Cultural Hybridity* (London, 1997); and B. Moore-Gilbert, *Postcolonial Theory* (London, 1997).

[10] For a powerful argument about the *intrinsic* entanglement of race and class issues with gender inequalities, see E. V. Spelman, *Inessential Woman* (Boston, MA, 1988); for an analysis of the potentially fruitful interplay between critical theory, feminist theory and feminist theology in the highlighting of multiple oppressions, see M. A. Hewitt, *Critical Theory of Religion* (Minneapolis, MN, 1995).

Even as this philosophical debate on power and submission has complexified, however, consumerist individualism has, on the wings of the Web, spiralled out to entice the 'two-thirds world', still itself in painful economic and political subjugation to the West, and increasingly crippled by the Aids pandemic. Whilst academics have been announcing the advent of 'postmodernity', and professedly sounding the death knell of all hegemonic 'grand narratives', global capitalism has insidiously established its power as perhaps the most rapacious grand narrative in the history of the West.[11] Rarely have philosophical discussion and economic reality been in such painful dislocation. The original Enlightenment resistance to 'submission' has ultimately spawned, it seems, an economic system that ironically guarantees the continuation of multiple forms of oppression.

For the *theologian* in this climate, the continuing cultural fear of 'heteronomy' – of submission, dependency or vulnerability – represents not just an intellectual, but also a spiritual, crisis of some magnitude. For how, in the wake of the twentieth century's shocking technocratic genocides,[12] and in the conditions of this new century's frighteningly globalized economic power and ever-more devastating fragilities (political, medical, ecological), is *divine* power to be seen as alluring and sustaining human (dependent) responsibility? Here we confront an unexpected twist, a seeming acknowledgement of theological defeat in the face of secularism's despair. For whilst some Jewish theodocy, unsurprisingly, has embraced the notion of a *finite* divinity, one intrinsically unable to effect a supernatural intervention in the face of grave human wickedness,[13] post-War Christian thought has tended more often to take a different turn: the most influential conglomerate of 'neo-orthodox' and 'post-liberal' (male) theologians has effected a new *valorization* of Christic 'vulnerability', an admission of divine self-limitation and exposure in the face of human cruelty.[14] Rather than deflecting human

---

[11] On these themes, see the trenchant essays by N. Boyle, in *Who are We Now?* (Notre Dame, IN, 1998).

[12] See Z. Bauman, *Modernity and the Holocaust* (Ithaca, NY, 1989), for an analysis of the essentially modern, technocractic 'achievement' of the Holocaust.

[13] For a useful survey of Jewish theological responses to the Holocaust, including that of the rejection of the traditional belief in a providential God who acts in history, see D. Cohn-Sherbok, *Holocaust Theology* (London, 1989).

[14] This tendency is prominently found – with somewhat different outworkings – in the work of Karl Barth, Hans Urs von Balthasar and Jürgen Moltmann, amongst others. For Barth see *Church Dogmatics* IV/1 (Edinburgh, 1956), esp. §59; for von Balthasar, see *Mysterium Paschale* (Edinburgh, 1990); for Moltmann, *The Crucified God* (London, 1964). A 'post-liberal' account of the 'vulnerable' God, which owes much to Barth, is to be found in W. Placher, *Narratives of a Vulnerable God* (Louisville, KY, 1994), who does – briefly – raise the problem of a gendered notion of 'suffering' for this approach (see ibid., 115–20).

weakness, this trend has embraced it – even into the trinitarian heart of God. Submission has become paradoxically *identified* with divine 'power'.

Yet for the feminist theologian, we must note, this highly prized tactic has proved double-edged; indeed the question of power and submission has become yet further fraught in the light of this popular male theological strategy. For how can the call for the liberation of the powerless and oppressed, especially of women, possibly coexist with a revalorization of *any* form of 'submission' – divine or otherwise?[15] Precisely as male theology has wallowed in a new adulation of 'vulnerability' and 'receptivity' (perhaps aiming – consciously or unconsciously – to incorporate a repressed 'femininity' into its dogmatic system), feminist theology has emerged to make its rightful protest. Such a strategy, it has urged, merely reinstantiates, in legitimated doctrinal form, the sexual, physical and emotional abuse that feminism seeks to expose. An abused God merely legitimates abuse.[16]

It is with these tangled questions of power and submission, both human and divine, that this book is centrally concerned. At the heart of the book is an insistence that the apparently forced choice between dependent 'vulnerability' and liberative 'power' is a false one. But the terms of the debate – the different possible meanings of 'power' and 'submission' (whether human or divine), and their semantic cultural admixtures – are what are crucially at stake.

Things would be simpler if there were any agreement on what human 'power' was in the first place; but the academic disputes over its meanings in recent years rival in complexity – and arguably replicate in secular form – the debates that might in a pre-modern age have been held over the nature and purpose of divine 'acts'.[17] Is power a force, a commodity, a hereditary deposit, a form of exchange, an authority, a means of 'discipline', sheer domination, or a more nebulous 'circuit'? Must it necessarily involve intentionality, imply resistance, suppress freedom, or assume a 'hierarchy'? And where does it reside: in individuals, in institutions, in armies or police forces, in money, in political parties, or more generally and democratically

---

[15] This objection becomes particularly pointed from women who have suffered physical or sexual abuse, and whose capacity for *trusting* 'vulnerability' or 'receptivity' becomes severely damaged. See J. L. Herman, *Trauma and Recovery* (New York, 1992).

[16] I face this important feminist argument in my discussion of christological *kenōsis* in ch. 1, below.

[17] One of the clearest introductions to this complexity is to be found in the editor's introduction to Lukes (ed.), *Power* (see n. 1, above), 1–18. The account is strikingly devoid of any reference to God.

in every sort of subtle societal exchange?[18] There is no answer to these questions which is not also an implicit ideology, or at least a *recommendation*: this is nowhere more obvious than in the famous exchange between Foucault and Habermas on power, between the notion of inexorable local contestations of power/knowledge on the one hand (Foucault), and of an implicitly universalizable theory of 'communicative action' on the other (Habermas).[19] Thus, perhaps, as Steven Lukes has sagely put it, 'the very search for such a definition [of power] is a mistake. For the variations in what we are interested in when we are interested in power run deep . . . and what unites the various views of power is too thin and formal to provide a generally satisfying definition.'[20] In short, how we define 'power' will either be a charter of how *we* intend that it be used, or else a (more or less) despairing critique of what we see as its abuse.

Now it is strangely difficult to say how *divine* power could be reinstated in this complex and fascinating secular debate. Academic theologians are curiously coy about admitting their own institutional 'power', let alone inserting a rhetoric of God's power into an already-established secular discourse: the contrast with the explicit power language of the world of the New Testament, as Stephen Sykes has noted, is remarkable.[21] Whilst feminist theologians have made considerable use of the early Foucault (predominantly as a means of charting the 'genealogy' of repressive patri-archalism),[22] few theological commentators have ventured to describe the remarkable collapse of the secularization thesis as a sign of divine 'power' at work, or considered the notable success of Alchoholics Anonymous as an (actual) effect of a 'higher power', or – for that matter – wondered at the explosive recent growth of interest in 'spirituality' as anything else but another commodified 'leisure pursuit'.

---

[18] S. R. Clegg, *Frameworks of Power* (London, 1989), attempts a new account of power as 'circuit' or 'process' which does not necessarily throw these alternatives into a series of disjunctive choices.

[19] For a detailed account of this literary exchange (Foucault and Habermas never actually met), see Kelly (ed.), *Critique and Power* (n. 1, above).

[20] Lukes (ed.), *Power*, 4–5.

[21] S. W. Sykes, *The Identity of Christianity* (London, 1984), esp. 73–7.

[22] For a nuanced use of Foucault by a feminist theologian, see S. D. Welch, *A Feminist Ethic of Risk* (Minneapolis, MN, 1990). For assessments by secular feminists of the (somewhat mixed) blessing of a Foucaultian approach to power, see N. Hartsock, 'Foucault on Power: A Theory for Women?', in Nicholson (ed.), *Feminism/Postmodernism* (n. 3, above), 157–75; and L. McNay, *Foucault and Feminism* (Cambridge, 1992).

But what if this coyness proved, after all, to *be* a 'crime'?[23] What if divine power should not thus be short-changed, sidelined or embarrassedly left to the rhetoric of the new religious Right? It is to meet this challenge that the main arguments of this book are forged. In the essays in the first section of the book it is argued that a particular form of spiritual 'practice', known in the Christian West as 'contemplation', can – even in its humdrum 'acquired' form – be a graced means of human empowerment in the divine which the feminist movement ignores or derides at its peril. Certain previous tendencies in the feminist theological movement to belittle or downgrade the significance of ascetic practice are met and responded to: that such practice encourages societal 'submissiveness', disassociated introversion, apolitical anaesthesia, or the silencing of 'woman' are charges with which this book is familiar, and are already faced in chapter 1.[24] Chapters 2 and 3, however, acknowledge the deeply insidious ways in which such messages of trivialization and subordination can indeed be smuggled even into spiritual direction which is otherwise rife with wisdom; such a 'messy entanglement' is the stuff of adjudication for a new generation of feminist spiritual discernment.

But the alternative dangers of a busy pragmatism in matters of feminist reform are also underscored: to leap to the supposedly clear-cut goal of 'justice' without delicate training in *attending* to the 'other'; to impose programmes of reform without considering *self*-reform and *self*-knowledge; to up-end 'patriarchal' power without considering the possibility of the mimetic *feminist* abuse of power: such, we might say, are the looming dangers of feminist institutional 'success'. That most of the world has still not advanced even minimally towards the goals of 'Enlightenment' feminism[25] is no reason to suppress these questions and anxieties now; indeed the urgent matter of the integration of beliefs and 'practices' (now being advocated afresh in Western philosophy faculties by followers of the late Pierre Hadot[26]) is arguably more obvious to the emergent feminism of the

---

[23] My 'coy' allusion is of course to Andrew Marvell's 'To His Coy Mistress' (1681): 'Had we but world enough, and time,/This coyness, Lady, were no crime'.

[24] See pp. 32–9, below.

[25] On this see the important new book of M. C. Nussbaum, *Sex and Social Justice* (Oxford, 1999), a defence of 'justice' in an (adjusted, feminist) 'liberal' tradition.

[26] See P. Hadot, *Philosophy as a Way of Life: Spiritual Exercises from Socrates to Foucault* ([1]1987; Oxford, 1995), for the argument of the inseparability of belief and 'spiritual' practice in ancient philosophy.

'two-thirds' world than it is to the spiritually dessicated elite of the educated West.[27]

The message here is not, of course, one of submission to the 'world' – in the various senses of 'worldly' power that we have already entertained. On the contrary, it is about a very subtle, and one might say *sui generis*, response to the divine allure that allows one to meet the ambiguous forms of 'worldly' power in a new dimension, neither decrying them *in se* nor being enslaved to them, but rather facing, embracing, resisting or deflecting them with discernment. Whilst an earlier form of feminist theology tended undifferentiatedly to *identify* 'power' with ecclesiatical 'domination', this study makes no such simplistic assumptions. It does not of course deny that such domination has been a woeful part of Christian tradition, with heinous effects for women and other subordinates: many of the essays are concerned with unravelling and displaying such effects, ones often still hidden from the 'masculinist' gaze. But in the spirit of the late Foucault (though without his accompanying anarchic ethical presumptions) this work also takes the complex exchanges of societal power-relations to exclude very few of us from responsibility;[28] whilst institutions may indeed 'discipline' us (for good or ill), we also have the 'power' to discipline ourselves. It is as well to acknowledge how deeply unfashionable such a call may sound in a post-Freudian, post-Foucaultian generation (an issue with which chapter 9 later concerns itself).

Before that, in the second part of this volume we face the complicated question of the genesis of certain 'Enlightenment' visions of the self out of late medieval prototypes of 'spiritual practice' (this involves a somewhat novel argument),[29] and go on to indicate how attentiveness to such practice may cause us to make specifically feminist assessments of current philosophical trends more pointed. The 'Enlightenment', we argue (including one of its noted progeny: the discourse of 'analytic philosophy of religion'), is more double-edged in its implications for contemporary theological feminism than some would suggest.[30] The analysis in this section (see especially

---

[27] Post-colonial theorists tend to talk rather little of the deep religiosity of the cultures from which they spring, except where a *fracas* is caused over something like Salman Rushdie's *Satanic Verses*. For sage comments on the clash of cultures involved here between religious traditionalism and an (assumed) secularized 'liberalism', see Asad, *Genealogies* (n. 4, above), Chs 7 and 8.

[28] See M. Foucault, *Power/Knowledge* (Brighton, 1980), and the brief discussion of this in ch. 1, below.

[29] See ch. 4, below.

[30] This is the dominant theme of chs 5 and 6, below.

chapter 4) also indicates the falsity of the suggestion that 'contemplative practice' is narrowly introverted or apolitical: as 'Eastern' traditions of meditation have admittedly tended to make more explicit than has Christianity, the spiritual practitioner is a symbolic microcosm of the 'world' she inhabits (and transforms).[31]

And that brings us, finally, to the themes of politics and gender that infuse the more explicitly doctrinal essays of the last section of the book. Much has been written of late from a postmodern perspective about the 'subversive' nature of 'mystic' speech;[32] much less has been said – on account of current metaphysical scepticism – about the *encounter* with the divine that might sustain, if painfully and obscurely, such a subversion.[33] The treatment of 'trinitarian' speech about God in chapter 7 faces this question, and looks at how spiritual practice generates an apophaticism that (creatively) affects both doctrinal utterance and gender stability. Chapter 8 addresses the epistemological question that attends such noetic 'slippage': are these the conditions under which the 'risen Christ' can be recognized, and if so, how do we account for them in terms of bodily sensations and responses? Finally, the question of the 'eschatological' body is addressed head-on in the last essay (chapter 9), when we chart how current postmodern gender theory might have ironic foreshadowings in pre-modern intimations about the future, resurrected 'body'. Once again, the epistemological significance of a particular form of ascetic practice is given new coinage in conversation with contemporary theorizing about the politics of gender.

We started this 'Prologue' with some comments on the current cultural valency of the terms 'power' and 'submission', and noted the near-universal resistance to according the latter any positive value. By now we see that the already-mentioned move in post-War *Christian* theologies to incorporate 'vulnerability' into the trinitarian understanding of God evades the feminist

---

[31] See my edited volume, Sarah Coakley, *Religion and the Body* (Cambridge, 1997), for close examination of the theories of the societal – as well as individual – effects of 'meditation' practice in Buddhism, Daoism, Sikhism, Zoroastrianism and modern Japanese religion.

[32] See *inter alia*, M. Sells, *Mystical Languages of Unsaying* (Chicago, 1994); A. M. Hollywood, *The Soul as Virgin Wife: Mechthilde of Mageburg, Marguerite Porete, Meister Eckhart* (Notre Dame, IN, 1995).

[33] In a forthcoming book (given originally as Ferguson Lectures at the University of Manchester, 1997, under the title *Diotima and the Dispossessed*), I aim to provide a more extended philosophical 'justification' for theistic belief on the basis of an analysis of texts of 'negative theology' from the Carmelite tradition. Hints of the direction of the argument (in critical conversation with analytic philosophy of religion's treatment of 'religious experience') are given at the end of ch. 6, below.

issues we have here delineated if it merely adulates that 'vulnerability' and simultaneously returns the 'female' to a suitable biblical subordination (Barth),[34] or to a pedestalized place of suffering (von Balthasar).[35] That locus in Hegel of which we spoke earlier, however, in which our dependency on the 'other' for our very *selves* is acknowledged, need not be so parsed; if our fundamental and *practised* dependency is on God, there is the fulcrum from which our (often necessary) dependencies on others may be assessed with critical discernment, and the assumed binary gender-associations of such dependencies called into question. Such is the logic that we have explored in these pages.

Western 'liberal' theology has been accused of late of a 'false humility', and the accusation has justice.[36] The danger, however, is that any less wimpish theological alternative will itself insidiously fall prey to the Nietzschian will-to-power that it ostensibly criticizes: theology is triumphantly returned to the public sphere of discussion, but essentially as *polemics*. (At the same time, interestingly, feminist agendas may be curiously sidelined.[37]) How then can a bold new rhetoric of peace ensure its own peacefulness? It is the burden of this book to insist that no such utopia will be achieved merely by taking thought; the means of peace, and indeed of the final gender equity that must attend it, are patient *practices* of transparency to God, by whose light political strategies must ultimately also be illuminated.

Let us then reinvite the gentleness of divine 'power' into this quest for peace and equity.

---

[34] See the discussion of the subordinate position of 'woman' in K. Barth, *Church Dogmatics* III/2 (Edinburgh, 1960), esp. §45.

[35] See H. U. von Balthasar, *First Glance at Adrienne von Speyr* (San Francisco, 1981), for his indebtedness to von Speyr for her experiences of the suffering of 'Holy Saturday'.

[36] See J. Milbank, *Theology and Social Theory* (Oxford, 1990), 1: 'The pathos of modern theology is its false humility.'

[37] The problem of *gender* equity is barely addressed in Milbank's *Theology and Social Theory*; one might argue about the reasons, but the scathing treatment of 'liberation theology' (ibid., Ch. 8) gives pause for thought, and opens his position to a neo-conservative adulation that can easily repress feminist concerns. Milbank's brilliant and archetectonic rethinking of the place of theology in intellectual affairs is certainly *capable* of adjustment to face more explicitly the issues of gender and subordination I raise here; his 'Augustianian' theology of right 'desire' also begs the question of the 'practices' that alone can realign desire, and so enable a dispensation of non-violence (see ibid., Ch. 12).

Part I

THE CONTEMPLATIVE MATRIX

Chapter 1

Kenōsis and Subversion: On the Repression of 'Vulnerability' in Christian Feminist Writing

In an important passage in *Theology and Feminism*, Daphne Hampson tackles the question of christological *kenōsis*, or 'voluntary self-emptying on the part of the second person of the Trinity'.[1] Citing Rosemary Radford Ruether's view that Jesus' self-emptying offers a challenge to patriarchy,[2] she counters with the thought that 'it is far from clear that the theme of *kenōsis* is the way in which monotheism would need to be qualified in order to bring the understanding of God more into line with feminist values'. She goes on:

> That it [*kenōsis*] should have featured prominently in Christian thought is perhaps an indication of the fact that men have understood what the male problem, in thinking in terms of hierarchy and domination, has been. It may well be a model which men need to appropriate and which may helpfully be built into the male understanding of God. *But . . . for women, the theme of self-emptying and self-abnegation is far from helpful as a paradigm.*[3]

What are we to make of Hampson's rejection of *kenōsis* and Ruether's equally staunch – though brief – defence of it? The matter clearly cuts close to the heart of what separates Christian and post-Christian feminism; and hence my focus on it in this essay. For Hampson, female 'autonomy' is a supreme good which kenotic Christology can only undermine, not enhance. In contrast, for me, what rightly distinguishes Christian feminism from various secular versions of it must necessarily lie in this disputed

Originally published in Daphne Hampson (ed.), *Swallowing a Fishbone? Feminist Theologians Debate Christianity* (London, SPCK, 1996), pp. 82–111. Reprinted with permission from SPCK, with light revisions.

[1] D. Hampson, *Theology and Feminism* (Oxford, Basil Blackwell, 1990), p. 155.

[2] See R. R. Ruether, *Sexism and God-Talk* (London, SCM Press, 1983), pp. 137–8.

[3] Hampson, *Theology and Feminism*, p. 155 (my emphasis).

christological realm: here, if anywhere, Christian feminism has something corrective to offer secular feminism.

It will be the burden of this essay, then, to offer a defence of some version of *kenōsis* as not only compatible with feminism, but vital to a distinctively Christian manifestation of it, a manifestation which does not eschew, but embraces, the spiritual paradoxes of 'losing one's life in order to save it'. But in order to arrive at the point where I can justify such a 'loss' for Christian feminism (an ostensibly implausible move, one might think), I first have to unravel some semantic and historical confusions about the very meaning of *kenōsis*, a word that has had a bewildering number of different evocations in different contexts in the Christian tradition. Indeed it is a misunderstanding on this score which is partly responsible for the divergence between Hampson and Ruether, as we shall see.

The value of this unravelling task will not, I believe, be merely pedantic. For it is central to what I am attempting in this essay to demonstrate that the rhetoric of *kenōsis* has not simply constituted the all-too-familiar exhortation to women to submit to lives of self-destructive subordination; and nor (as Hampson believes) can it be discarded solely as a compensatory reaction to 'the male problem'. The evocations of the term have been much more complex and confusing even than that; just as the Christian tradition is in so many respects complex, confusing and (as I believe), continually creative. Thus by showing briefly in this piece how New Testament, patristic, post-Reformation Lutheran, early twentieth-century British, and contemporary analytic philosophy of religion discourses on *kenōsis* fail to mesh or concur at crucial points (and even use the term in straightforwardly contradictory ways), we shall be able to make some finer distinctions than those in the exchange between Hampson and Ruether about what form of *kenōsis* would be compatible with feminist interests, and what not. We shall also be able to distinguish, without disconnecting, the specifically christological meaning of *kenōsis* from the more broadly spiritual meaning. Moreover, since debates about christological *kenōsis* distil for us the more fundamental philosophical problem of how, normatively, to construe the relationship between the divine and the human *tout court*, it will be instructive to note how gender preconceptions, or gender anxieties, tend to lurk in this discussion. (To this extent Hampson's passing remarks about gender and *kenōsis* are certainly suggestive, and have yet to be applied to the philosophical dimensions of the issue.)

Finally, I shall enquire why themes of 'fragility', 'vulnerability' or 'self-emptying' have been relatively muted in white Christian feminist writing up till now, when secular feminism, and non-white or Black womanist theology have in a variety of ways tackled these themes more directly. I shall end with a suggestion for 'right' *kenōsis* founded on an analysis of the activity of Christian silent prayer (or 'contemplation'[4]), an activity characterized by a rather special form of 'vulnerability' or 'self-effacement'. My aim here is to show how wordless prayer can enable one, paradoxically, to hold vulnerability and personal empowerment *together*, precisely by creating the 'space' in which non-coercive divine power manifests itself, and I take this to be crucial for my understanding of a specifically Christian form of feminism. Or to put it more boldly and autobiographically: if I could not make spiritual and theological sense of this *special* form of power-in-vulnerability (*kenōsis* in one sense to be defined), I would see little point in continuing the tortured battle to bring feminism and Christianity together. In this sense, I am not sure that I want to pick the bones out of the Christic 'fish' before I begin; for it could be that in so doing I had removed the backbone that structures the central mystery of Christian salvation. Our first task, then, will be to turn back to the New Testament in search of Paul's meaning of *kenōsis*. It will be illuminating to discover how little this has to do with Hampson's critique.

I

The word *kenōsis* does not appear as a noun in the New Testament at all, and the entire debate about 'self-emptying' goes back to an isolated appearance of the verb *kenoō* (I empty) in Philippians 2.7. To choose to cite one English translation over others here is already to beg significant questions of interpretation; but the Revised Standard Version of Philippians 2.5–11 runs:

> [5]Have this mind among yourselves, which you have in Christ Jesus, [6]who, though he was in the form of God, did not count equality with God a thing to be grasped, [7]but emptied himself [*heauton ekenōsen*], taking the form of a servant, being born in the likeness of men [*anthrōpōn*, i.e., of humans]. [8]And being found in human form he humbled himself and became obedient unto death, even death on a cross. [9]Therefore God has highly exalted him and bestowed on him the name which is above every other name, [10]that at the name of Jesus every knee shall bow, in heaven and on earth and under the

---

[4] It is important to underscore at the outset that I do not use this word in an elitist sense, but rather to denote any (relatively) wordless form of prayer in which discursive thought is reduced to the minimum. For more on this, and its centrality to the essay, see section VI below.

earth, [11]and every tongue confess that Jesus Christ is Lord, to the glory of God the Father.

Without in any sense committing the 'genetic fallacy' of presuming that the 'original' meaning of this passage is now binding on us, it is nonetheless intriguing to enquire what the 'emptying' here did connote at the outset. The matter is, however, one of the most convoluted (and disputed) in New Testament exegesis. Since Ernst Lohmeyer's influential analysis of the strophic structure of the passage in the late 1920s,[5] commentators have been virtually agreed that the passage was originally used liturgically as a hymn (possibly in either a baptismal or eucharistic setting); and the probability that the passage therefore represents pre-Pauline material taken over by Paul for his own purposes in this letter complexifies the issue of interpretation at the outset. (For we thus already have a double layer of meaning within the text as we have received it.) Waves of fashion in this century's New Testament scholarship have dictated widely divergent readings of Paul's (and his shadowy forebear's) intent. At one extreme there have been the (mainly German) exponents of the 'gnostic redeemer' theory,[6] who argue, under the influence of 'history of religions' analysis, that Paul has taken over, and modified, a soteriological framework from (what are taken to be) pre-Christian gnostic circles, in which the archetypal *Urmensch*, or 'original Man', descends to earth and simulates human existence in order to impart secret saving *gnosis* to his select followers. According to this view, *some* form of divine (or quasi-divine) 'pre-existence' is assumed for the Christ redeemer, and the 'emptying' connotes his appearance on earth. The emphasis, however, is not on the precise metaphysical speculation of later patristic Christology, on Christ's full and substantial divinity (or otherwise), as in the debates surrounding the Council of Nicaea (325); rather, it is

[5]   See E. Lohmeyer, *Kyrios Jesus: Eine Untersuchung zu Phil.* 2, 5–11 (Heidelberg, C. Winter, 1961 (1928)). Lohmeyer was, however, not the first to detect a strophic construction to the passage, and the debate continues on how to divide the *strophēs*: see (for example) J. Jeremias, 'Zu Phil. ii. 7: *heauton ekenōsen*', *Novum Testamentum* 6 (1963), pp. 184–8, for a discussion and analysis of this problem, with criticism of earlier solutions.
[6]   See R. P. Martin, *Carmen Christi: Philippians ii. 5–11 in Recent Interpretation and in the Setting of Early Christian Worship* (Cambridge, Cambridge University Press, 1967), pp. 74–84, 89–93, for a brief account of this theory as maintained by various members of the Bultmannian school. (Martin's book remains the best general introduction to the exegetical problems of Philippians 2.) M. Hengel, *The Son of God* (London, SCM Press, 1976), esp. pp. 1–2, represents the most impenitent recent reassertion of the view that Philippians 2 is speaking of Christ's pre-existent *divinity*. As such, Hengel's exegesis falls outside the two major contemporary 'types' of interpretation I am here sketching.

on the mythological rhythm of salvific intervention and release. As Käsemann put it, 'Philippians 2 tells us what Christ *did*, not what he *was*.'[7]

At the other end of the spectrum lies a more straightforwardly ethical
interpretation of the passage,[8] with no clear implications at all of Christ's
pre-existence. Such an interpretation may at first sight seem surprising, even
suspiciously artful, accustomed as we are to reading this passage through the
lens of later credal orthodoxy: is not the 'emptying' of v. 7 most obviously
seen as a reference to the incarnation? But there are a number of reasons
why this alternative reading might seem more consistent with earliest
Christianity in general, and Pauline theology in particular. First, the notion
of substantial pre-existence does not otherwise feature in (proto-) Pauline
settings. Second, the crucial preceding participle clause ('though he was
in the form of God'), which triggers our train of thought towards pre-
existence and incarnation, may in context more appropriately be read as a
piece of Adam typology (already a characteristic of Paul's Christology in
Romans 5 and 1 Corinthians 15). On this view the 'form of God' is a
reference to the creation of the *human* race; Genesis 1.26–7, after all, speaks
of God creating 'man' 'in his own image'. So now Christ, as second Adam
(also in 'the form of God'), revokes the penalty of Eden by undoing Adam's
primal disobedience. Thus, third, the 'thing to be grasped', as the RSV has it
(the *harpagmon*, v. 6), becomes quite possibly an allusion to Adam's first sin
in making himself 'like God' (Genesis 3.5, 22), again here recapitulated and
reversed in Christ's life and example.[9] We are not on this view, then, talking
about a set of (pre-existent) divine attributes which could have been held
onto by Christ, but instead were relinquished. Rather, the 'grasping' is a
form of moral turpitude and arrogance that Jesus avoids right from the start
of his ministry. And so, fourth, then, the 'emptying' on this interpretation

---

[7]   E. Käsemann, *Exegetische Versuche and Besinnungen: erste Band* (Göttingen, Vandenhoeck
und Ruprecht, 1960), p. 70 (cited in Martin, *Carmen Christi*, p. 83).

[8]   See (for example) Jeremias, 'Zu Phil. ii.7' (by implication); and more fully in J. A. T.
Robinson, *The Human Face of God* (London, SCM Press, 1973), pp. 162–6, and J. D. G.
Dunn, *Christology in the Making* (London, SCM Press, 1980), pp. 114–21. Martin, *Carmen
Christi*, pp. 68–74, provides a brief discussion of earlier twentieth-century exponents of this
'ethical example' interpretation.

[9]   See Dunn, *Christology*, ch. 4, *passim*, for this line of argument on Adam typology. (The
matter is, however, not uncontentious: it is not *clear* from the original Hebrew text of Genesis
2 that being 'equal with God' is deemed to be either a 'snatching' or a 'sin'. I am grateful to
Robert Murray, SJ for a number of illuminating discussions on this point.) N. T. Wright, *The
Climax of the Covenant: Christ and the Law in Pauline Theology* (Minneapolis, Fortress Press,
1992), *passim* (see esp. the chart on p. 81 as résumé), contains an exhaustive survey of the
possible meanings of *harpagmos* in this context.

now denotes not incarnation, but rather the 'servant-like' example set by
Jesus' demeanour throughout his life (with possible overtones of the Isaianic
'suffering servant'), an 'empty-ing' which finds its ultimate end in the events
of the cross (v. 8). Thus, on this 'ethical' reading, the 'emptying' of v. 7 is
parallel to the 'humbling' of v. 8;[10] both take place within Jesus' earthly
existence, rather than the 'emptying' being a precondition of the earthly life
(as on the 'pre-existence' reading).

To sketch out these two dominant schools of interpretation of Philippians 2
in broad outline is to give only a crude account of the complexity of the New
Testament hermeneutical debates on this passage over recent decades. The
two basic views sketched both have remaining problems, and some scholars
have argued that it is a false move to force a disjunctive choice between
them.[11] Debates continue about the contextual background of the passage:
are the allusions mainly to the Hebrew Scriptures, or to gnostic and pagan
themes? But one striking point of unanimity in the modern New Testament
discussion (amidst all this dissent) has been the virtual ruling out of a 'dogmatic'
or 'metaphysical' reading of Paul's interests in this passage. It is not, in other
words, a prefiguration of second-century Logos speculation (in the mode of
Justin Martyr, for instance), let alone a preview of fourth-century Nicaean
orthodoxy (which takes the Son to share all divine characteristics with the
Father in advance of the incarnation). Rather, *if* 'pre-existence' (of a sort) is
implied here, it is of a 'mythological' or soteriologically oriented kind, as in
gnostic redeemer narratives; and it is this *narrative* structure which the Philippians are being asked to enter into, to make their own 'mind' (v. 5).

This ostensibly 'anti-dogmatic' tenor of the New Testament discussion of
kenōsis contrasts forcibly with discussions of Philippians 2 in other circles, as
we shall see, especially the contemporary analytic philosophy of religion
writing on the matter (which appears strangely ignorant of the New Testament debates). And yet, despite the conscious preference of many twentieth-century New Testament scholars for existential rather than metaphysical
categories, we may, I suggest, nonetheless detect ways in which concern
about 'incarnation' and the 'two natures' problem has (more or less covertly)
fuelled their concerns and fashions, whether in criticism or redirection of
traditional patristic options. To expose this rather buried dimension of the

---

[10]   So Jeremias, 'Zu Phil. ii.7', p. 187; Dunn, *Christology*, p. 118.

[11]   This is the conclusion of Wright's complex argument (*The Climax of the Covenant*, p. 97),
which picks up some dimensions of an influential earlier article by C. F. D. Moule ('Further
Reflexions on Philippians 2:5–11' in W. W. Gasque and R. P. Martin (eds.), *Apostolic History
and the Gospel* (Grand Rapids, Eerdmans, 1970), pp. 264–76; see esp. pp. 264–5). I treat of
Moule's position in some more detail below.

New Testament hermeneutical question will also prove illuminating in relation to our central, feminist concern (though, tellingly, I can find no explicit feminist analysis in the voluminous New Testament secondary literature concerning Philippians 2 itself).

Of the two broad tendencies in New Testament interpretation of Philippians 2 I have described, the first, influenced as it was by 'history of religions' methodology, and thus anxious to locate earliest Christology within a broad stratum of Middle Eastern mythology and ritual practice, explicitly thrust aside what it saw as the metaphysical clamps of later doctrinal 'orthodoxy' in search of a more direct, 'existential' response of faith. This, after all, was the hallmark of Bultmann's Heideggerian theology. As a result, and as we have just seen, even though 'pre-existence' of a 'mythical' form was presumed in the interpretation of Philippians 2, the 'emptying' here was not seen to imply the *divesting* of some clearly defined set of divine characteristics, otherwise uniquely shared with the 'Father'. Rather, if anything, the docetism of the gnostic redeemer mythology still hung over its Pauline reworking: the Christ figure appeared only 'in the *form* of man', feigning human weakness for the purposes of salvific activity. This being the case, we can now see that Daphne Hampson's charge against *kenōsis* with which we opened (as a masculinist ploy, beset by conscience), does not clearly score at all against this form of New Testament interpretation of Philippians 2. That is, precisely because the later 'two natures' gloss on pre-existence has, for theological or ideological reasons, been rejected by this school of thinking from the outset, so too it never considers the kind of compensatory 'emptying' that Hampson is attacking.[12] If anything, the quasi-gnostic redeemer of the pre-Pauline hymn merely pretends to abandon his divine powers, rather than actually doing so.

So Hampson's critique does not really touch this form of New Testament analysis; but even less, significantly, does it bite against the alternative, 'ethical' reading favoured by a different school of New Testament scholarship. For here, if I am right, an even more far-reaching questioning of later Nicene or Chalcedonian 'orthodoxy' may be driving the theological direction taken. If, that is, substantial pre-existence of *no* sort is found in the Pauline text, then there is no clear charter here for later Nicene 'orthodoxy', and no full range of divine characteristics to be abandoned or otherwise.[13] So once again Hampson's criticisms are deflected.

If, on the other hand, another variant of the 'ethical' interpretation is preferred, as suggested by C. F. D. Moule, then more far-reaching metaphys-

---

[12] The one major exception to this rule would be Hengel, *Son of God*. See n. 6 above.

[13] See again Dunn, *Christology*, pp. 114–21, for the clearest enunciation of these points.

ical implications are involved, though not the ones normally associated with Chalcedonian 'orthodoxy'. On this 'ethical' view Jesus' 'emptying' is seen not just as the blueprint for a perfect human moral response, but as revelatory of the 'humility' of the *divine* nature. As Moule puts it: '. . . Jesus displayed the self-giving humility which is the *essence of divinity*'.[14] Moule's interpretation, we note, involves a strange combination of factors. Unlike other interpreters of our 'ethical' type, he appears to take Christ's pre-existence, and certainly his full divinity, as given in the passage; but *like* other 'ethical' readings he finds the 'emptying' not to refer to an effect on either of these, nor to his incarnation, but rather to his humanly 'humble' and 'non-grasping' nature – which, however, he then casts as the distinctively *divine* characteristic. Thus Moule combines a remaining 'orthodox' commitment to pre-existence and incarnation with a significant relocation of the attribute of 'humility'. This (new) metaphysical gloss was one taken up more systematically by Moule's Cambridge colleague, J. A. T. Robinson, and we shall return to consider its coherence a little later. The point to be made for our immediate purposes here is how *complex* is the entanglement of hermeneutical and dogmatic questions where this passage is concerned, even when questions of christological speculation in the patristic mode have ostensibly been abandoned (and that, too, before we get to the subtler issues of gender subtext). What is at stake is nothing less than our fundamental presumptions about divine and human nature, and the possibility, or otherwise, of their complete concurrence. In Moule's artful reworking of the 'ethical' interpretation, we note, Hampson's critique of *kenōsis* is again averted, but this time in yet another (and third) way: Jesus' 'emptying' involves no compensatory loss of 'masculinist' divine powers, because his example shows us that divinity is 'humble' *rather than* 'powerful' (whatever this means). His way to the cross is the revelation of an unchanging, but consistently 'humble', divinity. Thus, Moule's interpretation is somewhat closer to what Ruether seems to mean by *kenōsis* when she asserts that Jesus' message and example represent 'patriarchy's' *kenōsis*: that is (or so I read her), Jesus promoted values quite different from those of *machismo* or worldly power. In his ethical example patriarchy was emptied out (not, we note, Christ himself emptied out).

We come away from the New Testament debate, then, with a host of questions, only partially resolved. All commentators (or nearly all) concur that it is an anachronism to see Paul or his source expressing anything like the 'two nature' Christology of later 'orthodoxy'; yet disagreements about

---

[14]   Moule, 'Further Reflexions', p. 265 (my emphasis).

the original context, religious genre, and aims of the Christic hymn of Philippians 2 still lead to different (implicit) dogmatic conclusions about the normative relation of divine 'powers' to the human here expressed. Let us consider the range of possibilities we have already generated. Is the christological blueprint of Philippians 2 a matter of: (1) temporarily *relinquishing* divine powers which are Christ's by right (as cosmic redeemer); or (2) *pretending* to relinquish divine powers whilst actually retaining them (as gnostic redeemer); or (3) choosing *never to have* certain (false and worldly) forms of power − forms sometimes wrongly construed as 'divine'; or (4) *revealing* 'divine power' to be intrinsically 'humble' rather than 'grasping'? Of these four alternatives already in play, Hampson would presumably only regard (1) − or possibly also (2) − as falling under her critique of masculinist *kenōsis*; and I have argued that even they, if framed in the terms of the 'history of religions' approach, are less obviously subject to her criticism than if they had been formulated on the presumptions of later patristic categories. For my own part, for the reasons sketched above, I am mo convinced by the third interpretation than the others (at least as far the New Testament debate is concerned), and I shall return to this option again when I regather my systematic conclusions at the end of the essay. Hampson, however, might justifiably here object that she had none of this New Testament complexity in mind when she made her charge. Rather, her target is the much later form of speculative 'kenoticism' devised by early twentieth-century British theologians of privileged backgrounds, exercising their (perhaps guilty) social consciences. In this she is right; but in order to see how we get from the New Testament to these exponents, some interim historical material is worthy of review. Again, as we shall see, ironic results arise from trying to bring different notions of *kenōsis* into consistent focus, especially where a feminist analysis is concerned. But at least we are beginning to see why Hampson and Ruether do not agree: it is because, in all this historical and semantic complexity over *kenōsis*, their views do not even properly *connect*. Ruether is promoting a view of *kenōsis* that Hampson does not seriously consider.

II

The patristic exegesis of Philippians 2, and of the term *kenōsis* in particular, makes very different hermeneutical and philosophical presumptions from those of the modern New Testament discussions we have just surveyed. Yet, strangely − as shown in a now-classic coverage of the patristic material by Friedrich Loofs[15] – the range of options presented (from 'ethical' to 'incarnational', with various stopping-points or combinations in between), is uncannily similar to the modern-day alternatives endlessly rejigged by New Testament scholars with (often) very little knowledge of 'pre-critical' exegesis. I do not, however, here want to focus on the 'ethical' (or what Loofs terms the 'Pelagian') variant, which in any case did not ultimately emerge as regnant in the patristic period. Rather, what I wish to underscore is the *irony* of the reversal of presumptions about *kenōsis* between the time of Paul and the triumph of Chalcedonian 'orthodoxy' in the fifth century – an orthodoxy highly influenced by the demanding paradoxes of the Christology of Cyril of Alexandria (d. 444).

Whereas Paul's views on *kenōsis*, as we have seen, were largely non-'speculative', non-'dogmatic', and arguably not even asserting substantial pre-existence at all, the formative christological discussions of the fourth and fifth centuries (in the wake of the hard-won battles over the Council of Nicaea) take Christ's substantial pre-existence and essential divinity *for granted*. The problem then resides in explicating what 'emptying' can *mean* in Philippians 2, assuming now that it is somehow coextensive with the event of incarnation, but granted that characteristics such as omniscience and omnipotence are taken (unquestioningly) to be unchanging aspects of the divine nature.[16] Thus Hilary of Poitiers, in the fourth century, could talk rather daringly – and indeed confusingly – of an 'evacuation of the form of God', whilst yet denying that Christ's divinity had been dislodged in any sense; while Cyril of Alexandria, in the fifth century, went on to make Philippians 2 the narrative focus of his entire Logos Christology, clarifying that the pre-existent divine Logos was – albeit paradoxically – also the personal or 'hypostatic' subject of Christ's human states, but without any impairment or restriction of the divine attributes.[17] For Cyril, then, the word *kenōsis* signified no loss or abnegation, but simply

---

[15]   As presented in English in F. Loofs, 'Kenōsis', *Encyclopaedia of Religion and Ethics*, ed. J. Hastings, vol. VII (Edinburgh, T. & T. Clark, 1914), pp. 680–7.

[16]   A glance at the entry '*Kenōsis*' in G. W. H. Lampe, *A Patristic Greek Lexicon* (Oxford, Clarendon Press, 1961), with its various sub-categories, is revealing here, showing a prevalence of patristic discussions of Philippians 2 concerned to defend the unchanging nature of the divine essence in spite of the biblical language of 'emptying'.

[17]   There is a brief, but clarifying, discussion of Hilary of Poitiers' position in W. Pannenberg, *Jesus – God and Man* (London, SCM Press, 1968), pp. 307–8. Cyril's distinctive approach to *kenōsis* is well charted in F. Young, *From Nicaea to Chalcedon* (London, SCM Press, 1983), pp. 260–3, drawing on an important earlier article by R. A. Norris, 'Christological Models in Cyril of Alexandria', *Studia Patristica* 13 (1975), pp. 255–68.

the so-called 'abasements' involved in the taking of flesh. He was finally at a loss how to *explain* how this assumption of flesh could occur without detriment or change to the divine Logos; it led him, for instance, to glory in such famously paradoxical expressions about Christ's passion as 'He suffered unsufferingly'.[18] But he achieved his theological goals by seeing the *kenōsis* of incarnation not as loss, but rather as an addition of human flesh and blood to the abiding and unchanging characteristics of divinity. As he writes: 'The Only begotten Word ... came down for the sake of our salva- tion and abased Himself into emptying [*kenōsis*] and was incarnate ... not indeed casting off what He was, but even though He became Man by the assumption of flesh and blood He still remained God in nature [*physis*] and in truth.'[19]

Now, if we again adjust the hermeneutical lens in a feminist direction, we immediately see the further ironies – for a feminist critique such as Hamp- son's – of the shift out of the New Testament discussion into the patristic one. For in Cyril's theology of *kenōsis* there is no question of any aspects of unchanging divinity being abandoned, restricted, or never taken up in the incarnation; whatever else one may accuse Cyril of, it cannot be that his vision of *kenōsis* signifies a compensatory exercise of masculinist guilt. Far as his metaphysical presumptions may be from Paul's in Philippians 2, then, his deflection of Hampson's charge is as complete: no *actual* 'self-emptying' can occur in Christ, since none of his pre-existent divine attributes could, by definition, be surrendered or modified. Whilst some feminists might wish to question the very construction of divine 'omnipotence' which Cyril is assuming (a point to which I shall return),[20] his theory of *kenōsis* scarcely suffers from squirmings of 'self-abnegation'. Cyril's Christ abandons no 'power' whatever. Thus, to our four-point list of possible interpretations

---

[18]   Again see the discussion and references in Young, *Nicaea to Chalcedon*, p. 261.

[19]   From Cyril's third letter to Nestorius, translated in T. H. Bindley and F. W. Green (eds.), *The Oecumenical Documents of the Faith* (London, Methuen, 1950), pp. 213–14. (This is also cited and helpfully discussed by S. W. Sykes in his article, 'The Strange Persistence of Kenotic Christology' in A. Kee and E. T. Long (eds.), *Being and Truth: Essays in Honour of John Macquarrie* (London, SCM Press, 1986), pp. 350–1.)

[20]   Thus Frankenberry's feminist analysis of different forms of theism rejects 'classical theism's' definition of God as hopelessly incoherent from the outset, even in advance of feminist critique (see N. Frankenberry, 'Classical Theism, Panentheism, and Pantheism: On the Relation Between God Construction and Gender Construction', *Zygon* 28 (1993), pp. 30–3). My own (feminist) view, whilst criticizing particular 'masculinist' thematizations of God's nature, is, for philosophical and theological reasons adumbrated in this chapter, more accepting of the 'classical' divine attributes such as omnipotence, omniscience, immutability and timelessness (see below, section V).

of *kenōsis* gleaned from the New Testament discussion above, we must now add a fifth, and classically 'Alexandrian', one of very different presumptions. The meaning is indeed in straightforward contradiction with some of our earlier definitions, for here *kenōsis* connotes: (5) the divine Logos's *taking on* of human flesh in the incarnation, but without loss, impairment, or restriction of divine powers.

The christological paradoxes heightened thus by Cyril, and to some ill-defined extent taken over into Chalcedonian 'orthodoxy' a little later,[21] arguably achieved a form of theological coherence at the cost of some strained credibility about the form of Christ's earthly life, and certainly left many points of christological detail unanswered. We shall attempt to show in the remainder of this essay how these points have direct or indirect feminist implications. In particular, the idea of Cyril and others that, in virtue of the union of natures in Christ's *hypostasis* ('person'), one could appropriately 'predicate' attributes of one nature to the other (the so-called *communicatio idomatum*),[22] left question marks about how, precisely and metaphysically, the all-too-human states of anxiety, weakness and ignorance occasionally displayed by Jesus in the gospel narratives could be explained. What effect, if any, should these have on one's perception of the nature of divinity? Could the classical notions of divine omniscience or omnipotence really remain unimpaired? (We note how the particular problems of *kenōsis* here become problems about the nature of incarnation *in general*.) This last, and radical, question was one not adequately faced at all in the patristic, or

---

[21]   The extent to which Cyril's 'Alexandrian' Christology is endorsed in the Chalcedonian Definition of 451 remains a matter for dispute. The Definition represented a compromise between the rival christological schools of Alexandria and Antioch; but it is also a subtle exegetical matter whether we should read it as straightforwardly *identifying* the pre-existent Logos with the *hypostasis* ('person') who unites divine and human 'natures'. Such would be a 'Cyrilline' reading; but it can be challenged. (See A. Baxter, 'Chalcedon, and the Subject in Christ', *Downside Review* 107 (1989), pp. 1–21, and see n. 81 below.) The *Tome* of Pope Leo, which was officially endorsed at Chalcedon, does contain a view of *kenōsis* (*exinanitio* in Latin) comparable to Cyril's; that is, the 'self-emptying' involved is not seen as implying any detraction from Christ's divine characteristics. (On this point, see Sykes, 'The Strange Persistence', p. 351.)

[22]   This is a common, if loose, definition of *communicatio idiomatum* (as given, for example, in Young, *Nicaea to Chalcedon*, p. 238), but it is not as technically precise as we might wish. Quite how the 'communication' is deemed to operate – in which direction (or both), whether only in virtue of the *hypostasis* or directly from one nature to the other, and if merely by verbal attribution or *in re* – were matters for later dispute (see, for example, Pannenberg, *Jesus*, pp. 296–307, and my further discussion below). None of the patristic authors, however, argued that *human* attributes could be directly attributed to the divine nature.

even scholastic, discussion. Indeed Cyril's solution, as we have intimated, hovered uncomfortably close to our second definition of *kenōsis* given above (though he would doubtless have vigorously denied any suggestion of docetism): that is, Christ, he said, at 'times' in the incarnation '*permitted* his own flesh to experience its proper affections, [and] *permitted* [his human] soul to experience its proper affections';[23] but this was a 'permission' operated all along, it seems, from the unshakeable base of the Logos's unchanging divinity. Thus, since no revision of the notion of divinity was envisaged in the light of the gospel narrative on these points (or in the light of the 'attributed' *communicatio*), and no substantial change to the idea of humanity either, it was hard to see how these manifestations of the so-called *kenōsis* were not, in effect, only an *appearance* in the human nature, and that somewhat sporadic. As christological thought was further developed in the patristic East after Cyril and Chalcedon, a clarification was achieved (by the eighth-century Greek theologian John of Damascus, most significantly) about the metaphysical implications of the *communicatio*. If anything, however, it heightened the quasi-docetic tendencies of Cyril's views: the 'communication' was now explicitly said to operate only *one way* (from the divine to the human), the divine fully permeating the human nature of Christ by an act of 'coinherence' (*perichōrēsis*). What space, then, for those dimensions of Christ's passion most poignantly demonstrating human anxiety, weakness and desolation? Were those to be obliterated by the invasive leakage of divine power into Christ's human nature? If so, the kenotic act of the incarnation could now only signify 'emptying' in the most Pickwickian sense: 'a condescension *inexpressible and inconceivable*', as John of Damascus put it in one of his more revealingly tortured sentences on the matter.[24] Whilst many christological commentators have remarked on the discomforts of this position for the integrity of Christ's human nature *tout court*, our own more pressing (and novel) concerns in this essay are over the implications for a gender analysis of normative human–divine relations. The spectre raised here of a divine force that takes on humanity by controlling and partly *obliterating* it (and all, seductively, in the name of '*kenōsis*') is thus the issue that should properly concern us where the further outworkings of the 'Alexandrian' tradition are concerned: it is a matter of how divine 'power' is construed in relation to the human, and how this could insidiously fuel masculinist purposes, masculinist visions of the subduing of the

---

23   Cyril, *De recta fide* II.55, cited in Young, *Nicaea to Chalcedon*, p. 262 (my emphasis).
24   *De recta orthodoxa* III.1, cited in A. B. Bruce, *The Humiliation of Christ* (Edinburgh, T. & T. Clark, 1881), p. 73 (my emphasis).

weaker by the stronger. Thus, while we are still far away from Hampson's initial critique of (one meaning of) *kenōsis*, we may nonetheless here be facing a philosophical issue of more fundamental import. How, that is, are Christian feminists to construe the *hypostatic* 'concurrence' of the human and the divine in Christ (if indeed they wish to defend the Chalcedonian tradition at all) without endorsing a vision of divine power as forceful obliteration?

III

This matter was to take some new turns within early Protestantism. Many centuries later than John of Damascus, in the aftermath of the Lutheran reform in Germany, the question of the *communicatio idiomatum* again became contentious in the light of the interpretation of Philippians 2. This time the issue of the *precise* form of interpenetration between the natures, and especially the implications for expounding the significance of the human nature of Christ with integrity, could no longer be kept at bay. Luther's Christology stressed the extreme vulnerability of Christ on the cross; but at the same time he gave new reinforcement (for reasons to do with his defence of the 'real presence' of Christ in the eucharist) to the doctrine of the *communicatio idiomatum*: the divine had to permeate the human in Christ sufficiently to allow his 'real' (not merely spiritual) presence in multitudinous – and simultaneous – celebrations of the Lord's Supper. But how, then, could Christ's *divinity* be said to be operative in, for instance, his cry of despair at death?[25]

Once this question was pressed, the main European Reformers fell into different camps on the issue, correlated to their divergent views on the Eucharist. Zwingli saw the 'communication' of attributes as no more than a hyperbolic figure of speech; Calvin (in the tradition of the school of Antioch and many of the western Scholastics) saw the attributes of the natures communicating in the *person* of the Saviour, but not interpenetrating directly; whilst the Lutherans, in the Formula of Concord (1577), clarified their preference for the Greek tradition of John of Damascus, insisting that

---

[25]   Luther's own position on the *communicatio* is somewhat hard to discern; but it may be deduced from his eucharistic writings and some other texts that he *does* hazard a metaphysically daring 'two-way' understanding of the communication (a position from which followers such as Melanchthon drew back). On this problem of exegesis see esp. E. Metzke, 'Sakrament und Metaphysik. Ein Lutherstudie über das Verhältnis des christlichen Denkens zum Leiblich-Materiellen' in K. Gründer (ed.), *Coincidentia Oppositorum* (Witten, Luther-Verlag, 1961), pp. 158–204. I am grateful to Wilfried Härle for an illuminating discussion on this point.

attributes of divinity such as omnipresence and omnipotence fully pervaded the human nature of Christ. But the Lutheran position was still clearly problematic; to arrive back at an 'Alexandrian' solution of the *communicatio* (dictated by the needs of the high eucharistic theology) was merely to beg the question of Christ's human brokenness with which Luther had begun.

A school of seventeenth-century Lutherans from Giessen later proposed a solution which returned to Philippians 2 with a slightly novel twist,[26] and one that I wish to suggest might have some life in it as far as a feminist reconstruction is concerned. These theologians suggested that Christ's ostensible weaknesses could be explained in terms of a *kenōsis* operative on his *human* nature, whilst his divine nature retained its powers. The position was thus subtly, though importantly, different from the much earlier Cyrilline one, granted the relocation of the site of 'emptying': whilst Cyril and his Greek successors saw no actual loss in the so-called 'abasements' of incarnation (a *kenōsis* only in name), the Giessen school proposed that the *human* nature of Christ was in effect 'empty' of the possession of such divine attributes as omnipresence and omnipotence during the incarnation – though they added that in virtue of the *union* of the natures there remained the 'possibility' of their reactivation. This last admission was not of course a very happy one (*was* the human nature 'emptied' or not?); and one might well argue that this whole Lutheran debate was being propelled by its unfortunate earlier decision to opt for an interpretation of the *communicatio* that allowed total permeation of the human nature by the divine in the first place (here partially revoked).[27] But one can nonetheless see the good *intentions* of the Giessen school. They were grappling with the crisis of explanation both of Christ's human psychological growth and of his weakness and anxiety in the face of death (a crisis that could only become the more intense with the emergence of modern historiography); and they were doing so within the constraints of a broadly 'Alexandrian' reading of Christology, one that, as we have seen, always teetered towards the 'docetic' in its assumption that the ultimate point of personal identity in Christ could be *identified* with the pre-existent divine Logos. Thus we may perhaps see the Giessen school's vision of *kenōsis* as a variant on our third definition, above (Christ choosing *never to have* certain forms of power in his incarnate

---

[26]   There are brief discussions in English of this school's position in J. A. Dorner, *History of the Development of the Doctrine of the Person of Christ* (Edinburgh, T. & T. Clark, 1870), II.2, pp. 282–6; Bruce, *Humiliation*, pp. 106–14; Sykes, 'The Strange Persistence', p. 352.

[27]   See the criticisms from a Reformed perspective in Bruce, *Humiliation*, Lecture III, esp. pp. 106–14.

life, never to 'grasp'), the difference being that this approach is now linked
to a 'two natures' Christology and the 'emptying' applied to the human
nature *alone*. That this solution fitted uneasily into its presumed 'Alexandrian' framework we have just indicated; but the possibility raised here of a
vision of christological *kenōsis* uniting human 'vulnerability' with authentic
divine power (as opposed to worldly or 'patriarchal' visions of power), and
uniting them such that the human was wholly translucent to the divine, is I
believe of some continuing relevance to Christian feminism, and an issue to
which I shall return shortly. For the meantime, let us note that we have at
last reached one version, at least, of what Hampson may be rejecting when
she accuses 'kenoticism' of being a 'male problem'. That is, if we take
something like the Giessen form of *kenōsis* as read, is the 'abandonment'
of certain forms of control or power seen here in Christ's human realm to be
regarded as of imitative spiritual significance only to *men*? Is Hampson
objecting to 'self-emptying', 'vulnerability', or surrendering of 'control'
featuring in *any* form in her vision of women's spiritual flourishing?[28]

Perhaps we can answer this with full clarity only when we have the final
version of (nineteenth- and twentieth-century) *kenōsis* also in mind. For here
I think is Hampson's real butt: not the relatively obscure post-Reformation
reflections on the *communicatio* and the union of the two natures, but the
much more daring – and distinctively modern – idea that even the pre-
existent *divine* Logos is 'emptied' (in some sense) in the incarnation, actually
relinquishing or 'retracting' certain attributes of divinity such as omnipotence or omniscience. It was another Lutheran (the late nineteenth-century
Gottfried Thomasius) who took this bold step, and so tackled the remaining
difficulties of the *communicatio* head on. As he acutely saw, they were
rendered more problematic by the evolving disciplines of biblical criticism
and developmental psychology. Did Jesus develop ordinarily as a human
child? Was he aware of a pre-existent divine life? Thomasius felt unable to
hold on to the orthodox notion of a personal unity of the divine and human
in Christ 'without the supposition of a *self-limitation of the divine Logos*
coincident with the Incarnation'.[29]

---

[28]   Such would appear to be the clear implication of Hampson's adjunct essay 'On Power
and Gender', *Modern Theology* 4 (1988), pp. 234–50, esp. p. 239: 'I want to suggest that this
paradigm [the paradigm of self-giving to another], which men may have found useful, is
inappropriate for women. Feminist women seemingly reject it with unanimity.' This is of
course precisely the point I am questioning.
[29]   An extract from G. Thomasius, *Christi Person und Werk*, II (2nd edn, 1857), translated in
C. Welch (ed.), *God and Incarnation in Mid-Nineteenth Century German Theology: G. Thomasius,
I. A. Dorner, A. E. Biedermann* (New York, Oxford University Press, 1965), p. 89 (my
emphasis).

This, then, was a real *novum*: the idea of a self-limitation of the *divine* realm; but the attempt to express it without incoherence, within a broadly 'Alexandrian' reading of Chalcedon, was to prove at least as difficult (and I believe ultimately more difficult) than the earlier efforts to explicate the 'kenotic' act of incarnation. According to Thomasius, certain divine properties (omnipotence, omniscience, omnipresence) were in Christ shown to be only 'relative' divine characteristics, withdrawn to a condition of 'potency' during the incarnate life of Jesus. This position is somewhat close to our first definition of *kenōsis* given above (the temporary *relinquishing* of divine powers in the incarnation); and yet to say it was a straightforward version of this type would clearly be to mislead: to withdraw *some* divine properties into 'potency' for a while (leaving aside for the moment whether this idea is cogent or not), is clearly not the same thing as a *total* – albeit temporary – relinquishing of divine powers. The distinction is significant, for it has proved useful to a number of distinguished critics of this modern form of *kenōsis* to tar it with the brush of complete, if temporary, abandonment of divine powers (or even of the divine nature),[30] thus mightily confusing this already convoluted problem of definition. In order to avoid this muddle, we shall need to generate a sixth definition of *kenōsis* for Thomasius and his ilk, thus: (6) a temporary retracting (or withdrawing into 'potency') of *certain* characteristics of divinity during the incarnate life. We are now in a position to consider the feminist implications of this development.

IV

The challenge of expressing views like Thomasius' in pictorial imagery vivid to minds of the time was taken up by a range of British kenoticists in the early part of the twentieth century. It is surely these writers that Hampson has in mind when she launches her attack on *kenōsis* as a 'male' expression of compensatory need or guilt; and she is certainly right to suggest that a gender analysis of their work is long overdue. Frank Weston's *The One Christ*, for instance (originally published in 1907), employs a revealing set of analogies in order to express the 'law of self-restraint' that the Son imposed upon his

---

[30] So (misleadingly) J. M. Creed, in his essay 'Recent Tendencies in English Theology' in G. K. A. Bell and A. Deissmann (eds.), *Mysterium Christi* (London, Longman's Green, 1930), p. 133; Donald Baillie in *God Was In Christ* (London, Faber & Faber, 1948), pp. 94–5, 96–7; and David Brown in *The Divine Trinity* (London, Duckworth, 1985), p. 231.

own divinity in the incarnation. Christ was like 'St Francis de Sales', first, acting in a professional role as priest and confessor to his parents (a role seen here as restricted), but in another, wider, role as their son. (We note how, for the purposes of this analogy, the position of 'priest' is seen as involving partial 'limitation' and restriction of knowledge. This is a far cry from the debates between the sexes over priestly powers in this century; Weston can take a certain form of male priestly authority for granted, but then focus on the professional 'limitation' that the confessional imposes.) The next analogy utilized by Weston (Canon of Zanzibar Cathedral at the time) is of an 'African king' who is reduced to slavery; another is of a 'favourite son of a commanding officer', who has to exercise pretence or filial restraint when he is transferred to his father's own regiment; and the final suggestion is the analogy of a 'king's son' who leaves his palace and 'dwell[s] a workman amongst workmen . . . [passing] through all the troubles and vicissitudes of the life of a manual labourer. . .'.[31] *Autres temps, autres moeurs*: one can hardly suppress a smirk of embarrassment at this catalogue of class and gender assumptions. As Hampson indicates, the privileged male can afford to seek some compensatory 'loss' in such ways (though, tellingly, only the 'African king' seems to lose out substantially in these heart-warming tales of noble self-abnegation). To be fair, Weston is well aware of the fallibility and partiality of his analogues; but far from his mind – naturally enough – is the social and sexual subtext of what he proposes.[32]

In the slightly earlier writing of Charles Gore, the kenotic analogy was (not much more reassuringly, perhaps, to a feminist) that of empathetic identification with the circumstances of an 'inferior': the child, the uneducated, or the 'savage'. Again, as in Weston, Gore's christological analysis in *The Incarnation of the Son of God* (1891) and *Dissertations on Subjects Connected with the Incarnation* (1895) is both intricate and profound: there is no denying the originality and sophistication of these writers, for all the (new) problems of coherence they present. Yet Gore, rather bemusingly, could hardly be called a consistent 'kenoticist' according to the sixth definition we have just generated. Despite his fairly imprecise talk here about 'abandonment' of divine powers in the act of 'empathy', his work elsewhere suggests a

[31]   See F. Weston, *The One Christ* (London, Longman's Green, 1914 (1907)), ch. 6, esp. (for these analogies) pp. 166–87. This quotation is from p. 182.

[32]   Weston admits the inadequacy of each of his analogies as he discusses them, and esp. on p. 185 of *The One Christ*: 'these analogies have not taken us very far . . .'. J. Hick, *The Metaphor of God Incarnate* (London, SCM Press, 1993), ch. 6, has recently presented a clear analysis of modern 'kenoticist' positions, with philosophical critique, but makes no remark on what I have here termed the 'social and sexual subtext' of their accounts.

retention of all divine characteristics, according to a 'two levels of consciousness' model (ironically the one now promulgated by analytic defenders of high Chalcedonian 'orthodoxy').[33] If a bishop understands an
'uneducated' [woman?] or a 'savage', then, he does so without any final
ontological change to his privileged make-up.

In the writings of P. T. Forsyth, however (significantly the only Non-
conformist of this group of British kenoticists), the tone is somewhat
different. *The Person and Place of Jesus Christ* (1909) presents us with a
range of analogies to the 'kenotic' act which involve much greater and
more permanent loss than those rehearsed by Gore and Weston (so much so
that Forsyth's position veers closer to our first definition of *kenōsis* than our
sixth); but the analogies are no less embedded in the presumptions of male
social and intellectual superiority. Here we have a 'venerable vizier' who
takes poison in the place of a 'foolish young Sultan', and suffers consequent
debilitation; a Russian concert violinist who is so committed to the poor (in
pre-Revolutionary times) that he undergoes exile and loss of his musical
career; and a promising philosophy student who sets aside an academic
career to support his family, and so submits to 'drudgery' in 'modern
industrial conditions' (which of course blunts his intellectual brilliance!).
Forsyth's point, and it is movingly and even persuasively argued, is that a
restriction on human freedom, consciously and resolutely accepted by an act
of 'supernatural' will, can in due course be seen as a means of glory.[34] But
what of those (women, 'workmen', 'African slaves') who arguably do not
enjoy the capacity of 'supernatural' freedom in the first place? As with Gore
and Weston, the extent to which the assumed 'masculinism' of the vital
imagery employed affects the *cogency* or *coherence* of the theological picture is
a nice point. The issue of the technical coherence of divine *kenōsis* might
seem to be one removed from the precise evocations of a particular thought
experiment, to be a matter merely of logic and consistency. Yet it is
sometimes only when a range of controlling images or 'intuition pumps'

---

[33]   For Gore's analogies for christological *kenōsis*, see C. Gore, *The Incarnation of the Son of
God* (London, J. Murray, 1891), pp. 159–62 (and note the talk of 'real abandonment' of divine
properties, p. 161). In C. Gore, *Dissertations on Subjects Connected with the Incarnation* (New
York, C. Scribner's, 1895), p. 93, however, Gore adopts what is now called a 'two centres of
consciousness' model, which denies any actual loss of 'divine and cosmic functions' during the
incarnation. (R. Swinburne, *The Christian God* (Oxford, Clarendon Press, 1994), p. 230, n. 32,
comments illuminatingly on the confusion caused by dubbing Gore's position straightforwardly 'kenotic'.) See section V, below, for further discussion of the contemporary 'two
centres of consciousness' defence of Chalcedonianism, which is predominantly anti-'kenotic'.
[34]   See P. T. Forsyth, *The Person and Place of Jesus Christ* (London, Hodder & Stoughton,
1909), pp. 296–300.

break down (often for reasons beyond those of pure logic) that we realize that we have been obsessed with the wrong questions.[35]

The early twentieth-century kenoticists, as we have shown, struggled to express divine self-limitation within an 'Alexandrian' reading of Chalcedon. It never occurred to them to question, more radically, whether that particular gloss on Chalcedon (which located the personal identity of Christ undiffer-entiatedly in the pre-existent divine life of the Logos) was either theologically necessary or textually obvious; just as it never occurred to them to reflect on the gender and class evocations of their analogies (which just as clearly started from a presumption of possessed power and influence). Yet these are the very assumptions we shall shortly wish to question. Oddly, however, Daphne Hampson's critique of *kenōsis* also appears to make some similar gender presumptions. Thus, for her, 'males' (all males, including 'workmen' and 'slaves'?) need to compensate for their tendency to 'dominate' by means of an act of self-emptying; whereas 'women' (all women, including university professors?) do not. The question that now presses, therefore, is whether Hampson may not, in her perceptive critique of early twentieth-century kenoticists, have fallen into the trap of her own gender stereotypes. Has she not assumed, that is, that 'vulnerability' or 'self-effacement' are prescriptively 'female' (though regrettably so), and thus only 'helpful' as a secondary or compensatory addition to 'male' power and dominance; whereas such ('male') power ought now *rightly* to be pursued (also by way of compensation) by feminist women? But why should we continue with these outworn gender presumptions in the first place? Is there not, we might ask, a more creative theological way through our dilemma via a *reformulation* of the very notion of divine 'power' and its relation to the human?

Since Gore, Weston and Forsyth, the discussion of *kenōsis* has taken one more twist – in my view a misleading twist – which may nonetheless help us confront this question more directly and clearly. This is the form of 'kenoti-cism' aligned to the 'ethical' interpretation of Philippians 2 favoured by C. F. D. Moule (discussed above), but then given a more overt philosophical expression which was to undercut the 'two natures' structure still implicitly retained by Moule. Moule, we recall, spoke of the 'form of the servant' actually revealing the 'nature of God': 'the self-giving humility which *is* the *essence of divinity*'.[36] In line with this kind of exegesis of Philippians 2, John

---

[35]   This point is well made (in relation to the question of how misleading images may dominate philosophical discussion of free will) by D. C. Dennett in *Elbow Room: The Varieties of Free Will Worth Wanting* (Oxford, Clarendon Press, 1984), pp. 169–71.
[36]   See again Moule, 'Further Reflexions', p. 265 (my emphasis).

Robinson was to develop a more metaphysically enunciated notion of *kenōsis as 'plērōsis'*.[37] Instead, that is, of presuming a substantial pre-existence for Christ and then wondering how a 'human nature' could be compatible with it (the 'Alexandrian' problem, as we have seen, from the start), Robinson proposed a reversal of the traditional directionality of the *communicatio*, and thus a radical seepage of the *human* characteristics into the *divine* – such, indeed, as to collapse the apparatus of the 'two natures' doctrine altogether. Thus the human limitations of Jesus were seen as a positive expression of his divinity rather than as a curtailment of it. In somewhat similar mode, John Macquarrie has written of a 'new-style kenoticism', in which 'the self-emptying of Jesus Christ has not only opened up the depth of a true humanity, but has made known to us the final reality as likewise self-emptying, self-giving and self-limiting'.[38]

Now, it is important to underscore the radicality of what has occurred here. We are no longer speculating about the paradoxical *relationship* of human and divine 'natures' (and then arguing about the possible accommo-dations necessary when bringing them into 'concurrence'). Rather, it is being urged that the 'limitations' of Jesus' human life are in some sense directly *equatable* with what it is to be 'God'. But can we make coherent sense of this? It is obviously the final philosophical terminus of the 'Tho-masian' road; but it goes far beyond anything Thomasius himself envisaged or desired – the *identification* of 'God' as permanently 'limited'. Does this not then also make God intrinsically non-omnipotent and non-omniscient (as opposed to temporally non-omnipotent and non-omniscient under the conditions of incarnation)? And how, then, could such a being be 'God'?

Interestingly, one of the rare *analytic* philosophers of religion to favour kenoticism today, S. T. Davis, seemingly takes these implications to follow from a 'kenotic' approach to Christology too, and in exploring this avenue of approach he parts company with most of his colleagues in the discourse of analytic religious philosophy. His reflections are therefore worthy of some comment. Unlike Robinson, Davis maintains the Chalcedonian structure of pre-existence and the 'two natures' doctrine, but argues that, if the incarnate Christ as depicted in the biblical narrative shows signs of non-omniscience, then an implication may be that omniscience is not, after all, an *essential* property of the divine.[39] But then Davis wavers on this point: it seems he is

---

[37] Robinson, *Human Face*, p. 208, citing Moule with approval: '*kenōsis* actually *is plērōsis*'.

[38] See J. Macquarrie, 'Kenoticism Reconsidered', *Theology* 77 (1974), pp. 115–24; this quotation from p. 124.

[39] See S. T. Davis, *Logic and the Nature of God* (Grand Rapids, Eerdmans, 1983), pp. 123–4.

not familiar with the history of the doctrine of the *communicatio idiomatum*, and which form of it he wishes to espouse. Insofar as he considers allowing this permanent revelatory status for the human life of Christ as a window onto the divine, he is joining hands with Robinson and the other 'new kenoticists' (who embrace the fourth definition of *kenōsis* given above); but insofar as he also talks of Christ's failure in omniscience as only 'temporary' (like a 'skilled tennis player [choosing] to play a game with their weak hand'![40]), he is closer to our first definition of *kenōsis*, where divine characteristics are only briefly set aside for the purposes of the incarnation. The result is not a very happy compromise, and only questionably coherent.[41] Yet the 'new kenoticists', in contrast, seem in even deeper waters metaphysically, as we have intimated. Perhaps it is they, after all, who represent the final outworkings of the liberal 'masculinist' guilt derided by Hampson? Their God, it seems, becomes intrinsically devoid of omniscience and omnipotence (at least in anything like the traditional definitions). Yet it is one thing, of course, to *redefine* divine 'power' creatively, another to shear God down to human size, to make God intrinsically power*less*, incapable of sustaining the creation in being.[42]

But how then does this recent, or 'new', kenoticism throw light on our feminist agendas? What one sees so interestingly in writers such as Moule, Robinson (and to some degree Davis) is a primary commitment to the given *narrative* of the New Testament, and especially of the gospel accounts of Jesus' life; and this takes precedence even over philosophical questions of apparent coherence, or of traditional *a priori* assumptions about the unchanging divine attributes. Such narrative commitment is a feature of post-War theology in general (especially continental theology), and indeed could be said to be the point at which contemporary theology and analytic

[40]   Davis, *Logic*, p. 125. (Playing tennis with one's weak hand may be an analogy laudably free from *sexist* overtones, but it is scarcely calculated to inspire spiritually.)

[41]   For recent criticism of Davis's position on grounds of coherence, see Hick, *Metaphor of God*, ch. 7. Relevant comments on Davis in a mode more sympathetic to 'kenoticism' are to be found in R. J. Feenstra, 'Reconsidering Kenotic Christology' in R. J. Feenstra and C. Plantinga (eds.), *Trinity, Incarnation, and Atonement* (South Bend, IN, Notre Dame Press, 1989), pp. 128–52.

[42]   See Sykes in Kee and Long (eds.), *Being and Truth*, pp. 358–60, for critical reflection on this point. (A 'process' view of theism would of course more willingly embrace these implications. See again Frankenberry, 'Classical Theism', pp. 34–9, for a view of Hartsthornian 'panentheism' that is read positively by her in terms of gender issues. The full case for my own maintenance of a more 'classical' perception of God is unfortunately impossible within the constraints of this chapter, although some of the main lines of argument are sketched here.)

philosophy of religion divide most painfully in their fundamental assumptions. What for Barthian theologians, for instance, is seen as the inexplicable
and 'absolute paradox' of the incarnation *given* in the irreducible narrative of
the biblical text, is for most analytic philosophers of religion (bar, here, in
some respects, Davis) instead a matter of the *logical* demonstration of the
coherence of the traditional christological formulae, granted certain *a priori*
presumptions about the nature of God and humanity.[43] Where the question
of gender then insidiously inserts itself into this scholarly divide is in the
willingness, or otherwise, to construe forms of 'weakness', 'passivity' or
'vulnerability' (all traditionally demerits for the 'male', but manifestly present in Jesus' passion) as either normatively human or even revelatorily
divine. Most philosophers of religion would resist both of these options;
some theologians, as we have shown, would consider one or both. If either
of the latter positions is sustained, however (and I have already intimated
that I prefer the former), then a traditional gender stereotype starts to
crumble. That is, if Jesus' 'vulnerability' is a primary narrative given, rather
than a philosophical embarrassment to explain away, then precisely the
question is raised whether 'vulnerability' *need* be seen as a 'female' weakness
rather than a (special sort of) 'human' strength. As in Ruether's standpoint,
so here: Jesus may be the male messenger to *empty* 'patriarchal' values.

V

Such narrative commitment amongst theologians is thus in striking contrast
to the general assumptions of mainstream analytical philosophy of religion
(with which, as we have shown, Stephen Davis is in somewhat problematic
conversation). Here it tends to be assumed that we know, either *a priori* or
else via the authority of tradition, what 'God' must look like, as possessing a
certain form of omniscience, omnipotence, omnipresence, immutability
and perfect goodness.[44] It also tends to be assumed (especially where the
problem of evil dictates the terms of the discussion), that a normatively

---

[43]   For one of the testier examples of the latter approach, see Thomas V. Morris, *The Logic of
God Incarnate* (Ithaca, NY, Cornell University Press, 1986) esp. ch. 3 and 4. Morris insists that
'the figure of the God-man is in no way at all even a paradox for faith' (p. 74).
[44]   See, for example, the much-quoted opening paragraph of R. Swinburne, *The Coherence of
Theism* (Oxford, Clarendon Press, 1977), p. I: 'By a theist I understand a man who believes that
there is a God. By a "God" he understands something like a "person without a body (i.e. a spirit)
who is eternal, free, able to do anything, knows everything, is perfectly good, is the proper
object of human worship and obedience, the creator and sustainer of the universe".'

'human' trait is the possession of 'libertarian' freedom, that is, a sovereign self-possession and autonomy that is capable of rising above the weaknesses and distractions of human desires and human tragedy.[45] On this view, then, as in the patristic discussion, the gospel stories of Jesus' vulnerability and anxiety in the face of the cross present a problem to be negotiated, not a narrative prototype to be philosophically explained. But the christological difficulties are, I believe, here sharpened even beyond what Cyril and his ilk confronted. For the sovereignly-free 'individualism' of the Enlightenment 'man of reason',[46] is, when smuggled into christological construction, even more hard to square with the assumed notion of divinity inherited from the 'classical' tradition than the understandings of 'humanity' with which the Fathers themselves operated. Indeed, even the supposedly 'classical' view of God just mentioned shows suspicious signs of bearing the masculinist projections of writers already committed to an Enlightenment view of 'man'. He, too, is another 'individual', a *very large* disembodied spirit with ultimate directive power and freedom.[47] How can the natures of *two* such 'individuals' concur christologically?

This point deserves a little more explication, because it shows how gender presumptions and anxieties are, I believe, lurking in the staunchly conservative – and for the most part staunchly anti-'kenotic' – defence of Chalcedonian orthodoxy found in recent analytical philosophy of religion. (I think here especially of the work of Thomas V. Morris, David Brown and Richard Swinburne.[48]) The first point to note is the

---

[45]   M. McC. Adams and R. M. Adams (eds.), *The Problem of Evil* (Oxford, Oxford University Press, 1990), esp. the editors' introduction, pp. 10–16, shows with clarity how problems of theodicy have propelled modern philosophers of religion (even Calvinists) towards a 'libertarian' view of freedom (since without such an explanation, the divine responsibility for appalling levels of evil in the world would appear impossible to square with the notion of perfect divine goodness). Adams and Adams do not discuss the question, raised here in my essay, of whether these Christian philosophers are already predisposed towards a 'libertarian' view of freedom on account of their Enlightenment heritage. (For what the masculinist implications of such a view might be, see Frankenberry, 'Classical Theism', pp. 33–4, who comments on the gender presumptions smuggled into discussions of divine power in current analytic philosophy of religion.)

[46]   For a discussion of the gendered nature of this Enlightenment figure, in his various forms, see G. Lloyd, *The Man of Reason: 'Male' and 'Female' in Western Philosophy* (Minneapolis, University of Minnesota Press, 1984), esp. ch. 3–5.

[47]   See again Swinburne, *Coherence*, esp. pp. 1–7: God is a 'person' ... 'in the modern sense' (p. I and n. I). The revised edition of the book (1993), more conscious of trinitarian issues, omits n. I.

[48]   See Morris, *Logic*; Brown, *Divine Trinity*; Swinburne, *Christian God*.

defensive resistance to any form of feminist critique evident in the discourse of analytic philosophy of religion in general. With striking disregard for the developments of feminist theology, analytic philosophers of religion have shown almost no cognizance of the profound critique of 'masculinist' notions of God which is now almost taken for granted in theological discussions. Nor have they heeded the rigorous challenges of feminist philosophy, where a complex debate has grown up about the construal of the self and of 'human' freedom in post-Enlightenment philosophy, and the extent to which the notion of either a disembodied soul, or a sovereignly 'free individual', may be masculinist abstractions with little regard for bodily life, feelings or imagination – much less the lessons of child psychology or the formative matrix of primary family relationships.[49] So far, then, analytic philosophy of religion has been remarkable for its resistance to feminist questionings. The silence, we might say, is deafening.

But it is precisely in christological discussion that we can see these basic philosophical assumptions made by analytic philosophy of religion beginning to come under strain. S. T. Davis's probing, if uncertain, questionings about *kenōsis* are one sign; another (as with the early twentieth-century 'kenoticists' we discussed earlier) is the revealing analogues that analytic 'anti-kenoticists' bring to bear in their attempt to give clear expression to the humanity and divinity in Christ. Their favourite, significantly, is the analogy of the Freudian 'divided mind'.[50] The idea is that, as in modern psychoanalytic accounts of the self, unconscious forces may be operating – even operating more powerfully – than conscious forces, so too in Christ we may hold up an image of an 'individual' with not one, but two 'centres of consciousness' – one, however (the divine) more powerful and all-encompassing than the other. Thomas Morris talks of an 'asymmetric accessing relation' between 'two minds', the divine encompassing the human; Richard Swinburne of 'two systems of belief to some extent

---

[49]   For discussion of the potential importance of feminist and psychological considerations for contemporary epistemology, see N. Schemann, 'Individualism and Objects of Psychology', and J. Flax, 'Political Philosophy and the Patriarchal Unconscious: A Psychoanalytic Perspective on Epistemology and Metaphysics' in S. Harding and M. B. Hintikka (eds.), *Discovering Reality: Feminist Perspectives on Epistemology, Metaphysics, Methodology and Philosophy of Science* (Dordrecht, D. Reidel, 1983), pp. 225–44 and 245–81, respectively.

[50]   Utilized in a variety of ways by Brown, *Divine Trinity*; Morris, *Logic*; Swinburne in his article 'Could God Become Man?' in G. Vesey (ed.), *The Philosophy in Christianity* (Cambridge, Cambridge University Press, 1989), pp. 53–70; and (in somewhat revised form) Swinburne, *Christian God*.

independent of one another'; David Brown, rather differently, of a 'dialogue between . . . conscious and subconscious selves'.[51] However, this basic analogue is a revealing one for a number of reasons. For a start, the very invocation here of the unconscious (or 'subconscious': they are not clearly distinguished), let alone the appeal to Freud, with his messages of deep sexual motivations,[52] is a sign that the more normative 'Enlightenment man' of analytic philosophy of religion is wading out of his depth. For analytic philosophy of religion *properly* to take on Freudian issues of the unconscious or the dream-world, of primary parental relations and of sexuality, would I suspect be to transform its discourse about 'man' and 'God' almost out of all recognition; certainly it would drive it much more closely towards appreciation of feminist theological and philosophical critiques of its basic assumptions. (Contemporary continental philosophy's assimilation of Freud into its categories of discussion is a clear witness to that.[53])

But there are other uneasy aspects of this newly constructed 'orthodox' Christology.[54] For the resistance to raising previously held views about 'God' and 'man' in the light of the gospel passion narratives still shows itself in a number of ways. As in Cyril, we do not *start* from the constraints of the gospel story. Thus, since the dominating idea is that the divine pre-existent Logos must be able to *control* a (possibly resistant?) human nature, there is sometimes a covert 'Apollinarianism' lurking in the discussion, that is, the suggestion that there is a ready-made 'individual' who is the Logos and who, *qua* 'soul', simply has to join with, or take over, a human body. This kind of talk fits ill with the *two* 'centres of consciousness'

---

[51]   See Morris, *Logic*, p. 103; Swinburne in Vesey (ed.), *Philosophy*, p. 65; Brown, *Divine Trinity*, p. 262.

[52]   For the most part the 'divided mind' christologians wholly ignore this dimension of their own analogy, though – if one pressed it – Freud's deeper sexual motivations would presumably have to be associated with the *divine* nature in Christ (i.e., that 'mind' kept somewhat in the background during Christ's earthly existence). Swinburne's brief exploration of the sexual analogy in Vesey (ed.), *Philosophy*, p. 62, however, sees sexual desire as a *human* temptation which some stronger dimension, analogous to the divine (i.e., the will), should overcome. Perhaps significantly, Swinburne omits this element of the 'two minds' analogy from his more recent (parallel) discussion: Swinburne, *Christian God*, ch. 9.

[53]   Thus contemporary French feminisms can build on an existing discussion in French postmodern philosophy of Freud and Lacan: see, by way of introduction, the useful discussion of French feminist writers in C. Weedon, *Feminist Practice and Post-Structuralist Theory* (Oxford, Basil Blackwell), 1987.

[54]   See Hick, *Metaphor*, ch. 5, for a clearly expressed critique (motivated *against* traditional Chalcedonianism).

otherwise promoted.[55] In Morris's work, too, there is a strange mixture, in his account of the two 'wills' in Christ, of a remaining commitment to a 'libertarian' view of human freedom, combined with an underlying concept of the divine as wholly *controlling* it.[56] Thus, as a feminist, I am not particularly consoled or inspired by the thought that Jesus' unique human–divine sinlessness was perhaps rather like a man 'Jones', who, unbeknownst to him, has electrodes implanted in his brain by a big-brother figure, which can then prevent him from doing things that he ought not to do. In fact, however, the electrodes do not have to be operated if Jones does what he should on his own account. This rather chilling parallel is meant to give us an idea of how Jesus could be truly 'free' in a libertarian sense but at the same time 'necessarily good, unable to sin'.[57] Instead, to me as a feminist commentator, the Morrisian fantasy of one who achieves complete 'control' over someone else without that person even realizing it summons up every sort of political and sexual nightmare.

Another sign of strain to these prevalent analytic assumptions about the 'human' emerges in Richard Swinburne's insistence that human and divine natures be kept somewhat 'separate' in Christ (a strangely un-Chalcedonian form of expression[58]), lest the divine nature permeate the human in such a way as to undermine its integrity. The soteriological motivation for this point is admirable, of course, and fully in line with what we have argued above about the dangers of an eastern (or Lutheran) perception of the *communicatio idiomatum* inviting 'obliteration' of the human. What is more revealing in Swinburne's case, however, is his assumption that any sign of minor ignorance, frailty or 'desire' in Jesus is an indication of his *less-than-perfect* 'humanity'. (Indeed, this is perhaps the more profound reason why Swinburne wants to keep Jesus' humanity 'separate' from his divinity.)

---

[55]   See Swinburne in Vesey (ed.), *Philosophy*, p. 59 ('[Christ's] soul which is subsequently the human soul'), and, more clearly, p. 61 ('joining his [Christ's] soul to an unowned human body'). In Swinburne, *Christian God*, ch. 9, these phrases are repeated (pp. 194, 196), but the suggestion of quasi-Apollinarianism is corrected by a clarification that the 'reasonable [human] soul' of Christ (defended at Chalcedon against Apollinarianism) is not to be seen as an identifiable substance, like Christ's pre-existent divine soul, but rather as 'a human *way of thinking and acting*' (p. 197, my emphasis). This adjustment is arguably still not very comfortable, however, importing as it does a Cartesian notion of 'soul' into the ('Alexandrian') reading of the pre-existent Logos as *identical* with Christ's *hypostasis*.

[56]   See Morris, *Logic*, pp. 150–3 (esp. pp. 151–2, drawing on a well-known thought-experiment devised by Harry Frankfurt).

[57]   Morris, *Logic*, p. 153.

[58]   Recall the injunctions of the Chalcedonian Definition: '...in two natures, without confusion, without change, without division, *without separation* ...'.

Thus events like Gethsemane and Golgotha seem to show Jesus' humanity, according to Swinburne, as in some sense *defective* from its true, heavenly norm.[59] But what, we may ask, if the frailty, vulnerability and 'self-effacement' of these narratives *is* what shows us 'perfect humanity'? The resistance to such a possibility is itself, I suggest, one shot through with gender implications; for to admit such would be to start to cut away the ground on which the 'man of reason' stands. But then analytic philosophy of religion is hardly noted, as we have seen, for its positive attention to states of 'passivity', 'vulnerability' or the ceding of 'control' – states, one suspects, that could normally be delegated to the subordinate (and wholly unmentioned) 'female'.[60]

Let me now sum up the results of this complex account of historic debates about *kenōsis* and its gender inflections. What we should underscore, first, about our recent comparative discussion of 'new' (theological) 'kenoticism' on the one hand, and analytic (philosophical) 'anti-kenoticism' on the other, is that both have severe – though very different – drawbacks from a feminist perspective. Whereas the 'new kenoticism' appears to make 'God' both limited and weak (by a process of direct transference from Jesus' human life to the divine), and so endanger the very capacity for divine transformative 'power', the analytic 'orthodoxy' clings ferociously to a vision of divine 'omnipotence' and 'control' which is merely the counterpart of the sexist 'man' made in his (libertarian) image. One model seems propelled by masculinist guilt; the other by unexamined masculinist assumptions. Neither

---

[59]   See Swinburne, *Christian God*, p. 208: 'the "divided mind" view...allows the human nature of Christ to be not a nature as perfect as a human nature could be', etc.

[60]   There are occasional, and interesting, exceptions to this rule in the discourses of analytic philosophy of religion. R. M. Adams's profound spiritual questioning of the 'lust for control of my own life and its circumstances', in *The Virtue of Faith and Other Essays in Philosophical Theology* (New York, Oxford University Press, 1987), pp. 18–20, is an important counter-instance (though, significantly, he remarks in a note, p. I, that he owes this insight in large part to his wife). In a christological context, J. R. Lucas has argued (in 'Foreknowledge and the Vulnerability of God' in Vesey (ed.), *Philosophy*, pp. 119–28) that – *contra* Swinburne et al. – the 'Christian God' (as opposed to 'an impersonal Neoplatonist Absolute') is necessarily a 'suffering', 'fallible' and 'vulnerable' God. Ironically, these conclusions seem to arise less from a conviction of the priority of the New Testament narrative (though the passion is briefly mentioned in closing), than from an outworking of philosophical presumptions also shared by Swinburne (and *not* shared by 'classical theists' in the Thomist tradition): the 'libertarian' freewill of the individual, and the en-timed nature of the divine.

   Neither Adams nor Lucas, we might note, raises gender issues in making these points about 'vulnerability' and loss of 'control'.

considers – any more than does Hampson – the possibility of a 'strength made perfect *in* (human) weakness' (2 Corinthians 12.9), of the normative concurrence in Christ of non-bullying divine 'power' *with* 'self-effaced' humanity. It is here that the remaining potential of the third definition of *kenōsis* given earlier in our New Testament discussion (a choosing *never to have* 'worldly' forms of power), may yet, I suggest, join hands with the Giessen school's insight that *kenōsis* pertains appropriately to the *human* in a 'two natures' model. Yet we still have to confront the problems, both philosophical and feminist, that we have highlighted about the dominance of the 'Alexandrian' reading of Chalcedon, and to these issues we must now return in our final section. Can we after all locate a systematic alternative, both christological and spiritual, which finds an appropriate place for human *kenōsis* without merely reinforcing gender stereotype or sexist compliance?

As Stephen Sykes has well observed, the lessons of what he calls 'the strange persistence of kenotic christology' are mainly about failures in *anthropomorphism*.[61] What we tend (unwittingly, often) to read on to God from our human perspective will surely be revealed when we start to think about questions of *kenōsis*. And hence the extraordinary complexity of this historical tale I have just told, and the entanglement of gender themes with metaphysical and semantic choices. Before going on to explicate a feminist version of *kenōsis* which will, I believe, show a way beyond the Ruether–Hampson exchange (and also retrieve those strands in the story which are capable of contemporary application), it may therefore be worth pausing to recapitulate some of the ironies and confusions that have been laid bare in this account.

By distinguishing six different meanings of *kenōsis*, and highlighting the lack of clear interconnections between different discourses on the matter, we have demonstrated how various exponents of *kenōsis* can disagree on even such basic matters as: whether *kenōsis* involves pre-existence (or not); whether it implies a temporary loss of all or some divine characteristics (or neither); whether the 'emptying' applies to the divine nature or the human (or alternatively rejects 'two natures' Christology altogether); and whether the effects of *kenōsis* pass to the eternal nature of the Godhead (or not). Thus, further, when charges of 'kenoticism' are levelled by such as oppose it, they may often turn out to be shadow-boxing, to be attributing to the 'enemy' a position she or he never occupied (the total, if temporary, loss of the divine nature, for instance);[62] and, conversely, someone who (like Gore)

---

[61] See Sykes in Kee and Long (eds.), *Being and Truth*, p. 357. (Sykes is not, however, considering gendered anthropomorphism.)
[62] See again n. 30, above.

embraces the *title* 'kenoticist' may actually hold a position on 'two centres of consciousness' almost indistinguishable from an 'anti-kenotic' defender of Chalcedon.[63]

As if this complexity were not enough, we have attempted to weave into it a thoroughgoing feminist analysis of the different options. What we now see even more clearly, I trust, is that Hampson's critique scores only against relatively modern forms of *kenōsis*, and in particular those where the 'emptying' is regarded as compensating for an existing set of gender presumptions that might be called 'masculinist'.[64] Thus in the course of our discussion we have detected two fundamental problems with the generalizing tone of Hampson's original criticism of *kenōsis*. First, it does not apply to notions of human *kenōsis* where 'masculinist' (or 'worldly', bullying) forms of power are eschewed *from the outset* by Jesus (and this, it seems, is closer to Ruether's position); and second, it appears to presume the very questions it is begging about gender stereotypes: the alignment of 'males' with achieved, worldly power, and women with lack of it. The presumption is that women *need* 'power' – but of what sort? How are they to avoid aping the 'masculinism' they criticize? In taking up these two points in my closing section I want to sketch out an alternative that Hampson seems not to have considered. For what – as I have hinted several times – if true divine 'empowerment' occurs most unimpededly in the context of a *special* form of human 'vulnerability'?

VI

But what form should this human vulnerability take? It is no secret why 'vulnerability' has been such a taboo subject in Christian feminist writing up

---

[63]   See again n. 33, above.

[64]   I am aware of the regrettable looseness with which I have wielded the term 'masculinism' in this chapter. In feminist writing the word tends to be used as a shorthand, to denote attitudes and actions derogatory to women and women's flourishing, but often encouraged or condoned in the population at large, especially amongst men. (Such a definition, however, begs many questions itself. For example: how are such attitudes promoted and sustained? Are women themselves immune from them? What *is* 'women's flourishing'?) For a clear, and critical, introduction to some philosophical issues encountered here, see J. Grimshaw, *Feminist Philosophers: Women's Perspectives on Philosophical Traditions* (London, Harvester Wheatsheaf, 1986), esp. ch. 2 and 7. I hope it will be clear from what I have written that I do not share Hampson's (apparently) essentialist and universalizing views (expressed in Hampson, 'On Power and Gender' and *Theology and Feminism*) that there are fixed 'male' and 'female' approaches to God, human nature, 'power', etc.

till now.[65] The (rightful) concentration in the literature on the profound, and continuing, damage to women from sexual and physical abuse, even in 'Christian' families and churches, and on the seeming legitimation of this by men otherwise committed to disciplined religious practice and the rhetoric of cruciform redemption,[66] shows what a perilous path we are treading here. An undiscriminating adulation of 'vulnerability' might appear to condone, or even invite, such evils. I do not in any way underestimate these difficulties; nor do I wish to make a straightforward *identification* between 'vulnerability' in general (often a dangerous or regrettable state) and the particular notion of spiritual *kenōsis* here under discussion. But what I am suggesting is that there is another, and longer-term, danger to Christian feminism in the *repression* of all forms of 'vulnerability', and in a concomitant failure to confront issues of fragility, suffering or 'self-emptying' except in terms of victimology. And that is ultimately the failure to embrace a feminist reconceptualizing of the power of the cross and resurrection. Only, I suggest, by facing – and giving new expression to – the paradoxes of 'losing one's life in order to save it', can feminists hope to construct a vision of the Christic 'self' that transcends the gender stereotypes we are seeking to up-end.

But what can I mean by this? I know of no better way to express it than by reflection on the practice of prayer, and especially wordless prayer or 'contemplation'.[67] This is to take a few leaps beyond the notion of *kenōsis* as a speculative christological theory about the incarnate life of Jesus; but if the

---

[65]   It would be misleading to suggest it has been completely taboo; indeed, 'vulnerability' in 'mutual relation' (see I. C. Heyward, *The Redemption of God: A Theology of Mutual Relation* (Lanham, MD, University Press of America, 1982); and R. N. Brock, *Journeys by Heart: A Christology of Erotic Power* (New York, Crossroad, 1988)), suffering as purposive (see D. Soelle, *Suffering* (Philadelphia, Fortress Press, 1975)), and ethical 'risk' (S. D. Welch, *A Feminist Ethic of Risk* (Minneapolis, Fortress Press, 1990)) have been significant, though not dominant, themes in recent feminist theological writing. There has also been one specific discussion of *kenōsis* from a feminist dialogue with Buddhism: see C. Keller, 'Scoop Up the Water and the Moon in Your Hands: On Feminist Theology and Dynamic Self-Emptying' in J. B. Cobb and C. Ives (eds.), *The Emptying God: A Buddhist-Jewish-Christian Conversation* (Maryknoll, NY, Orbis, 1990), pp. 102–15.

Much more common in feminist literature, however, is the (wholly understandable) emphasis on 'vulnerability' as an opportunity for masculinist *abuse*: see, for example, M. P. Engel, 'Evil, Sin, and the Violation of the Vulnerable' in S. B. Thistlewaite and M. P. Engel (eds.), *Lift Every Voice: Constructing Christian Theologies from the Underside* (San Francisco, Harper & Row, 1990), pp. 152–64.

[66]   See the chilling cases of abusive Christian fathers documented in A. Imbens and I. Jonker, *Christianity and Incest* (London, Burns & Oates, 1992).

[67]   This dimension of my argument is spelled out in more detail in my forthcoming book on the Trinity, *God, Sexuality and the Self: An Essay 'On the Trinity'* (Cambridge, Cambridge University Press).

majority of New Testament commentators are correct, then the 'hymn' of Philippians 2 was, from the start, an invitation to enter into Christ's extended life in the church, not just to speculate dispassionately on his nature.[68] The 'spiritual' extension of Christic *kenōsis*, then (if we can now favour our third definition from above, that is, the avoidance of all 'snatching' from the outset), involves an ascetical commitment of some subtlety, a regular and willed *practice* of ceding and responding to the divine. The rhythm of this *askēsis* is already inscribed ritually and symbolically in the sacraments of baptism and eucharist; but in prayer (especially the defenceless prayer of silent waiting on God) it is 'internalized' over time in a peculiarly demanding and transformative fashion. If I am asked, then, what Christian feminism must do to avoid emulating the very forms of 'worldly' power we criticize in 'masculinism', I point to this *askēsis*. It might be objected (by an extension of Hampson's original argument, though not one she herself applies), that such a danger is not one confronted by women less fortunate, less affluent and less 'powerful' than such as me. But I do wonder about this. Foucault has shown us that we all wield 'power' in *some* area,[69] however insignificant it may appear to the outside world (power over our children, our aged dependants, even our domestic animals). If 'abusive' human power is thus always potentially within our grasp, how can we best approach the healing resources of a non-abusive divine power? How can we hope to invite and channel it, if not by a patient opening of the self to its transformation?

What I have elsewhere called the 'paradox of power and vulnerability'[70] is I believe uniquely focused in this act of silent waiting on the divine in prayer. This is because we can only be properly 'empowered' here if we cease to set the agenda, if we 'make space' for God to be God. Prayer which makes this 'space' may take a variety of forms, and should not be conceived in an élitist way; indeed, the debarring of 'ordinary' Christians from 'contemplation' has been one of the most sophisticated – and spiritually mischievous – ways of keeping lay women (and men) from exercising religious influence in the western church.[71] Such prayer may use a repeated phrase to

[68]   This point is well made in Sykes' essay in Kee and Long (eds.), *Being and Truth*, esp. pp. 361–5, though Sykes applies it mainly to the practice of the sacraments.
[69]   See Foucault's late essays on power in M. Foucault, *Power/Knowledge* (Brighton, Harvester Press, 1980).
[70]   In Oxford Faculty Lectures, 1991 and 1992; further discussed in my forthcoming book *God, Sexuality and the Self*.
[71]   This is the theme of Tugwell's anti-élitist arguments in S. Tugwell, *Ways of Imperfection* (London, Darton, Longman & Todd, 1984), esp. chs. 9–11. Tugwell is not, however, especially interested in the gender dimensions of his subject matter, and, whilst lauding Julian of Norwich's theology, is deeply scornful of Margery Kempe (see ch. 16 and pp. 109–10).

ward off distractions, or be wholly silent; it may be simple Quaker attentiveness, or take a charismatic expression (such as the use of quiet rhythmic
'tongues'). What is sure, however, is that engaging in any such regular and
repeated 'waiting on the divine' will involve great personal commitment
and (apparently) great personal risk; to put it in psychological terms, the
dangers of a too-sudden uprush of material from the unconscious, too
immediate a contact of the thus disarmed self with God, are not inconsider-
able. To this extent the careful driving of wedges – which began to appear in
the western church from the twelfth century on – between 'meditation'
(discursive reflection on Scripture) and 'contemplation' (this more vulnerable activity of 'space-making'), were not all cynical in their attempts to
keep contemplation 'special'.[72] But whilst risky, this practice is profoundly
transformative, 'empowering' in a mysterious 'Christic' sense; for it is a
feature of the *special* 'self-effacement' of this gentle space-making – this
yielding to divine power which is no worldly power – that it marks one's
willed engagement in the pattern of cross and resurrection, one's deeper
rooting and grafting into the 'body of Christ'. 'Have *this* mind in you',
wrote Paul, 'which was also in Christ Jesus'; the meaning of that elliptical
phrase in Greek still remains obscure, but I am far from being the first
to interpret it in this spiritual sense, as a 'hidden self-emptying of the
heart'.[73]

If, then, these traditions of Christian 'contemplation' are to be trusted,
this rather special form of 'vulnerability' is not an invitation to be battered;
nor is its silence a silenc*ing*. (If anything, if builds one in the courage to give
prophetic voice.) By choosing to 'make space' in this way, one 'practises'
the 'presence of God' – the subtle but enabling presence of a God who
neither shouts nor forces, let alone 'obliterates'. No one can *make* one
'contemplate' (though the grace of God invites it); but it is the simplest

---

[72]   The word 'special' is used by the author of the fourteenth-century *The Cloud of
Unknowing* (ed. J. Walsh (London, SPCK, 1981), p. 115) in this context of entry into
'contemplation'. The work of the sixteenth-century Carmelites, Teresa of Ávila and John
of the Cross, is marked by a particular interest in charting the appropriate moment of
transition from 'meditation' to 'contemplation'. On this, see my discussion in 'Traditions of
Spiritual Guidance: Dom John Chapman OSB (1865–1933) on the Meaning of "Contemplation"' (ch. 2, below) which contains some remarks about the gendered dimension of the
issue.
[73]   This phrase is from the opening sentence of the Syriac *Book of Steps* (fourth to fifth
century), translated in S. Brock (ed.), *The Syriac Fathers on Prayer and the Spiritual Life*
(Kalamazoo, Cistercian Publications, 1987), p. 45. I am grateful to Sebastian Brock for a
helpful discussion of early Syriac treatments of Philippians 2.

thing in the world *not* to 'contemplate', to turn away from that grace. Thus the 'vulnerability' that is its human condition is not about asking for unnecessary and unjust suffering (though increased self-knowledge can indeed be painful); nor is it (in Hampson's words) a 'self-abnegation'. On the contrary, this special 'self-emptying' is not a negation of self, but the place of the self's transformation and expansion into God.

To make such claims as these is clearly to beg many questions. A number of possible misunderstandings (that this prayer is élitist, or the luxury of a leisured class, or an invitation to abuse, or a recipe for political passivity) I have already tried to avert. The 'mystics' of the church have often been from surprising backgrounds, and their messages rightly construed as subversive; their insights have regularly chafed at the edges of doctrinal 'orthodoxy', and they have rejoiced in the coining of startling (sometimes erotically startling) new metaphors to describe their experiences of God. Those who have appealed to a 'dark' knowing beyond speech have thus challenged the smugness of accepted anthropomorphisms for God, have probed (to use the language of contemporary French feminism) to the subversive place of the 'semiotic'.[74]

But no human, contemplative or otherwise, is beyond the reach of either self-deception or manipulation by others; and the spiritual literature of the Christian tradition is rife with examples of male directors who have chosen to confuse this special contemplative 'vulnerability' to the divine with enforced female submission to priestly authority, or to undeserved and unnecessary physical and mental suffering.[75] These problems and dangers can only be confronted, however, by the making of fine, but important, distinctions: between this 'right' vulnerability and mere invitation to abuse;[76] between this contemplative 'self-effacement' and self-destruction or self-repression;[77] between the productive suffering of self-disclosure and

---

[74]   For Kristeva's (Lacanian) appeal to a time preceding the development of language as a source of creativity and feminist subversion, see J. Kristeva, *Desire in Language: A Semiotic Approach to Literature and Art* (Oxford, Basil Blackwell, 1980), and T. Moi's helpful introduction to Kristeva, *The Kristeva Reader* (New York, Columbia University Press, 1986), esp. pp. 12–15.

[75]   See my discussion of this problem in relation to the spritual direction of J.-P. de Caussade, in ' "Femininity" and the Holy Spirit', in M. Furlong (ed.), *Mirror to the Church: Reflections on Sexism* (London, SPCK, 1988), pp. 128–30.

[76]   See the discussion of this point by C. Keller in Cobb and Ives (eds.), *The Emptying God*, pp. 105–6.

[77]   See Soelle's attempt at this in relation to Eckhart's theology in her lecture 'Mysticism-Liberation-Feminism' in D. Soelle, *The Strength of the Weak: Toward a Christian Feminist Identity* (Philadelphia, Westminster Press, 1984), pp. 79–105.

the decentring torture of pain for pain's sake.[78] That the making of these 'crucial' distinctions (and I use the word advisedly) is itself powerful,[79] is a lesson only gradually being learned in white feminist theology – such has been the repression of a productive 'theology of the cross' in the face of continuing disclosures of women's abuse in the *name* of the 'cross'. It is striking, indeed, how much less coy is Black womanist theology about naming the 'difference' between abusive 'suffering' on the one hand, and a productive or empowering form of 'pain' on the other;[80] for Black theology has necessarily never evaded the theological problems of undeserved suffering.

Where, then, finally, does gender find its place in the 'contemplative' reception to the divine I have tried to describe? The answer is in one sense obvious: is not such willed 'passivity' a traditionally 'female' trait? Is not this precisely why 'mystical' literature has so greatly emphasized the huge psychic reversals for men engaged in such 'submission' to the divine? And hence, is not the obvious danger here the one with which we started, that is, Hampson's charge that *kenōsis* may only be 'useful' to men, as a complement to their masculinism? But I have already tried to hint at a way in which I believe the contemplative exercise may take us beyond such existing gender stereotypes, up-ending them in its gradual undermining of *all* previous certainties and dogmatisms. Here, if I am right, is 'power-in-vulnerability', the willed effacement to a gentle omnipotence which, far from 'complementing' masculinism, acts as its undoing. And whilst spiritual *kenōsis*, thus construed, may, in our current cultural climate, be easy for men to avoid altogether, and even easier, perhaps, for women seriously to misconstrue (as 'appropriate' sexual submission), we cannot rest while such implied 'essentialist' visions of gender still exercise us. When Hampson talks of the 'male' God I fear she is thus resting.

---

[78]   For a perceptive – and politically astute – discussion of the deliberate destruction of both language and the personality in the act of torture (in distinction from other forms of productive and religiously motivated suffering), see E. Scarry, *The Body in Pain* (New York, Oxford University Press, 1985), esp. pp. 34–5.

[79]   This is a point made by Nussbaum in her discussion of 'fragility', 'vulnerability', and 'luck' in Greek thought. See M. C. Nussbaum, *The Fragility of Goodness* (Cambridge, Cambridge University Press, 1986), esp. p. xv: 'It occurred to me to ask whether the act of writing about the beauty of human vulnerability is not, paradoxically, a way of rendering oneself less vulnerable and more in control of the uncontrolled elements of life.'

[80]   On this point, see Townes' essay, 'Living in the New Jerusalem' in E. M. Townes (ed.), *A Troubling in My Soul: Womanist Perspectives on Evil and Suffering* (Maryknoll NY, Orbis, 1993), esp. pp. 83–6.

If, moreover, the more speculative christological counterpart of this appeal to *kenōsis* is to be laid bare, it must, as I have hinted, take a form not radically dissimilar from that of the Giessen theologians of the seventeenth century, that is, a form in which the 'emptying' applies to Christ's human nature rather than to the divine. To choose otherwise would be to fall into the manifold incoherencies and difficulties of Thomasius and his descendants, or, with the 'new kenoticists', to reduce God's 'power' to an inherent powerlessness. Yet if we are to avoid the lurking 'docetism' of the Alexandrian tradition, we shall also have to embrace a reading of Chalcedon that owes more to the Christology of the rival school of Antioch, that is, one in which Christ's personal identity (his *hypostasis*) is *confected out* of the 'concurrence' of the human and the divine, not simply *identified with* the invulnerable pre-existent Logos.[81] In other words, what Christ on this view instantiates is the very 'mind' that we ourselves enact, or enter into, in prayer: the unique intersection of vulnerable, 'non-grasping' humanity and authentic divine power, itself 'made perfect in weakness'.

Ultimately, of course, Christian virtue is known by its 'fruits'. Perhaps this is the only final and safe test of 'contemplation', in which activity – I freely admit – so much self-deception, and so much bewilderment and uncertainty, can attend even faithful and regular practice. Strangely, I think this – my practical conclusion about 'fruits' – is the point at which Hampson is most likely to agree with me: our theological conceptions and institutional commitments diverge at many points, but our sense of what feminism aims to gain and display is curiously convergent. What then do we seek in feminist *discretio spirituum*? Love, joy, peace – yes, and all the other Pauline spiritual fruits and gifts; but especially we must add to these: personal empowerment, prophetic resistance, courage in the face of oppression, and the destruction of false idolatry. What Hampson and other post-

---

[81]   This is, I believe, a legitimate (though 'Antiochene' leaning) way of reading the Chalcedonian Definition, granted that the word *hypostasis* does not appear in the Definition until the phrase relating to the 'concurrence' of the natures, and is not explicitly identified with the pre-existent Logos. On the significance of this 'Antiochene' reading, see the important article by A. Baxter, 'Chalcedon, and the Subject in Christ', *Downside Review* 107 (1989), pp. 1–21. The full implications, philosophical and theological, of developing this interpretation of Chalcedon, can unfortunately not be spelled out here; but it is instructive to note that feminist writers on Christology have so far been divided on whether the 'Alexandrian' or 'Antiochene' traditions hold more promise for a feminist standpoint. See P. Wilson-Kastner, *Faith, Feminism, and the Christ* (Philadelphia, Fortress Press, 1983), esp. pp. 83–4, for a position sympathetic to the 'Alexandrian' reading of Chalcedon, and Heyward, *Redemption of God*, esp. pp. 189–92, for a champion of the 'Antiochene' school.

Christians do not believe in any more, however, is the importance of what we may call the narrative 'gap', the *hiatus* of expectant waiting, that is, the precondition of our assimilation of Christ's 'kenotic' cross and resurrection. That this form of waiting often brings bewilderment and pain as the new 'self' struggles to birth, I cannot deny; that it is also transformative and empowering, I affirm; that Christian feminism ignores it at its peril, I have here tried to suggest; and that it is what finally keeps me a Christian as well as a feminist, it has been the task of this chapter to explore.

But what, then, is this 'contemplation' whose exercise proves so vital to the particular form of human empowerment I have here discussed? To a more severely practical consideration of this matter we now turn.

Chapter 2

Traditions of Spiritual Guidance: Dom John Chapman osb (1865–1933) on the Meaning of 'Contemplation'

Few spiritual directors of the modern period[1] have approached the topic of 'contemplation' with such eminently practical and acute insight as the English Benedictine John Chapman, Abbot of Downside 1929–33, and author of the still-influential *Spiritual Letters* (London, 1935; hereafter *SL*).[2] Chapman was primarily a scholar of the New Testament and church history, and his letters of direction were only posthumously collected and published. Moreover, he was a reluctant director: formal spiritual guidance in Counter-Reformation mode is not a traditionally Benedictine occupation, and Chapman's stated aim was to intervene only to the extent of helping another to 'walk unaided'. In practice, however, he was a man with certain distinctive, if controversial, messages about 'contemplative' prayer, and his letters promulgate them with almost missionary force. In what

Originally published in *The Way* 30, 1990, pp. 243–57. Reprinted with permission from the Editors of *The Way*; with light revisions.

I am grateful to Andrew Louth, Phoebe-Ann Caldwell, Janet Morley and Rowan Williams for stray conversations that have helped me in the preparation of this chapter.

[1] Dom Jean Leclercq has identified Chapman as one of the three most important Benedictine spiritual guides of the twentieth century ('Spiritual direction in the Benedictine tradition', *The Way* 27, 1987, 54–64; see p. 61). Whilst more recent (Cistercian) exponents of the 'Centering Prayer' movement have undeniably influenced more souls than Chapman – mainly as the result of developments in communication and the cultural commodification of 'spirituality' – it is striking that their teaching on *The Cloud of Unknowing* and on John of the Cross also owes a great deal to Chapman's influence: see, e.g., Thomas Keating, *Intimacy with God* (New York, 1995).

[2] The pagination given in this chapter is that of the 1976 Sheed and Ward edition. On the details of Chapman's life I cannot here expatiate, although they are obviously of significance for his theory of prayer. Dom Roger Hudleston provided a somewhat hagiographical portrait in the introduction to *SL*; a biography was promised (p. xi) but did not eventuate. It is worth comparing Dom Roger's account with the more critical portrait of Chapman that emerges from Dom Adrian Morey, *David Knowles: A Memoir* (London, 1979), esp. ch 5.

follows I shall enumerate these distinctive theories, and comment on them both appreciatively and critically.

The gender dimensions of Chapman's views – some more covert than others – will also not escape our notice. Chapman is, to be sure, a decidedly odd hero for feminists: his notable distaste for the entire affective realm causes him – as we shall chart – to denigrate 'female mysticism' (so-called) and to misread even his beloved John of the Cross in strangely distorting ways. Yet his evident respect for the many women he directed – not only enclosed contemplative nuns, but also powerful lay women such as Evelyn Underhill – is another dimension of his complex character. His spiritual teaching is thus – simultaneously and paradoxically – *both* an intensely practical guide to the often-bewildering contemplative state of 'empowered vulnerability' (and one that takes women's important part in this activity very seriously indeed), *and* an object lesson in the potentially destructive interpretative manipulation of this guidance for the puposes of reinstantiating a denigratory vision of the stereotypical 'female'. How subtle and complicated is this mixture in Chapman we shall now explore; far from 'feminizing' the peculiarly passive state of 'contemplation' itself, however, Chapman makes 'feminine' precisely what he sees as a false and misleading alternative. But let us start our exegesis from Chapman's own first principles.

Running through Chapman's correspondence are two eminently simple but practical maxims, which one could say form the basis of everything else that he teaches. One is: '*Pray as you can, and do not try to pray as you can't*' (*SL*, 109). An adjunct of this first maxim is not even to 'wish for any other prayer than what God gives'; nor should one struggle to read any books about prayer that do not immediately appeal or speak to one's current state (*SL*, 57). The second maxim is: '*The more you pray, the better it goes*', the converse of which ('the less you pray, the worse it goes') underlines that if prayer stops for any reason, it will be the surest sign that something is amiss. In the case of the 'contemplative' prayer that Chapman describes with such un-canny perceptiveness, 'a very little distraction by worldly things, and quite tiny unfaithfulnesses make it stop suddenly, and it may mean some humiliation and some time before getting it back again' (*SL*, 135; cf. 181).

If these basic maxims of Chapman's are unexceptional (albeit always worthy of repetition), his further views on 'contemplation' involve a de-cidedly controversial – some would say idiosyncratic – reading of John of the Cross, whose views Chapman takes to be normative. The controversy here revolves around the extent to which 'contemplation' (in John of the Cross's sense of a divine infusion of prayer into a passive recipient) may be the preserve of relative 'beginners'; and if so, what are the signs that the pray-er may appropriately abandon discursive scriptural meditation and adopt a simpler and more passive prayer, devoid of mental effort.

Chapman's line on these issues was the following. First, looking afresh at the three crucial passages in John of the Cross where the signs of the onset of 'contemplation' are charted,[3] Chapman points out, quite rightly, that John acknowledges that this shift can occur to some 'recollected' beginners (see *Dark Night* I, viii, 4). However, Chapman then significantly reinterprets and eases the apparently forbidding requirements for the entry into contemplation. For whereas John of the Cross insists, for instance, on a failure of any sense of pleasure (whether over divine or created things), and a continual 'painful care and solicitude about God' (*Dark Night* I, ix), Chapman is inclined to require only two of John's other signs: an inability to meditate, and a persistent sense of dryness (*SL*, 287–8). Already, then, Chapman has 'democratized' contemplation, by subtly redefining the 'essential marks'. He does so, as emerges from the *Letters*, on the basis of years of intensely curious observation of enclosed religious, both men and women, and other lay correspondents (an investigation he approached dispassionately, 'like chemistry'). On this basis Chapman is convinced that 'most Benedictines', 'virtually all contemplative orders', and a goodly number of 'pious' lay people are, whether wittingly or not, already in what John of the Cross calls the 'night of sense'.

What this means is that such people have embarked on the first stages of 'contemplative' prayer, characterized by an arid, emotionally unsatisfying, desire for God. They can no longer 'meditate' (as, for instance, in Ignatius's methods of imaginative or reflective use of scripture); this is no longer possible for them *qua* prayer. This is not to say that they cannot still work out a sermon or essay, say, on the basis of scripture, which Chapman insists that they should continue to do; scriptural reading is never to be abandoned. But discursive and imaginative meditation as a *method of prayer* will not suit all. Anyway, writes Chapman, 'There was little of all this before the 16th century, and none before the 13th' (*SL*, 104). He is right, of course, but no wonder he aroused some feelings of suspicion in Jesuit circles.

The main point at issue here, and the point where Chapman's theory was totally at odds with the Jesuit Poulain's widely-acclaimed *Graces of Interior Prayer* (Eng. tr. London, 1910), is over the indications of this caesura of John of the Cross's between 'meditation' and 'contemplation' – the 'ligature', in

---

[3]   *Ascent of Mt Carmel* II, xiii; *Dark Night* I, ix; *Living Flame of Love* III, 32–6. The English translation used here is that of E. Allison Peers, *The Complete Works of Saint John of the Cross* (London, 1953).

Poulain's parlance. Chapman derides Poulain's suggestion that there needs to be some linking stage, and that increasingly simplified *affective* states lead on – eventually, but rarely – into the 'night of sense' and miraculously high 'mystical' states.[4] On the contrary, says Chapman, it is a simple matter: 'affective' (meditative) prayer stops, because something else – the 'night of sense' is already starting:

> Either the imagination works or it doesn't. If it does, you can meditate; if it won't, you can't. The stoppage IS the Night of the Senses, and the Night of the Senses is *nothing more* than this stoppage, and *nothing else* (SL, 281).

Moreover, insists Chapman, this is a relatively commonplace occurrence. Indeed all of the *Letters* are addressed to people who similarly 'cannot meditate', and yet are equally clearly not in particularly 'high' or 'miraculous' states.

Chapman's controversial views on the onset of 'contemplation' are aligned with a concomitant attitude to that 'hateful, modern and ambiguous' word 'mysticism' (see SL, 297–321, Appendix II: 'What is Mysticism?'). Acknowledging that it *is* a modern word (in contradistinction from 'mystical theology'), Chapman nonetheless chooses to use it in a particular, and again 'democratizing', sense, based on his interpretation of Thomas Aquinas's epistemology. Thus Chapman holds that we all have some dim memory of the 'angelic' cognition Adam possessed before the fall, which was direct intellectual knowledge of God, without reference to material beings through the use of sense and imagination. In 'mysticism' these direct powers of perception are – albeit dimly – reactivated. When this happens (and Chapman claims it can in principle happen to anyone) it is not *necessarily* a 'supernatural' act, that is, a special grace or initiative from God. Rather, it can just be what Chapman calls 'praeternatural mysticism', the (admittedly unusual) re-arousal of that original Adamic cognition. Chapman places the 'nature mysticism' of such as Tennyson and Wordsworth in this category.

However, in the 'contemplation' of the 'night of sense' just discussed, God can and does use the reactivation of this faculty for God's own purposes:

> Consequently, though neither the mystical act nor the mystical faculty are 'supernatural', God can make them the vehicle of supernatural communication . . . a wire along which God can speak to the soul (SL, 309).

---

[4]   See Poulain, *op. cit.*, ch. XIV on the 'ligature', and ch. XV on the 'night of sense'. For Chapman's critique see (in more detail) SL, 280ff.

It may be clear by now that what I have called Chapman's 'democratizing' theories on 'contemplation' and 'mysticism' involved no mere semantic quibbles. They were to find some echoes, certainly, in Abbot Butler's rather differently nuanced *Western Mysticism*, which came out in 1922;[5] but they still flew in the face of the prevalent understanding of John of the Cross at the time, which preserved even the first of his 'dark nights' for a minority élite.[6] To the recipients of Chapman's letters, however, his analysis must have brought immense relief and encouragement; for many of them had, according to him, already spent long and painful years in the 'night of sense', inappropriately berating themselves for their lack of fervour and inattentiveness to meditation. For them, meditation was a 'physical impossibility'; but Chapman could reassure them that their prayer had probably already turned into something else, so 'delicate' and 'obscure', however (to use John of the Cross's language), as even to elude their notice.

It is at this point that Chapman bequeaths his greatest legacy; for unlike John of the Cross, whose practical advice here is consummately vague (if full of pregnant hints), Chapman actually tells his correspondents *precisely what to do*, what to expect, and how not to become disillusioned, in the prayer of the 'night of sense'. In the West, perhaps only the author of the fourteenth-century *Cloud of Unknowing* (whose practical hints Chapman also commends) approaches Chapman's specificity and acute psychological insights in this area. Again, however, we have to admit, as Chapman appears not to,[7] that his advice is both far more precise than that of John of the Cross, and at points close to contradicting him. Thus, while Chapman *spells out* – well beyond what John does – how one can be praying in the most intense way whilst simultaneously appearing to be 'doing nothing and wasting [one's] time' (*Dark Night*, I, x, 4), he also instructs the pray-er in a technique for dealing with *distractions*, of which John tells nothing, at least nothing explicit. Indeed, John gives the impression that the soul should fall naturally into a state of complete passivity, peace and inactivity, *devoid* of all anxiety and

---

[5]   Butler's work shared with Chapman's the stress on the relative ordinariness of contemplation, but there their agreement largely stops. (See *SL*, 67, 278–9, 328 n.1, for hints of Chapman's departure from Butler). For a detailed account of Butler's book and its reception, see Rowan Williams, 'Butler's *Western mysticism*: towards an assessment', *The Downside Review* 102, 1984, 197–215.

[6]   See Chapman's remarks *SL*, 71; and more fully in his art. 'Mysticism (Christian, Roman Catholic)' in ed. J. Hastings, *Encyclopaedia of Religion and Ethics* (Edinburgh, 1908–26), esp. cols. 100a–101b.

[7]   See esp. 'Mysticism', cols. 98a–100a, where Chapman simply weaves his own views and observations into his comparative account of Teresa and John of the Cross.

distraction (ibid.; and *Ascent of Mt Carmel*, II, xv; *Living Flame of Love* III, 34, 35, 38). No wonder then that Chapman's correspondents (who could not meditate) doubted that they could 'contemplate' either. Such ease of transition would indeed be rare.

Chapman's advice, in contrast, runs thus. First establish that your inability to meditate is not just 'laziness' or 'lukewarmness' (*SL*, 289, following *Dark Night* I, ix, 1). A good test here, says Chapman, is to try and say the 'Our Father' slowly, as a prayer, and really think out what each phrase means. If this is impossible (at any rate without feeling that one has stopped *praying* in order to think), then one should stop trying to meditate: the 'night of sense' has begun.

However it is quite impossible, Chapman acknowledges (as John of the Cross does not), to wish oneself without further ado into a state of complete passivity to God's 'delicate' act of contemplation. The active, analytical part of the mind and the ever-ebullient imagination bring their different sorts of distractions, and these Chapman is careful to distinguish (*SL*, 290). In the first case there are the distractions which 'take one right away', that is, stop the prayer by causing one actively to start thinking about them, and so detach the faculty which was communing with God from its undertaking. In the second case, however, there is another, and different, sort of distraction: the 'harmless meanderings of the *imagination alone*, while the intellect [remains] . . . idle and empty, and the will is fixed on God'.

How, then, to ignore the meaningless meanderings of the imagination, yet also avert the more serious and substantive distractions? Here Chapman gives his invaluable advice for 'beginners' (and he adds, 'Let us be thankful if we are like this for no more than twenty years' (*SL*, 289)!). The idea is to use repetitive but mechanical 'acts' (a phrase from a psalm, or just a general expression of wanting God), not *as* the prayer, but as a sort of accompanying 'drone' to keep the imagination occupied. Elsewhere, Chapman describes this as like throwing a bone to a dog – 'a sop to Cerberus' (*SL*, 60). Not only is the imagination thus mechanically stilled, but the 'drone' also helps prevent the mind from operating discursively; thus the (empty) intellect is left facing a 'blank', with the will gently holding it there. This 'blank', or 'nothing in particular' is, as Chapman likes to put it to startle, 'God, of course; for we *know* really that "nothing" [in this case] means "the ALL"' (*SL*, 94). The imagination naturally still tends to run around chaotically; but with a bit of practice with the (unfeeling) 'acts', can be largely ignored. Anyway, 'Provided these imaginations are not *wilful* they don't matter in the least' (*SL*, 58).

The prayer then consists in cleaving to God in what does indeed seem a mindless and 'idiotic' state; as when one is trying to fall asleep, and attempting to avoid thinking of anything in particular, so too then the imagination throws up a similar jumble of random images.

Now this sort of advice about distractions in 'contemplation' is of course not unfamiliar to readers of *The Cloud of Unknowing* (chs. 32, 36–40), or to those cognizant of the traditions and techniques of the Eastern Jesus prayer (to which Chapman does not allude, since this material was little known in the West at the time). What Chapman does do, however, is to align his advice very precisely to John of the Cross's epistemology, which, unlike the *Cloud*'s[8] locates the faculty of prayer and communion with God in the non-discursive 'higher' intellect, supported by the will. The body, the senses, the imagination and all 'feelings' associated with them, are seen as radically disjunct, and wholly insignificant to the workings of this prayer (a point to which we shall return later). 'Aridity', that is, *dry* emotionally unsatisfying conditions, are likely to be the norm (Chapman jokes about 'God's "Infra-red" rays', *SL*, 72); and the more distracted and unsatisfied, even 'anxious', one feels about one's prayer, the better, for thence comes humility. The 'night of sense' is, after all, according to John of the Cross, the *purgation* of sense, of the reliance on positive feeling states in prayer.

What Chapman has done, then, is to gloss and amplify John of the Cross's themes of 'darkness', 'dryness' and 'strangeness' (*Dark Night* I, ix–x) with the explicit admission that the 'lower' part of the self will still be disconcertingly chaotic and active in this prayer, producing distinct feelings of 'worry', 'anxiety' and 'bewilderment' (see *SL*, 42); on none of this does John himself expatiate. At the same time, however, and at some indefinable 'higher' level, there will be what Chapman calls the 'blank' (or, as John himself phrases it, not 'being able to think of any particular thing': *Dark Night* I, ix, 6). This, according to Chapman, will in time, or just sporadically, give way to a state more close to that described by John of the Cross: a 'peaceful and loving attentiveness toward God...*without anxiety*' (*Dark Night* I, x, 4, my emphasis). Thus will emerge, says Chapman, at least for some people, a consciousness 'of being in the presence of Something undefinable, yet above all things desirable, without any the more arriving at being able to think about it or speak about it...' (*SL*, 291). There will be other observable effects, too, though ones probably perceived more outside the time of prayer or indeed by others: a unifying sense of all things being directed to

---

[8]   *The Cloud* (see esp. ch. 4) makes a different sort of disjunction in the self from that of John of the Cross, dividing the *will* (which is the faculty of loving and contemplating) from the *intellect* (to which 'God is forever unknowable'). Chapman sometimes passes over this crucial difference (see *SL*, 149–50), but at *SL*, 257 points it out.

the will of God, a cessation of 'multiple resolutions' (so that resolutions now 'make themselves'), and, above all, the fruits of the Christian virtues. This last point is Chapman's acid test: 'I have *always* said that I cannot admit *any other* criterion of prayer than its effects.'

But is this prayer demonstrably 'Christian'? The question is not lost on Chapman, who admits that in earlier years he himself thought John of the Cross more 'Buddhist' than 'Christian'. Moreover, to our own eclectic generation, the resemblances of Chapman's practical advice to (say) the techniques of Transcendental Meditation will be obvious. Chapman's background theory of 'praeternatural' mysticism made him, of course, relaxed about such inter-religious comparisons (see, e.g. *SL* 65–6, 253). Yet he was also convinced, rightly or wrongly, that the prayer he described made people into 'good Catholics', even doctrinally (see *SL*, 66, 123–4), and that far from leading one away from 'Christ's humanity', as it might seem to do, this prayer was actually an imitation of Jesus's own evident need for solitude and extended time in prayer (see *SL*, 78, 314–15). As for the duty of Christian petitionary prayer, Chapman says little, and most surprisingly for him, offers no precise theory of its relation to the 'contemplation' he is describing. But he admits that 'more and more' he has come to the conclusion that 'contemplation' makes one bolder in one's petitions, and that one should ask God for 'everything' necessary for oneself and others; and 'make up your mind that you will get it (not because you deserve it, but because God is good)' (*SL*, 99).

I have dealt at length with Chapman's theory and description of 'beginners'' contemplation in the prayer of the purgation of sense, for the greater part of his correspondence is concerned with it. There are a number of letters, however (specifically nos. XXVI–XXVII and LVII) which deal with the symptoms and effects of the much more rare 'night of spirit', in which, according to John of the Cross, the higher realm of spirit is purged with disorienting and sometimes terrible effects (see *Dark Night*, Bk II). The 'darkness' now designates not merely noetic blankness (as in the Eastern Dionysian tradition inherited here), but a new, personal sense of 'affliction and torment' (*Dark Night* II, v, 2).[9]

Most of Chapman's remarks here are simple reassurance. 'What you describe seems to be not *abnormal* but *unusual*' (*SL*, 85), or, 'It is all right.... Don't worry' (*SL*, 140). But also he underlines: 'No one goes in

---

[9]   See Andrew Louth's illuminating discussion on the differences between the sanjuanist and earlier Eastern views of divine 'darkness' in *The Origins of the Christian Mystical Tradition* (Oxford, 1981), ch. 9.

for contemplative prayer without violent trials' – whether externally or internally presented (*SL*, 84). Working from John of the Cross's own analysis in Book II of the *Dark Night* (esp. chs. v–viii), Chapman again both gives practical amplification of it, and also further emphasizes the message of a fundamental division in the self. Thus, two characteristic signs of the 'night of spirit' – the feelings of 'being off the main road, or isolated' (*SL*, 86) and of 'personal impurity' and 'nothingness' (ibid.) – are fully to be expected here (see *Dark Night*, II, vii, for example). But, according to Chapman's reading of John, the 'real ME' is 'above all feelings of discomfort, or despondency or doubt'. Consequently, if you have such feelings, causing depression or anxiety, disown them...' (*SL*, 87). Other symptoms will be a sense of stupidity or failure of concentration (see *Dark Night*, II, viii, 1), a sense of affliction by God (see ibid. II, vii, 7), and even despair and the fear of collapse (see ibid. II, vi, 5). Chapman treats of all these in letter LVII, and also of what he sees as a more modern symptom – 'temptations against the Faith' (*SL*, 142), Such humiliations are, however, all the intentional acts of the divine sculptor (one of Chapman's favoured images) 'carving us into the likeness of His son' (*SL*, 143).

We see here that Chapman's reflections on the 'night of spirit' can at times take a moving christological turn, and it is significant that it is only and precisely at these points that he softens his otherwise staunch demand to 'disown' feelings of any kind. For here he concedes that, though we ought to 'aim at' a contempt for suffering, such suffering is only real suffering if we hate it and wish it would go away (*SL*, 157). In this, Christ's example in the Garden of Gethsemane shows that such a hatred of suffering is not incompatible even with divine perfection: 'He prayed that the chalice might be taken away, – to show that the feeling of hating suffering, and feeling it unbearable, is a *part of perfection* for us, as it is a part of our weakness of nature' (ibid.). The appropriate and 'perfect' response to all such suffering, however, Chapman underlines, is a sort of 'abandonment to God'. For 'Everything that happens to us, inside and outside, is God's touch' (*SL*, 163). With this subject of 'abandonment' we turn to the last of Chapman's central themes.

In 1920 (see letter XVII) Chapman first wrote of having started to read the eighteenth-century Jesuit de Caussade's *L'Abandon à la Providence divine*. He describes it then as 'extraordinarily good' (*SL*, 62), and thereafter de Caussade's doctrine of *abandon* becomes the *Leitmotif* of Chapman's letters, a sort of summation of everything else he is trying to say. To agree thus with a Jesuit gave Chapman special satisfaction: he himself had not survived the Jesuit novitiate (perhaps unsurprisingly in the light of his lack of attraction to Ignatian methods of meditation, and his profound distrust of 'affectivity').

He had also at times, to his chagrin, been taken by Jesuit acquaintances to be 'run[ning] down the Exercises of St. Ignatius';[10] but in fact he underscores that de Caussade's doctrine of 'abandonment to divine providence' can be seen to be derived wholly from Ignatius's 'simple and sublime teaching ... : *Sume et suscipe, Domine, universam meam libertatem ...* ', the prayer in the *Exercises* which delivers the whole self into God's possession.[11]

But what did de Caussade mean by 'abandon' or 'the sacrament of the present moment' (his other celebrated phrase)? According to Chapman, the doctrine is not as simple as it seems. It is not, for instance, merely passive, apathetic (or 'quietistic') acceptance of everything that happens to one. Instead, it requires a positive and participative intention to will God's will for one at this moment, and to accept (just for *this* moment) that whatever is befalling one is indeed God's will. Thus:

> We can be perfect here and now by being exactly as God wishes us to be here and now: perfection is not an aim to be realized in a dim and doubtful future, but it is for this minute ... Here, I venture to think, is Père de Caussade's novel contribution to ascetical literature.[12]

This subtle but profound doctrine seems to inspire Chapman's own more colourful images for the inexhaustible and pervasive presence of God's love in all that we do. Thus we are as 'fish in water'; we are carried 'in God's arms', but 'so close to His Heart that [we] cannot see His Face'; in all things 'His hand [is] upon us'; so that finally 'It is one long act of love – not of my love to God, but of His to me. It is always going on – but in prayer you put yourself into it by an act of faith' (*SL*, 46).

I have dealt earlier with the contentious nature of Chapman's 'democratization' of contemplation and his reading of John of the Cross's signs of the 'ligature'. My own view is that Chapman gives what is certainly one *plausible* account of John of the Cross's views on the transition into contemplation (especially as read from *The Dark Night*), and that, by amplifying

---

[10]   The remark appears in Chapman's article 'J. P. de Caussade', *The Dublin Review* 188, 1931, 1–15; see the note on p. 12. The postscript about hating to make enemies among 'the S.J.s' (at *SL*, 81) is relevant here; Chapman however could also underscore that 'nothing could be more opposed than the Benedictine and Jesuit methods' (*SL*, 23).

[11]   The whole prayer, from the 'Contemplation for Achieving Love' runs: 'Take, Lord, into Your possession, my complete freedom of action, my memory, my understanding and my entire will, all that I have, all that I own: it is Your gift to me, I now return it to You. It is all Yours, to be used simply as you wish. Give me Your Love and Your grace; it is all I need' (*The Spiritual Exercises of Saint Ignatius*, tr. T. Corbishley, SJ (Wheathampstead, Herts., 1973), 80.)

[12]   Art. cit., *The Dublin Review* 188, 1931, 6.

the matter of how continous distractions are to be expected in 'beginners" contemplation, Chapman affords to many relieved correspondents the opportunity to give up fruitless and frustrating meditation. The more important issue here, then, is the good pastoral consequence of Chapman's advice, rather than the hermeneutical quibble over John of the Cross's precise meaning. However, it must be admitted that if we turn to such passages as *Ascent of Mt Carmel* II, xv, 1–2, we find advice that more readily supports Poulain's thesis of a sort of transition stage between meditation and contemplation, such that when contemplation proper begins it is '*without* [the soul] in any way exercising its faculties . . . with respect to particular acts' (ibid., 2, my emphasis; and see *Living Flame of Love* III, 32–4).[13] Perhaps we must simply concede a level of ambiguity in John of the Cross on this point. But does it matter? Surely not as much as Chapman's more fundamental maxim: 'Pray as you can and [not] . . . as you can't.' Moreover, it may be worth noting, from a feminist perspective, that the somewhat obsessive interest in qualifications for 'contemplation' (shown by John of the Cross and Chapman alike) is something almost exclusively found in male writers, and then only from roughly the thirteenth century on.[14] The reasons for the more continuous and integrative sense of progress found in women 'mystical theologians' such as Julian of Norwich or (very differently) Teresa of Ávila are complex. One might argue that the posture of 'passivity' was already assumed, culturally, for women of their times and thus involved no sudden or demarcated *reversal*. Although this may be part of the gender picture, the full reality could be more complex: Teresa, after all, was forced (by uncomprehending male directors) to continue with imaginative scriptural meditation long after it had ceased to be fruitful for her. In her case, it was seemingly a (male) resistance to her dangerous potential *empowerment* through simpler forms of prayer that kept her from being 'allowed' to pass through to 'contemplation', until, that is, she was forcefully flooded by it in powerful psycho-physical form. Of such physical manifestations, as we shall now see, Chapman is exceedingly scornful.

This brings us to an important point of debate and criticism of Chapman's views: his understanding of a radical bifurcation in the self, and his concomitant disavowal of any significance to 'feelings' or bodily effects in prayer. We have already touched on this briefly, but Chapman's position, again based

---

[13]   Chapman does admit there may sometimes be a 'wobbly' stage between meditation and contemplation (*SL*, 327) but insists it 'is not recognized by St John of the Cross' and 'I don't believe in it . . .'.

[14]   This Western development is illuminatingly charted by Simon Tugwell, *Ways of Imperfection* (London, 1984), chs. 9–11.

on a *selective* use of texts from John of the Cross, needs some further explication.

Appealing to John of the Cross's sharp distinction between 'sense' and 'spirit', and then, also with John, identifying the ('higher') intellect and supporting will as the receptors of contemplation, Chapman dismisses all 'images' and 'emotions' as 'peripheral' and 'not me' (*SL*, 76). As for bodily effects – visions, levitations, or the like – these are equally irrelevant; indeed, in a most revealing article on 'Mysticism' that Chapman was persuaded to write for Hastings' *Encyclopedia of Religion and Ethics*,[15] Teresa of Ávila is lengthily berated for confusing progress in prayer with changes in physical or psychological accompaniments, and so fares dismally in comparison with John of the Cross. In the same article, the twelfth-century visionary Hildegard of Bingen is damned with faint praise as 'attribut[ing] to a divine source much curious information'; and the fourteenth-century Julian of Norwich merits, extraordinarily, only a passing mention amongst other (quickly dismissed) women mystics: for 'Delusions are ... exceedingly common in such cases.' A connected package of assumptions thus begins to emerge: the dismissal of bodily effects of any sort, along with 'sentiment', 'emotions' and 'feelings' (all of which we note are undifferentiatedly identified), and the connection of all these with a denigrated 'female mysticism'. The 'real "me"', in contrast, is 'not feeling and sentiment and worry and suffering' (*SL*, 85), but exists at the '*highest* point of the soul' (ibid.), called variously the 'higher intellect', the 'ground' of the soul (as in Blosius) or its 'apex' (Francis de Sales) (*SL*, 260). It is on this understanding, of course, that Chapman can urge someone undergoing the 'night of spirit' to accept and '*despise*' even feelings of incipient madness as if they were happening to 'someone else' (*SL*, 84).

There are a number of points which need addressing here. At the practical level, first, there is the danger that Chapman's superbly effective method for dealing with 'harmless' distractions (and the method is based precisely on this dualistic notion of the self, as we saw), may become so mechanically established that material from the 'lower' part of the self, which on occasions may *need* to be attended to, is either ignored or repressed. Part of the trouble here is that Chapman has no cognizance of the psychoanalytic categories that we now tend to wield freely, and in which this objection has to be couched. In these terms, however, one could call the contemplation of the 'night of sense' a state of willed 'disassociation', in which the 'unconscious' is released almost as in a dream. Such unconscious material will – at least in a Jungian understanding – be deeply

---

[15] Art. cit. (n. 6 above), see cols. 98a–99a.

significant for the purposes of the 'integration' of the self, whether or not it is reflected upon during the time of prayer. But if, in that prayer, one is simultaneously courting the release of such unconscious material, and yet also refusing or even repressing it, there may be dangerous psychological consequences. Indeed one cannot help wondering whether the 'anxiety' of which Chapman constantly speaks is not a symptom of this. Yet to correspondents suffering anxiety-states, the message is simply repeated: 'Put up with them – they are not really "you"' (see *SL*, 89).

This is indeed a spirituality of lonely 'iron heroism'. But is it fully true to John of the Cross's intentions? This is our next question, and again, not a simple one to answer. There is certainly no doubt that John of the Cross makes dramatically disjunctive remarks about 'bodily sense' on the one hand and 'spiritual things' on the other: this forms the very basis of his theory of the two 'nights'. Thus, in a section of *The Ascent of Mt Carmel* to which Chapman regularly alludes, John can utter such remarks as '. . . the bodily sense is as ignorant of spiritual things as is a beast of rational things, and even more so' (*Ascent of Mt Carmel* II, xi, 2). All 'corporeal visions' and 'feeling in respect to . . . the senses' are thus to be 'rejected' (ibid. II, xi, 5–6), for they could equally well be of the devil as of God. Likewise, the workings of the 'interior bodily senses' (imagination and 'fancy') must be 'cast out from the soul' (ibid. II, xii, 3). John can even on occasion use the violent language of 'annihilation' of the lower faculties when discussing the entry into pure contemplation (*Dark Night* II, iv, 2).

But there is another side to John of the Cross's position which Chapman wholly fails to enunciate, perhaps because his reading of him focuses so exclusively on these transitional 'ligature' passages, with their admittedly stern disjunctions and warnings of self-delusion. Yet the whole point of the disjunction of sense and spirit is their successive and eventual purgation, so that in due time the soul may be transformed, 'clothed with the new man . . . in the *newness of sense*' (*Dark Night* II, iii, 3, my emphasis). Likewise, when John talks of the faculties of the soul being 'perfectly annihilated', we know he is using hyperbole, for the synonym for 'annihilated' is 'calmed'; the same passage ends with a vision of how all the 'energies and affections of the soul' are ultimately to be '*renewed* into a Divine temper and Divine delight' (*Dark Night* II, iv, 2, my emphasis).[16] Indeed, the whole of the *Spiritual Canticle* and *Living Flame of Love* (to which, significantly, Chapman makes very little allusion) are about how, once both the bodily senses and

[16]   The point is of course most famously expressed in the lines at *Ascent of Mt Carmel* I, xiii, 11: 'In order to arrive at having pleasure in everything, desire to have pleasure in nothing', etc.

the spiritual faculties of the soul are emptied and purged, the 'spiritual senses' come into their own in union, and the language of feeling returns at this higher level with all the daring force of erotic metaphor.

It has to be admitted, I think, that John remains fundamentally ambiguous about the ultimate significance of the body *per se* (though a fascinating treatment by Alain Cugno of 'bodily' themes in John of the Cross vividly illustrates how differently from Chapman one may read him given alternative philosophical presuppositions).[17] On the subject of 'senses' and 'feelings', however, John is infinitely more subtle, nuanced – and positive – than Chapman's analysis admits. For Chapman omits to see the whole matter in the light of the ultimate and integrative goal of the self's transformation into God.

For Chapman, however, as we have shown, 'feelings' are not only no necessary sign of progress in prayer, and thus on the whole better ignored (both of which points are indeed made by John of the Cross), but, more radically, they are not even part of 'me' (see *SL*, 175) – they have no ultimate significance in the constituency of the self. The *opprobrium* that Chapman accords to 'feelings', we note, allows him to make no convincing distinction between 'sentimentality' (for which Thérèse of Lisieux is chided), 'emotions' (passing states of tonality which may have various causes), and what might be called the core affective constituent of the soul – residing in the will, in the Western Augustinian tradition which John of the Cross inherits. Yet John himself devotes much of the last part of *The Ascent of Mt Carmel* (III, xvi ff.) to the subject of the *purgation* of this affective organ for the purposes of its divine transformation and proper 'rejoicing' in God. Chapman talks much of the transitional 'empty will', but not of the (affective) joy for which this emptiness is destined.

We know, of course, that something projective (indeed emotive!) is afflicting Chapman here in the negativity he accords to 'feeling'; for the subject becomes muddled up with two other objects of scorn – Protestants and women mystics. '*Feelings*,' he expostulates, 'Protestants depend upon them ... ' (*SL*, 99); as for 'ecstasies', they are 'commoner in women than in men, and are more frequent in persons of feeble intellect...'.[18] Nor is it a coincidence, surely, that the subject of sexuality at no point emerges into explicit discussion in Chapman's correspondence. We may put this down to

---

[17] See Alain Cugno, *St John of the Cross* (Eng. tr. London, 1982), ch. 6. The author at points acknowledges his debt to the Jewish philosopher Emmanuel Lévinas.

[18] Art. cit. 'Mysticism', col. 99a. See also the crushing end to a letter to a (woman) correspondent: 'As to visions, they are rarely to be trusted. Women have them...' (*SL*, 108). It is worth noting that the distrust of visions is *not* linked to a stereotyping of 'female mysticism' in John of the Cross himself.

the coyness of his age; but it is a startling omission, as anyone seriously engaged in non-discursive prayer will testify. It involves, of course, the most curious of all Chapman's *excerptions* from John of the Cross's writing; for at no point does Chapman even mention the poetry around which John's entire corpus is constructed, a poetry rejoicing in the erotic metaphors of the *Song of Songs*. Chapman has nothing whatever to tell us about the connection between sexual desire and the desire for God; John of the Cross has – at least implicitly – a great deal.

To conclude: Chapman's *Spiritual Letters* have been justly influential. His practical and perceptive advice on 'beginners'' contemplation is almost unmatched in its charting of the unchartable. 'The intellect is facing a blank and the will follows it' (*SL*, 76); this 'near nonsense' of Chapman's, as Sebastian Moore has described it, this love affair with a 'blank', probes to the heart of what the contemplative has to express if she/he is to speak in any way adequately of God.[19] More than one English generation, then, both Roman Catholic and Anglican, has taken Chapman's reading of John of the Cross as normative, has seen John through Chapman's lens. In this essay I have attempted to show at what points Chapman in fact adjusts, amplifies, excerpts from – even distorts – John's original meaning. True to his Benedictinism, Chapman is eclectic, forging his own synthesis.[20] It is a brilliant and insightful reading of John of the Cross; but it is not the whole picture. Let us call it 'sanjuanism with a stiff upper lip'.

What, then, has Chapman *not* told us? His account of 'contemplation' – for all its extraordinary practical acuity – requires a more deeply realistic excursus on the messy entanglement of authoritative claims to divine power, on the one hand, and of human abuses on the other; of frail human sexuality, on the one hand, and of the divine erotic allure on the other; of creative gender play, on the one hand, and of gender prescription on the other. Thus it is time to look more closely at this deep problem of discernment that we have unearthed: the profoundest levels of 'contemplative' activity do not escape the constraints (sometimes distorting or harmful constraints) of the 'frail earthern vessels' in which they are carried. To this task of discernment we now turn, adjusting our gaze to the more inclusive theme of human 'creaturehood' before God.

[19] See Sebastian Moore, 'Some principles for an adequate theism', *The Downside Review* 95, 1977, 201–13.
[20] See Jean Leclercq, art. cit. (n. 1 above), p. 63, and also the citation from Benedict's *Rule* on p 54. Chapman's *SL* draw on a wide range of authorities at points, including Evagrius, the Macarian homilies, Thomas Aquinas, *The Cloud*, Teresa of Ávila, Ignatius of Loyola, as well as John of the Cross and Père de Caussade.

Chapter 3

CREATUREHOOD BEFORE GOD: MALE AND FEMALE

'The human soul comes directly from God, and therefore finds its happiness by returning direct to God', writes Thomas Aquinas (X *Quodlibets*, viii. I). The Christian tradition presents no single normative understanding of what it means to be a creature; indeed it is not even clear to me that there exists a *uniquely* 'Christian' standpoint on creatureliness: the quotation from Aquinas is sufficient to remind us of the lasting entanglement of the Neoplatonic theme of 'return' with the Nicaean insistence on a free personal creation *ex nihilo*; and further paradoxes confront us with the realization that even creation *ex nihilo* is difficult to justify from Scripture alone.[1] But at the heart of any Christian doctrine of creaturehood must surely lie, as perhaps Aquinas' theology illuminates above all, the notion of a radical, and qualitatively distinct, *dependence* of the creature on God. It is this constellating theme of creaturely dependence, along with what I shall argue have been its fatal cultural admixtures for women in Christian patriarchal society, which I wish to explore in this chapter.

My analysis will employ what may seem to some an untidy combination of themes from Christian iconography and spirituality, psychoanalytic theory, and secular and theological feminism, as well as from the more usual resources of biblical and systematic theology. Such messiness is however nothing but the methodological counterpart of the equally messy entanglement of the theme of creaturely dependence on God with *different* sorts of human dependence. Official doctrinal formulations and theological discussion on 'creatureliness' traditionally ignore or repress reflection on these entanglements, and hence the need to probe to the 'soft underbelly' of the doctrine, to expose by reference to popular symbolism and spiritual

From *Theology* 93 (1990), pp. 343–53, with light revisions. © Sarah Coakley.
[1] The interpretation of 2 Macc. 7.28 is disputed.

practice the wider ramifications of the theme of 'dependence'. Dorothee Soelle has posed the necessary questions succinctly:

> It seems to me that at the core of all feminist philosophy or theology there lies this matter of 'dependency' ... Is it a good thing to make oneself emotionally independent, or would this only lead us to the position of the male with his superficial ties who would not dare attack the ideological independence of the male heroes? What does it mean anthropologically to be dependent? What does it mean in social life? The area covered by this inter-feminist debate is also the area where decisions have to be made in theory. Is this dependency only a repressive inheritance from the past or is it part of the simple fact that we are created?[2]

I have elsewhere[3] sought to describe and explicate – in trinitarian terms – the unique sense of creaturely dependence that silent prayer inculcates, a dependence unlike any other, for in it what is experienced as noetic blankness is theologically explained as 'that-without-which-there-would-be-nothing-at-all'.[4] This then is radical, absolute – and so intellectually ungraspable – creaturely dependence; to grasp it would be to make God into an entity. But God is by definition ungraspable, and towards God the dependent creature yearns inchoately, with 'the restless heart' of quasi-erotic unfulfilment. The recurring metaphor is that of 'ascent' to divine intimacy (whether Gregory of Nyssa's dark operation of the 'spiritual senses', for instance, or Bernard of Clairvaux's more openly erotic 'kiss of the mouth'); and the undeniable interconnection of sexual desire and contemplative desire for God is celebrated in the elaboration of the themes of the *Song of Songs* from Origen to St John of the Cross. But the unresolved antinomy between the (acceptable) erotic desire for the divine on the one hand, and actual relationships with people of the opposite sex on the other, is as tense, if not tenser, than in the Platonic writings from which Christianity inherited it.[5]

Now the paradox for the feminist who surveys this material, and who herself experiences the tug of the dependent heart on the divine, is this. The

---

[2]   In J.-B. Metz and E. Schillebeeckx (eds.), *God as Father?* (Edinburgh and New York 1981) pp. 73–4.
[3]   In *We Believe in God* (London 1987) ch.7, as a member of the Church of England Doctrine Commission.
[4]   Here I acknowledge my indebtedness to Sebastian Moore's argument in 'Some Principles for an Adequate Theism', *The Downside Review*, 95 (1977) pp. 201–13.
[5]   See for instance Diotima's speech in Plato's *Symposium*: one 'ascends' from actual love affairs finally to the vision of 'the beautiful'.

metaphor of 'ascent' is a metaphor of power and hierarchy; the Cappadocian doctrine of the Trinity announces on the one hand the absolute equality of the 'persons' according to the *homoousian* principle; but in describing the incorporation of the soul into the divine life through prayer, Basil of Caesarea's debt to Neoplatonic subordinationism is scarcely veiled:[6] the Spirit catches one *up* so that one may ascend to the level of the Son, and then via him glimpse something of the dizzier heights of the Father's glory. The Father, of course, is in this Eastern vision the convergent 'source' and 'cause' of the other two 'persons'. This hierarchical Godhead is however symbolically charged with social implications for women: for how is the ceding to the Spirit in the contemplative quest not also implicitly, for a woman, the ceding to potentially repressive and patriarchal structures in church and society?

In the medieval West, as we shall explore a little later, the same trend of dominance is associated with a particular, negative stereotyping of 'female mysticism', arising out of the male mystic's quest to transmute his sexual energy towards God. In search of the dependent creaturely perfection of his ('female') soul, the male contemplative projects onto the real women who might deflect him from this goal all the negativity of his still unresolved desires. Even Bernard of Clairvaux, lauded by Jean Leclercq for his won-drously healthy 'sublimation' of the erotic towards God,[7] can warn his monks that it is quite impossible to have a normal relationship with any woman without it ending in an illicit sexual liaison. This reflects the western Augustinian background we shall explore briefly below: if woman is per-ceived as intrinsically 'bodily', then she is either a temptress or a 'female' type of saint, also bodily, emotional, 'hysterical'.

We must attempt, then, to *distinguish* more clearly and consciously between different sorts of dependence; not, I believe, because we can ever hope finally to disentangle them, to arrive at the tidy isolation of a pure contemplative dependence on God; but because it is as well to bring to consciousness how easily one fades into another, how the infinitely 'subtle' and 'obscure' operation of the divine on the dependent creature is entwined with the deepest hopes and fears about family relationships, about sexuality, power and death.

Consider then the following distinguishable types of 'dependence'. Alongside what we have called the 'absolute dependence' of the creature on God brought to special consciousness in contemplation, we must range:

---

[6]   See *On the Holy Spirit* 9.23.
[7]   Jean Leclercq, *Monks and Love in Twelfth-Century France* (Oxford 1979).

the complete physical dependence of the newborn infant on the mother (or other primary caretaker) for nourishment, warmth and cleanliness; the no less significant emotional and psychological dependence of small, growing, and even grown-up children on parents and parental figures; the economic dependence of families (and so often women) on the wage-earner and bread-winner (or in the case of the unemployed or disabled, on the state or charity); the 'dependence' of servile subjugation or imprisonment in countries subject to oppressive regimes; the dependence of prisoners on their captors; of the tortured on their torturers; the emotional, psychological and sexual dependence of the spouse, the lover – or rather differently, the infatuated – on the beloved; the 'dependence' of slothful mental habit and failure in critical thinking which is the opposite of 'independence of mind'; the arrested infantilism of neurotic dependence; the dependence on drugs (of whatever kind); the dependence we are all subject to, in events beyond our control – the elements, accidents, disease; the dependence on others for sustenance and care in sickness, handicap or mental disturbance; and finally the yielding to the unknown in the 'dependence' of death.

These intertwined themes of dependence find powerful Christian icono-graphic expression.[8] A vivid example of the sense of the cosmic significance of the mother is to be found in Georgios Klotzas' icon of the Virgin and child at the heart of the world, the spirals of the mandala shape centring in on the supreme mother on whom all are dependent. The fragility of the baby Christ dandled on her knee presents another variation on this theme, whether the Virgin is portrayed as full of concern and foreboding or, more usually, as rapt in pure absorption. This theme may itself contain a pointed reminder of him on whom the Virgin in turn is dependent, and to whom she is submissive: consider, for instance, Stephan Lochner's 'Madonna in a Rose Bower' where the papal Father figure lurks half-hidden at the apex.

In the 'dependence' of death, the cycle comes full circle and the son is again cradled on his mother's knee; but in the Orthodox representation of the Virgin's 'Dormition' the roles are reversed, and the mother's soul is held by Christ as a dependent baby itself now, while the saints mourn over her physical body.

---

[8]   This chapter was originally presented as a paper at a meeting of the Society for the Study of Theology (St Andrews, April 1999), in which the slides alluded to here in the text were shown at the same time as the paper was read. Unfortunately production restrictions for this volume made it impossible to reproduce all the illustrations; the one exception is the Piero della Francesca 'Virgin of Mercy', which appears on the cover of this book and well represents the reality of an *empowered* but transparent female response to the divine.

Mary's role as protector and intermediary, a favourite theme of the late medieval West, suggests not only continuing dependence on the approachable maternal figure, but the desire to flee the dangers of the world and of a potentially vengeful Father God. Thus in the 'Virgin of Mercy' type Mary both shelters the faithful under her robe and acts as point of safe contact with the heavenly realm. In Piero della Francesca's unique representation of this theme, however (depicted on the cover of this volume), Mary achieves the stature of what one might call 'proto-feminist' assurance, and her followers, significantly, are more respectful than cowed. More common, however, are the distinctly neurotic overtones of the hierarchy in which the Virgin *replaces* the (ineffectual?) Spirit; the penitent may safely approach the awesome papal Father only via the Virgin and then the Son, both of whom plead to the Father by reference to their own points of vulnerability and tenderness (Christ's wounds and Mary's breast).

But the Virgin also can be a dominating, awesome, mother-type, to whom submission in turn is due, as powerful, perhaps as overwhelming, as some of the pagan Mother goddesses she replaces. She can also be herself dependent on her own mother, bespeaking that probably universal experience of new mothers of their own fundamental fragility and exhaustion, of their need for being mothered again upon their entry into the awesome responsibilities of motherhood. The chain of dependence creates another hierarchy (in the 'St Anne Trinity' of St Anne, the Virgin, and the Child), perhaps an unwitting pastiche of the visual form of the Eastern hierarchical Trinity discussed above; here, perhaps, is the *matriarchal* power-structure of the Greek extended family centred on the grandmother, a hierarchy no more releasing, I would argue – and doubtless more fearful to a man – than its counterpart in the 'male' Trinity. The tables are turned, only to repeat the subordinationist pathology in reverse.

The Virgin can be represented also as Christ's lover, sexually as well as religiously dependent on his superior divine status. According to Bernard, the Virgin 'ascends to the throne of glory', 'sings a nuptial hymn' and is greeted with 'kisses of [Christ's] mouth'.[9] On this however Marina Warner comments, more with sadness than bitterness, that 'The icon of Mary and Christ side by side is one of the Christian church's most polished deceptions: it is the very image and hope of earthly consummated love used to give that kind of love the lie.'[10] Likewise, the Assumption, greeted by C. G. Jung as

---

[9] *In Assumptione Beatae Mariae Virginis, PL*, 183, col. 996; quoted in Marina Warner, *Alone of all her Sex* (New York 1976) p. 130.
[10] Warner, op. cit., p. 133.

an implicit acknowledgment of the 'equality of women' and as a transformation of the Trinity into a properly balanced quaternity, is again not all that it seems. The Virgin is welcomed into the magic mandala, certainly, but it is visually clear in Fouquet's representation of this scene that she remains in a subordinate and fully dependent submissive position, again as 'befits' a woman.

Finally, but most symbolically redolent of all of Christian prayer and practice, we have the Annunciation, Mary's 'fiat' of ready submission and acceptance of divine will. Despite brave and promising efforts by contemporary feminist theologians to find in the Annunciation a symbol of right 'cooperation' and response to God,[11] or even, more backhandedly, an event at least without active intervention from a human father,[12] we can have no doubt of the implications of the more traditional interpretation for dependent women. Although there are many lovely exceptions, where for instance the Virgin exhibits self-composure as well as obedience, contemplative absorption rather than cowed submission before the angel, the themes of fear, humility and submission in the face of divine command are predominant, and a natural enough interpretation of Luke 1.26ff. Mary, recapitulating and reversing the disobedience and carnal knowledge of Eve, accepts the announcement of the Father God's intentions in obedient, and this time pure, sexual submission. Indeed, it is her willing *passivity* (whether or not this is wholly true to Luke's original intentions)[13] which has so exercised the proponents of 'dependent', contemplative prayer. In the eighteenth-century Père de Caussade's theory of 'abandonment to divine providence', for instance, the theme of contemplative acceptance is woven specifically around the Annunciation story.[14] It is worth remembering, as I have remarked elsewhere,[15] that de Caussade, a Jesuit director of considerable influence and intellectual flair, wrote for nuns already enjoined to a double submission: to their own superiors, and to male confessors and directors. It is not

---

[11]   See for example Rosemary Radford Ruether, *Sexism and God-Talk* (London 1983) ch. 6.

[12]   So (the earlier) Mary Daly, *Beyond God the Father* (Boston 1973), p. 84.

[13]   See the interesting argument to the contrary by Deborah Middleton, 'The Story of Mary: Luke's Version', *New Blackfriars* (December 1989) pp. 555–64. My own (critical) reflections on the possibilities for a feminist Mariology are to be found in Sarah Coakley, 'Mariology and "Romantic Feminism"' in Teresa Elwes (ed.), *Women's Voices* (London 1992) pp. 97–110.

[14]   See Jean-Pieore de Caussade, *Self-Abandonment to Divine Providence* (London 1971) p. 31 ff.

[15]   Sarah Coakley, '"Femininity" and the Holy Spirit?' in M. Furlong (ed.), *Mirror to the Church* (London 1988) p. 129.

particularly reassuring to find him warning them against 'intellectual curiosity' and recommending yet more 'humble submission'.

Thus we conclude: 'all creatures are dependent, but some are more dependent than others.' The message has had unchartable spiritually stultifying effects for women of many generations; but for men, too (and arguably most acutely since the creation of the Enlightenment cultural ideal of the heroic, lonely, cogitating self), the effects of this adage have been both equally dehumanizing and desiccating. In a brilliantly insightful essay, Mary Midgley has shown how the very creation of such a vision of the self could rest on *unconscious* dependences – in Kant's case, for instance, the domestic dependence on his man-servant![16] The *denial* of creaturely 'dependence', then, is as misleading as is its subordinationist misuse in human hands.

But what then of male creaturely dependence? Does not the Christian tradition provide resources for a riposte to the Enlightenment distortion of the self-sufficient (male) individual? We have already illustrated something of the double-sidedness of this theme in tradition: the urging of the submission of the (significantly 'female') soul to God or the Virgin on the one hand, but the implicit legitimation of male power over female subordination on the other. Jesus' ultimate yielding on the cross in death is the supreme locus for such a theme of male dependence, and as some Christian feminists have urged,[17] this symbolic *depotentiation* of male control, this breaking of societal stereotypes, is what makes for them the retention of a male saviour not only bearable but thoroughly pointed. But again, if we look to the iconographical evidence, especially from the West, we find this theme complicated by the (male) power-play implicit in the relationship between Father and Son at the point of Christ's death. Thus, in the late medieval *Gnadenstuhl* ('throne of grace') type of representation of the Trinity, the Father dispassionately holds up the Son at the moment of death, accepting the just punishment for human sin absorbed into the body of the Man of Sorrows. The paradoxes for the male beholder are evident, and indeed still being played out in modern Western theology. For with whom does the male (whether consciously or unconsciously) most easily identify? *Is* it with the yielding, depotentiated Son, or more truly with the impassive and all-powerful Father, bent on justice and punishment? The paradoxes are only partly relieved by the later reinterpretation of this type in the so-called *Not*

---

[16] Mary Midgley, 'Sex and Personal Identity: The Western Individualistic Tradition', *Encounter* (June 1984) pp. 50–5.
[17] Notably Angela West, 'A Faith for Feminists?', in J. Garcia and S. Maitland (eds.), *Walking on the Water* (London 1983) pp. 66–90.

Gottes representation of the Trinity:[18] here the Father, with increasingly compassionate visage, supports the dead body of his son, whom he has however still abandoned to a lonely and agonizing death.

Themes of male power and subordination are still lurking here then, as too, I believe, are sexual connotations. The symbolic connection between male sexual release and death is well documented in literature; and von Balthasar's argument in his essay 'The Christian and Chastity' is based precisely on this male sexual symbolism:

> In its origin [the New Testament] presents to man and woman a glorious picture of sexual integrity: the Son of God who has become man and flesh, knowing from inside his Father's work and perfecting it in the total self-giving of himself, not only of his spiritual but precisely also of his physical powers ... What else is his eucharist but, at a higher level, an endless act of fruitful outpouring of his whole flesh, such as a man can only achieve for a moment with a limited organ of his body?[19]

This line of connection, whatever one thinks of von Balthasar's particular argument here, is one that I suspect is worthy of bringing to greater consciousness.

Yet the seamier side of such a sexual connection is a tendency to sado-masochism; it is essential that we should expose any distorting and destructive aspects of spiritual practice that have been based on such hidden sexual agendas of a punitive type. Sara Maitland, reviewing some pertinent evidence from female saints (Rose of Lima, Margaret Mary Alacoque, and most worryingly, the canonized Maria Goretti, who chose death over loss of 'honour' at the hands of a rapist), poses the right question: 'What can possibly lead women [such as these] to believe that they are more "conformable", more lovable to the God of creation, love and mercy, bleeding, battered and self-mutilated, than they would be joyful, lovely and delighted?'[20] The question applies no less poignantly to men who have trodden this path; but, as Maitland's essay shows, the frenetic quality of some of the evidence relating to women in this area alerts us once more to the hierarchical context in which women have sought with desperation for spiritual equality and perfection.

---

[18]   For both these types see G. Schiller, *Iconography of Christian Art* II (London 1972).

[19]   Hans Urs von Balthasar, *Elucidations* (London 1975) p. 150.

[20]   Sara Maitland, 'Passionate Prayer: Masochistic Images in Women's Experience', in L. Hurcombe (ed.), *Sex and God: Some Varieties of Women's Religious Experience* (London 1987) p. 127.

But the 'hierarchy' – as we have already hinted – is differently enunciated in East and West Christendom, and it is well to be clear about this, if only to highlight the fallibility of some supposed corrections to the problem. In a now classic article, Rosemary Radford Ruether outlined the difference between Gregory of Nyssa's and Augustine's understanding of creation, and of the implications thereof for the place and understanding of female creatureliness.[21] According to Gregory, there is a double creation: in the first instance a non-sexual and purely spiritual creation (for it is assumed by Gregory that to be truly 'in the image of God' the creature must be angelic, non-physical); only in the second instance – and 'with a view to the Fall' – is bodily nature added, both male and female. On this view, then, the female creature is not regarded as intrinsically more physical or bodily than the male; but both the origins and goal of perfect creatureliness lie in a sort of humanoid state, where sexual differentiation is *irrelevant*. In Augustine, by contrast, the existence of the sexes is from the start 'intrinsic to creation', and sexual relations – without passion, however! – are part of God's good intentions. This might appear to be potentially a more promising picture for women, were it not for the sting in the tail: the disjunction of spirit and corporeality, with woman being fatally identified with the latter. Augustine sees the male, alone, as the proper and full image of God. He contains both 'male' spirit and 'female' bodiliness within himself, whereas the woman is *intrinsically* carnal, subordinate to the male, and in the image of God only insofar as she conjoins herself with her husband. The result, as Ruether avers, is that 'woman is not really seen as a self-sufficient, whole person with equal honor, as the image of God in her own right, but is seen, ethically, as dangerous to the male.'[22]

Now if we align this material with the insights already gleaned from attending to the different emphases of Eastern and Western trinitarianism,

---

[21]   Rosemary Radford Ruether, 'Misogynism and Virginal Feminism in the Fathers of the Church' in Rosemary Radford Ruether (ed.), *Religion and Sexism* (New York 1974) pp. 150–83. I concur with Ruether's general conclusions in this article as summarized here, but would want to urge that Augustine's position, especially in Book XII of the *De Trinitate*, is more complex and double-sided than Ruether allows. See the further treatment of this material in my forthcoming *God, Sexuality and the Self: An Essay 'On the Trinity'* (Cambridge, forthcoming) ch. 5; and also the important corrective article by K. E. Børresen, 'In Defence of Augustine: How *Femina is Homo?*', *Collecteana Augustiniana* (1990) pp. 411–28.

[22]   Op. cit. pp. 156–7. Much of the relevant material from Gregory and Augustine is conveniently available in Elizabeth A. Clark, *Women in the Early Church* (Wilmington, Delaware 1983).

we may arrive at some interesting results. In the East, first, there emerges a fascinating correlation between the *ideology* of *homoousian* equality in the 'persons' of the Godhead on the one hand, and creaturely equality of humanoid souls on the other. But we cannot help asking whether the *realities* are not in both cases actually more hierarchical and subordinationist than the ideology allows. For all its appeal to the natural and fortuitous inclusiveness of its *anthrōpos* language, the Greek Church – we could surely all agree – is not noted for its granting of equal ministerial roles to women; and it is these *practical* issues which are the acid test in the long run. Even such a moving visual correction of the hierarchical image as Rublev's icon – which employs what is indeed the older and for the East the mainstream, typology of Genesis 18 in attempting a visualization of God – still combines in subtler form the two distinctively Eastern characteristics we have highlighted; the de-sexed or humanoid view of the 'person', and the simultaneous bowing to the Father's monarchy, however delicately done in this case.[23] Thus too the apophaticism for which the East is justly lauded is sometimes capable of being a mask for complacency or a pat response to the feminist challenge. Let anyone who claims that he has passed well beyond the need for 'male' or 'female' images into God, or that (more ingeniously) 'Father' to him means nothing whatever to do with ordinary human fathering,[24] examine his actual relations with women in church and society. Things are not always what they seem.

In the West, however, one may suggest a different point of correlation between the trinitarian theology of Augustine and his views on male and female creatureliness, but one that is perhaps also telling. Running through the various different psychological analogies of the *De Trinitate* is the insistence on the right operation and *harmony* of the faculties of the soul (memory, understanding and will) which mirror the coinherent relations of the divine triad. It is not insignificant, I suggest, that what most offends Augustine about normal sexual activity is the failure of the male will to effect total dispassionate control over the phallus; the harmonious ordering of the soul is disrupted: the body revolts. (The contrast here with Gregory of Nyssa, as Peter Brown has recently illuminated, is of some importance: for Gregory the sexual act itself is apparently not intrinsically worrisome, but rather the implications of human reproduction for the continuing cycle of

---

[23]   It is usually assumed that the figure on the left of the icon is the Father (for this reason).

[24]   See the line of approach in *The Forgotten Trinity 1: The Report of the BCC Study Commission on Trinitarian Doctrine Today* (London 1989) p. 39. I was a member of this commission, but I was unconvinced by this particular argument.

births and deaths in a persisting social order.)[25] In Augustine, however, it is not the hope of eschatological flight to a non-sexual realm that is held before us, but rather *actual* sexual relations without loss of control. In this (somewhat joyless) vision of paradise the woman nonetheless remains intrinsically 'bodily' and subordinate to her husband's leading spirit. Now when such assumptions are carried over, much later, into the problematic inner-trinitarian relations of an Anselmian substitutionary atonement theory, a (bodily) female figure may occasionally be brought in visually as the *vinculum amoris*, effecting a *rapprochement* between Father and Son, whether directly as Holy Spirit or, more usually, as the Virgin replacing the Spirit and warding off the wrath of a visually vengeful Father. Christian feminists may again well ask, however, whether these spontaneous projections of female figures into the Godhead, retrieved and welcomed with enthusiasm by some, are really a viable way forward, recapitulating as they do the Western stereotype of bodily, subordinate dependence for women.

To sum up: if in the East we have detected at least a tendency to announce a spurious (and de-sexed) equality for female creatureliness, in the West a more explicit stereotype of subordinate female bodiliness has been the norm. From a Christian feminist standpoint clearly neither of these solutions is agreeable as a systematic view of female creatureliness. In concluding I shall make some brief programmatic suggestions about a way forward.

We may first note a suggestive convergence of themes from secular feminist psychoanalytic theory on the one hand, and Christian feminist atonement theory on the other. In the now classic work of Nancy J. Chodorow,[26] the Freudian theory of the 'castrated', incomplete female is turned on its head. By examining the different implications of the mother–child relationship for gender development in little boys and girls, Chodorow stresses that while girls are still encouraged, in contemporary Western culture, to continue in a state of relational identification with the mother, boys must forge an effective separation from her in order to develop as male 'individuals'. *Contra* Freud, it is this male urge to individuate that needs explaining, not the connectedness of the female identification with the mother. The results however are those gender characteristics thoroughly

---

[25]   Peter Brown, *The Body and Society* (New York 1988); see chs. 14 (on Gregory of Nyssa) and 19 (on Augustine). My own views on Nyssa's theological deposit and its potential contemporary significance are developed at greater length in chs. 7–9, below.

[26]   Nancy J. Chodorow, *The Reproduction of Mothering* (Berkeley and Los Angeles 1978) and *Feminism and Psychoanalytic Theory* (Oxford 1989).

sanctioned by our society: the 'relational' capacity for empathy and feeling in the female, and the propulsion to autonomy and control in the male. Chodorow's conclusions found interesting corroboration in Carol Gilligan's study of ethical decision-making.[27] Her surveys (on, for instance, decisions over abortion) brought to light in the 'different voice of women... an ethics of care, the tie between relationship and responsibility, and the origins of aggression in the *failure* of connection'[28] (my emphasis).

This line of approach – deeply contentious in contemporary secular feminism, for it has a strong tendency to smack of the essentialism it is trying to surmount[29] – finds its theological counterpart in the early pioneering Christian feminist work on 'female' sin and atonement. Thus, in an article originally published in 1960, Valerie Saving urged that the 'temptations of women *as women* are not the same as the temptations of men *as men*', and that whereas 'pride' and 'will-to-power' are the creaturely faults that come naturally to men, in women sinning is more likely to be associated with

> Frivolity, distractability, and diffuseness; lack of an organizing centre or focus; *dependence on others for one's own self-definition*; tolerance at the expense of

[27]   Carol Gilligan, *In a Different Voice* (Cambridge, Mass. 1982).

[28]   ibid. p. 175.

[29]   Waves of competing fashion in feminist theory – and differences of political contexts and practical goals – have tended to dictate whether a concentration on gender 'difference' (however construed), its effective obliteration into 'equality of opportunity', or its transmutation into gender 'fluidity', is what is deemed most worthy of pursuit. On the effects of these theoretical changes for feminist theology, see my long survey chapter, 'Feminist Theology' in James C. Livingston, Francis Schüssler Fiorenza, with Sarah Coakley and James H. Evans, *Modern Christian Thought* (rev. ed., Upper Saddle River, NJ, 2000) pp. 417–42. My own view is synthetic, as will be clear from the pages of this volume: the goals of 'liberal feminism' (with its roots in an Enlightenment vision of 'equality' for women) are still not met in most parts of the world and should not be lightly swept aside, for all that other aspects of Enlightenment 'individualism' are to be severely critiqued (on this see ch. 5, below); but the emphasis on 'difference' found (somewhat crudely) in the material just cited, and – more subtly and controversially – in the contemporary French feminists, is also of huge political, philosophical and spiritual significance (see below, ch. 6). It is a false move, in my view, to set these perspectives in ultimate logical diremption, despite all the theoretical difficulties of aligning the goals of 'equality' and 'difference'. Once 'difference' is yet further 'differentiated' – as, e.g., in the postmodern gender fluidity of Judith Butler's theories – we are asked to reconsider more critically the stereotypical gender *binaries* of the earlier feminist materials (without, in my view, altogether obliterating the *strategic* force of their rhetorical ploys). On Butler's recent work and the interesting parallelism with some themes in patristic ascetical theology, see ch. 9, below.

standards of excellence; inability to respect the boundaries of privacy; sentimentality; gossipy sociability, and mistrust of reason – in short, underdevelopment or *negation of the self*.[30]

Moreover, note again how the cultural effects for women are not just different but *negating*; as a Jungian psychotherapist recently remarked to me (and she deals with a substantial number of women religious): 'It is the combination of *overdependence* and self-*hatred* which is so fatal.'

If we still recognize even *some* aspects of the broad picture of modern female 'creatureliness' outlined here, then obviously a form of compensation for actual stereotyping is an urgent necessity. In part, but only in part, the Christian tradition has thrown up it own spontaneous corrections, and a comparison of the equally extraordinary twelfth-century figures Bernard of Clairvaux and Hildegard of Bingen is particularly instructive here. In Bernard we see a male saint asserting in a new way the importance of *feeling* in spiritual development; along with this goes a frank and even daring delight in the erotic metaphors of the *Song of Songs*: the soul is 'female' and passive before its lover; and in the iconography of St Bernard his devotion to the Virgin is celebrated as his feeding at her breast, returning, as Freudians would say, to a pre-Oedipal identification with the mother. In the connected Cistercian idea of *Christ* as mother, there is a similar turn to tenderness and passivity. Whatever one may make of this, these connected themes all indicate an unusual urge to 'relatedness'; whereas in the visions of Hildegard, Bernard's contemporary and correspondent, there is an opposite compensation towards female authority and power. Awesome female figures appear as Wisdom or 'Ecclesia'; conversely, however, the Spirit is celebrated not as submissive 'female' mediator but as a fiery (phallic) 'tower'. Yet, as Barbara Newman's brilliant analysis shows,[31] Hildegard's remarkable *sui generis* symbolism has its remaining gender paradoxes: just as Bernard's compensating themes break down at the point of accepting normal social relations with real women, so Hildegard too remains in thrall to societal assumptions about the 'weakness' and unreliability of women, whilst manifestly managing herself to be the exception that proves the rule.

To conclude: if we are to grope towards a more equitable representation of male and female creatureliness before God we shall indeed be doing a

[30]   Valerie Saiving, 'The Human Situation: A Feminine View' reprinted in Carol P. Christ and Judith Plaskow (eds.), *Womanspirit Rising* (New York, 1979) p. 37. My emphasis.
[31]   Barbara Newman, *Sister of Wisdom: St. Hildegard's Theology of the Feminine* (Berkeley and Los Angeles 1987).

new thing. Selective retrieval from the tradition will be instructive, but not, I suggest, wholly convincing without further critical reflection. Corrective 'androgynies' may still mask unacknowledged sexism;[32] the simple throwing up of compensating 'feminine' divine imagery may leave societal relationships between the sexes largely untouched; false apophaticism may leap to the place of 'unknowing', leaving curiously intact the sexual stereotypes it claims to overcome. The safer test for sexism overcome is not so much the purity or balance of an official doctrinal formulation, but the *practical* outworkings of the relationship between the sexes in society and Church.[33]

It has been the burden of this chapter to suggest – against the more radical of the post-Christian feminists[34] – that an 'absolute dependence' is indeed at the heart of true human creatureliness and the contemplative quest. But such *right* dependence is an elusive goal: the entanglements with themes of power, hierarchy, sexuality and death are probably inevitable but also best brought to consciousness; they are an appropriate reminder that our prayer is enfleshed. In that sense the lessons of such reflection may again be revealingly 'incarnational'.

---

[32] See the illuminating section in Reuther, *Sexism and God-Talk* pp. 127–30.

[33] See the remarks of Mary Daly in *Beyond God the Father* p. 20: 'Even when the basic assumptions of God-language appear to be non-sexist, and when language is somewhat purified of fixation upon maleness, it is damaging and implicitly compatible with sexism if it encourages detachment from the reality of the human struggle against oppression in its concrete manifestations.'

[34] See especially Mary Daly's trenchant and apposite remarks about Rom. 8 and Gal. 4 in *Pure Lust* (London 1984): 'We do not wish to be redeemed by a god, to be adopted as sons, or to have the spirit of a god's son artifically injected into our hearts, crying "father".'

Part II

Philosophical Interlocutions

Chapter 4

VISIONS OF THE SELF IN LATE MEDIEVAL CHRISTIANITY: SOME CROSS-DISCIPLINARY REFLECTIONS

So far in this volume we have been considering the ways in which the act of 'contemplation', whilst providing – I have argued – an acutely revealing point of reflection for the subtle intersection of divine power and responsive human vulnerability, is nonetheless, precisely in its subtlety, a place where cultural admixtures of every sort can vie for a presence: human 'principalities' and manipulations, gender distortions or prescriptions, abusive as well as liberating relationships. As so often, devilish perversities lurk around the arena of deepest truth.

On the one hand, in the face of this messy complexity, we would like to identify a 'pure' form of the *sui generis* intersection between the divine and the human; but although Christians may affirm in faith that the reality of 'Christ' is precisely that point of purity, it is a curiously elusive matter to encapsulate the exact nature of it: 'Christ' is not that easily caught and held. On the other hand, the necessary vigilance that the hermenutic of suspicion teaches us can itself become a dangerously blunt instrument, a newly destructive feminist 'instrument of torture'. For there is the reductive temptation – which we have so far strenuously resisted – to read classic texts on contemplation as *mere* invitations to abuse or sexist submission, programmes for a disassociated or an apolitical introversion.

In the three chapters that now follow, we subject some classic spiritual and philosophical material from the Christian tradition to a closer analysis in order to highlight further the dangers of such reductive readings. Here, in chapter 4, we reassess the spirituality of *The Cloud of Unknowing* (already

Originally published in Michael McGhee (ed.), *Philosophy, Religion, and the Spiritual Life: Royal Institute of Philosophy Supplement* (Cambridge, Cambridge University Press, 1992), pp. 89–103. Reprinted with permission from Cambridge University Press, with light revisions.

examined briefly in chapter 2), examine its cultural and historical context, and suggest a way in which it may itself be a remote ancestor of certain 'modern' philosophical developments in the West, developments which are in interesting contrast with what was happening, theologically and politically, at roughly the same time as *The Cloud* in the Byzantine East. One of the major implications of this essay lies in its acknowledgement of the social and political embeddedness of 'contemplation', its 'macrocosmic' implications as well as its 'microcosmic' effects on the individual soul/body.

Chapter 5 moves from here to examine the paradoxical heritage for feminist thought – both spiritual and philosophical – of Enlightenment and Romantic understandings of gender. Since chapter 4 has already established the continuities between pre-modern 'spirituality' and certain strands in modern 'philosophy', this is not a surprising leap; what is perhaps more unexpected is the sympathy with which certain (now regularly derided) Enlightenment thinkers are treated, the double-edged heritage of their thinking exposed to feminist assessment. Then, in chapter 6, another short step is taken to engage – again both critically and appreciatively – with the discourse of 'analytic philosophy of religion', itself deeply imbued with certain Enlightenment presumptions, but now increasingly under fire from feminist assault.

In all three of these essays we return, in different ways, to the alluring problem with which we began: how to explicate the particular nature of our deepest exposure to the divine presence, and how to assess the questions of power and gender that inevitably infiltrate this profound area of human desire and longing. What we find is that the *caesura* between 'pre-modern' and 'modern', deep as it is, is not so deep as to disallow significant points of continuity and retrieval; and that the 'postmodern', for all its bewildering novelty, is capable of reinstating both 'pre-modern' and 'modern' strands of spiritual tradition: once again, the 'spiritual' and the 'philosophical' can find a closer unity in *practice*.

In this first essay devoted to explicating the connections of philosophy, religion and the spiritual life, then, I would like to focus the latter part on a comparison of two Christian spiritual writings of the fourteenth century, the anonymous *Cloud of Unknowing* in the West (1981), and the *Triads* of Gregory Palamas in the Byzantine East (1983). Their examples, for reasons which I shall explain, seem to me rich with implications for some of our current philosophical and theological aporias on the nature of the self. Let me explain my thesis in skeletal form at the outset, for it is a complex one, and has several facets.

Outline of the Thesis

First, this comparison is I believe of some interest, historically and theologically, in its own right, for its witnesses to a fascinating divergence
between Western and Eastern Christendom at this point, the West driving
wedges between faculties in the self, the East arriving at a remarkable new
synthetic view of the person. If I am correct, *The Cloud*, on the one hand, is
one manifestation (one amongst the range of possibilities) of an emerging
sense of *optionality* in the West in this period about what constitutes the
ultimate locus of the self; the *perichoretic* co-operation of memory, understanding and will authoritatively found in Augustine, is, in various ways,
rent apart disjunctively in the spiritual texts of this time. No less is Aquinas's
integrative view of the 'composite of soul and body' under distinct threat, as
we shall see, and here the trend towards a new dualism between soul and
body is arguably more manifest in popular spiritual manuals in succeeding
generations than in official doctrinal formulations.[1]

As spiritual writers in the late medieval period in the West, then, were
driving wedges into classical Christian views of the person from their
tradition, Gregory Palamas, admittedly in the face of fierce public opposition from his critics, effected an extraordinary new *rapprochement* between
two views of the person that had previously in Eastern Christianity stood
somewhat apart, despite a few earlier synthesizing forays. The two views
were, first, the Platonizing view of the self as immortal mind, represented by
the fourth-century Evagrius, and the more biblically oriented spirituality of
the 'heart', 'body' and 'feeling', represented by the fifth-century *Macarian
Homilies*.[2] In short, while spiritual texts in the West were *dividing* the person,
peeling back to one indivisible point of reference, the East, in its public
acceptance of Palamas's viewpoint, was restructuring and resynthesizing it.

On any account, then, this fourteenth-century comparison is of some
historical interest (though not to my knowledge previously commented
upon in quite this way); and I shall dare to make some speculations a little
later about the cultural and social backcloth to such a divergence.

The two other parts of my argument apply some lessons of this comparison to our current debates about identity and immortality in philosophy of
religion, debates in which I believe a greater sensitivity to the diversity of

---

[1]   See Copleston, 1955, p. 152, who suggests the same point.
[2]   For this account of Palamas, see Meyendorff, 1964 (who admittedly over-schematizes the
dialectic between these two strands of tradition).

Christian traditions in spiritual practice would enrich our sense of *options*.[3] The first point here – my thesis 2 – concerns our current theological obsession with the supposed nastiness of Cartesianism, and whether or not we can blame Augustine for it. Rather than taking sides here either with those who find the unacceptable seeds of Descartes' individualism in Augustine, or with those, conversely, who seek to exonerate Descartes in relation to Augustine,[4] I wish instead to divert your attention to the long centuries in between. I want to ask whether the debate amongst medieval historians about whether the twelfth century (or the immediately succeeding period) invented the 'individual' is not of some considerable long-term background significance for our understanding of Descartes' 'sources of the self'. Curiously, even S. Lukes's magisterial little book *Individualism* (1973) only glancingly mentions this earlier period (p. 47). Moreover, current philosophical and theological critics of the Enlightenment understanding of the self have taken almost no account of it; nor have they heeded the claim of Colin Morris (1987) – and others – that it was neither the Renaissance, nor the Enlightenment, that invented the 'individual', but rather the rich period 1080–1150, which developed a peculiar 'self-awareness and self-expression', a freedom from 'excessive attention to convention or authority' (ibid. p. 7). I shall seek to build on this thesis, and highlight a tendency thereafter, in the later medieval period, to carve back to a unitary, solitary, and to a large extent disembodied sense of the self in the spiritual manuals of the thirteenth- and fourteenth-century West. Here are traits which I believe represent interesting foreshadowings of at least aspects of the Cartesian vision, despite all the remaining significant differences.[5]

Finally, and shifting to my comparative example of Gregory Palamas in the East, my third argument – thesis 3 – is that Palamas's integrative view of the Christian self, his understanding of the transformative possibilities of the embodied self in this life as an earnest of the next, and particularly his subtle view of the relation of 'body', 'soul', 'mind' and 'heart', all represent options worthy of serious consideration in our debates about personal identity and about life after death. Most important here, perhaps, is the lesson which

---

[3] My strategy here is not unlike that of Rorty, 1980, chs. 1 and 2, at least in exposing some of the presumptions of our current philosophical debate (see especially the relevant p. 44, n. 13).

[4] For the former position, see (e.g.) Gunton, 1985; for the latter, see Clark, 1992.

[5] My thesis is obviously less specific than that which links Descartes directly to scholastic predecessors (for which see Gilson, 1979); I concentrate here on what seem significant trends in more 'popular' spirituality.

surely should be more obvious than it is from any cursory survey of historical examples, that we should make no quick identification of 'soul' and 'mind' in our debates about the immortality of the soul. This point is of course already taken by sensitive reinterpreters of Aquinas' view of 'soul' and body; but more usually we are asked to make a choice based on smuggled Cartesian assumptions – *either* the immortality of the soul (=the mind) *or* the resurrection of the body (or neither).[6] Palamas represents just one figure here whose use of 'soul' language is more complicated and interesting than these disjunctions will allow.

Cartesian 'Individualism'

So much for a brief introduction of my main themes. I want now to include another brief preamble, this time on Descartes (and his modern critics and expositors), for it is important to clarify what *aspects* of 'individualism' we seek to highlight, and which may (perhaps) already be found in the earlier period to which I have alluded.

Fergus Kerr's illuminating book *Theology after Wittgenstein* (1986), for instance, opens with a brief, but fairly devastating assault on Descartes, who represents for him the veritable anti-hero of his whole volume. Descartes' self, he says, 'peels off' everything: 'previous beliefs, senses, body... the confidence even that the external world really exists' (ibid. p. 4). The accusations build up on this and succeeding pages: this 'peeled back' Cartesian 'I' is 'completely egocentric'; it is 'self-conscious', 'self-reliant', 'all responsible', but also has a capacity to recede towards ultimate emptiness (ibid. pp. 19–20); it is 'self-disembodying', 'solitary', 'detached', 'objective', 'seeking mastery', even perhaps seeking to be God. Charles Taylor, in his treatment of Descartes in *Sources of the Self* (1989), adds to a similar list of points the familiar charge that for Descartes God is merely an *inference* from '[rational] powers that... [he can] be quite certain of possessing' already (ibid. p. 157). 'What has happened', Taylor says, 'is... that God's existence has become a stage in *my* progress towards science through the methodical ordering of evident insight' (ibid.).

Now there are an awful lot of different things being claimed against Descartes here, which are often, and confusingly, allowed to heap up under the blanket accusation of Cartesian 'individualism': the usurpation

---

[6] One thinks, e.g., of the range of views represented in Penelhum, 1970; Lewis, 1973; Hick, 1976; and Swinburne, 1986.

of the divine realm, disembodiment, detachment and solitariness, egocentricity, self-consciousness and moral self-reliance; all these are rather different claims. Indeed, after a survey of such recent secondary views, I am struck by the unanalysed vehemence and passion with which Descartes is sometimes loaded with blame, especially by theologians. What is it, I wonder, about our current social and cultural circumstances, that makes Descartes such an easy target of scorn and loathing? Is it a need to purge out of the system something that we recognize all too clearly in ourselves? To this point I shall return briefly at the end of this chapter.

More closely at the level of text, however, I would want to suggest that some of these charges listed against Descartes stand up better under close scrutiny than others. I am not in the business of exonerating him from them *tout court*: that would be foolhardy indeed. But all too often Descartes is read only through selected purple passages, especially the 'peeling back' manoeuvres of *Meditation II*; a more rounded reading of his corpus, and specifically a more contextualized reading of the *Meditations*, reveal some surprising divergences from the archetypal figure with whom we have become familiar. For instance – to give just one or two examples – Michael Buckley (in his *At the Origins of Modern Atheism* (1987)) has elegantly shown that we ignore the intellectual context of Descartes' *cogito* at our peril; Descartes did not just arbitrarily and perversely *invent* his view of the self out of the blue: it arose in response to Montaigne's radical scepticism. The questions and options were thus already set up; Descartes reversed Montaigne's logic and moved *from* the radical scepticism served up to him *to* the certitude of his own existence, *from* the experience of his own imperfection *to* the idea of the all-perfect. 'What is never noted,' says Buckley (ibid. p. 69), 'yet is crucial for the interpretation of [Descartes'] project, is that he did not originate this conjunction between skepticism and the existence of God. It came to him already forged.'

Again, and on another point raised by the critics, the relation of soul and body in Descartes is often badly misunderstood. There is indeed a most radical *distinction* between them, the distinction between the material and the immaterial, the divisible and the indivisible. But Descartes devotes immense energies, especially in his later work, to charting their intrinsically close relation, insisting that the soul resides quite locatably in the pineal gland. Earlier, in *Meditation VI*, he had underscored: 'I am not lodged in my body only as a pilot in a vessel, I am very closely united with it.' And he was very aware, very bothered, that his account of how, precisely, the mind and body interacted, was possibly the weakest and most problematic link in his system. ('This', he wrote to the Princess Elizabeth, 'seems to me to be the question people have the most right to ask me in view of my published works.')[7]

Interestingly, too, under close feminist scrutiny of Enlightenment 'individualism', such as provided by Genevieve Lloyd's account in *The Man of Reason* (1984), Descartes fares – justifiably – rather better than his blatantly misogynist successor in the Enlightenment, Immanuel Kant. Descartes' view of the mind is at least not an intrinsically *sexist* form of 'individualism'. It is however the severe and demanding abstraction of Descartes' form of higher reasoning that bodes ill for those left to (complementary) activity in the kitchen, nursery or salon: 'The life I am constrained to lead', complained the Princess Elizabeth in a letter of 10/20 June 1643, 'does not allow me enough free time to acquire a habit of meditation in accordance with your rules.' Yet Descartes showed some awareness of this difficulty, and even saw its value: 'It is by availing oneself of life and ordinary conversations,' he replies, '... and studying things that exercise the imagination, that one learns to conceive the union of the soul and body' (letter of 28 June 1643). There is an ordinary, everyday reasoning, then, that rightly attends to the bodily, the imaginative and the passionate. Furthermore, Descartes is not quite the sustained *solitary* individual that he is often taken for: he does *start* from the individual, and he does say that our interests are 'in some way' distinct from others'; 'none the less ... one could not subsist alone and is, in effect, one of the parts of the earth, and more particularly, of this state, of this society, of this family to which one is joined' (letter of 15 September 1645).[8]

Wherein then lies the 'individualism' in Descartes that we seek to expose? It could still, I think we should admit, be located at a number of significant points; but the particular point which I seek to trace back to a much earlier period is this: it is the whittling away of the traditional Augustinian plurality in the faculties of the mind, the reduction to a single mental entity, and thereby the starker ranging of soul over against the body in a somewhat problematic relationship. The point is well illustrated by a passage from Descartes' fascinating late work, *The Passions of the Soul* (Part First, Article XL VII):

... there is within us but one soul, and this soul has not in itself any diversity of parts; the same part that is subject to sense impressions is rational, and all the soul's appetites are acts of will. The error which has been committed in

---

[7] These points are well brought out by Kenny, 1968, ch. 10.

[8] Quoted in Thomson, 1983, pp. 13–14, nn. 2–5, who provides interesting feminist commentary on this theme in Descartes.

making it play a part of various personages, usually in opposition to one another, only proceeds from the fact that we have not properly distinguished its functions from those of the body, to which alone we must attribute every thing which can be observed in us that is opposed to our reason.[9]

What I propose, then, is to turn back now to the late middle ages and see if we can find anything like *this* already in process of development at this earlier stage.

Twelfth-Century 'Individualism' and Succeeding Trends in Spirituality

The backcloth here, as I have already mentioned, is the debate about the apparent novelty in attitudes to the self that emerges in the twelfth century (or perhaps, as in Caroline Bynum's refinements of the thesis, a little later).[10] What is at stake here, in Colin Morris's now classic account (1987), is a concatenation of developments associated with the dramatic changes in European society from the period 1050 on, which I can here only summarize blandly and briefly. In this period, the cities assumed increasing significance, education became more widely available, and new classes of educated civil servant, lawyer, critical reformer, and ecclesiastical administrator emerged. In the country the aristocracy, too, was 'transformed in its structures' to allow greater new powers for local lordships, now founded in the principle of primogeniture. In sum, and to quote Morris, 'Twelfth-century society was thus disturbed by the rapid emergence of a whole series of new groups or classes, all of them requiring an idea on which to model themselves ... They thus created a conflict of values, and faced the individual with choices which in the year A.D. 1000 would have been unimaginable' (ibid. p. 47). The 'individualism' that Morris goes on to chart he defines initially rather inchoately as 'the sense of a clear distinction between my being and that of other people'. But evidence is then presented of various themes that cluster under this definition: a new sense of self-discovery, inwardness, self-expression, self-examination and intentionality, all to some extent manifest in the ethos and character of the Cistercian reform and in the

---

[9]   Haldane and Ross, 1931, vol. I, p. 353. It may be that Descartes has Plato closer to mind than Augustine in his objection to 'any diversity of parts' in the 'soul'; but my point about the *simplification* of the soul still stands.

[10]   See Bynum's essay, 'Did the Twelfth Century Discover the Individual?', in Bynum, 1984.

refinement of the penitential system at this time. Also there was a new freedom to contrast, choose between, and even defy, theological authorities and traditions (well expressed in Abelard's *Sic et Non*; it was one of Bernard's most vehement charges against Abelard that he (Abelard) assumed judgmental freedom over against tradition). And then, most importantly for our interests here, there also emerged a new fascination with the Augustinian faculty of will, reworked in terms of the affections and of erotic desire, which, one might argue, found its secular counterpart in the emerging rituals and attitudes of courtly love.

The crucial point for our purposes here, however, is that writers like Bernard of Clairvaux and his fellow Cistercian William of St. Thierry could give a new, indeed intense, value to feeling in their theology, whilst still, at this stage, holding a balance in their notion of the self between the faculties of knowing and feeling. 'Instruction makes people learned, but feeling makes them wise,' wrote Bernard in one of his *Sermons on the Song of Songs* (V. 14), a remark that might be read as already inviting a disjunction between the two faculties;[11] indeed Bernard does not very adequately explain how love and knowledge are related in moments of mystical union in this life. But he does also insist that love *is* a form of knowing: *amor ipse notitia est (De diversis* XXIX, 1); and in another of his *Sermons on the Song of Songs* (XLIX. 4) he describes ecstasy as incorporating both intellect and will.

The importance of all this as backcloth to the later, and significantly different, medieval mystical writers such as *The Cloud* is well brought out in an important recent article by Bernard McGinn (1987). McGinn argues thus. Whilst Bernard, William of St. Thierry, and the thirteenth-century Franciscan Bonaventure all held a balance (albeit somewhat differently enunciated) in their theories of mystical union between the newly emphasized feeling or will on the one hand and intellect or knowledge on the other, an important new sense of disjunction between the two faculties becomes apparent in the writing of a figure whose influence lies directly behind *The Cloud*. This is Thomas Gallus, who was the last great mystical writer of the Abbey of St Victor in Paris, who become abbot of Vercelli, and died in 1246. Gallus held the view that there are two quite *distinct* ways of relating to God corresponding to this difference between knowing and loving. There is the *theoricus intellectus*, by means of which we know things that are intelligible, and via them God as first cause; and there is the *affectio principalis*, which is, in contrast, the place where mystical union with God

---

[11] So Louth, 1976.

occurs. As McGinn expresses the novelty element here: 'Gallus's language about the relation of knowing to loving in the ascent to God stresses a rather sharp separation or cutting off of all intellectual operations... [Thus] For Gallus... affective union no longer seems as interested in subsuming the lower forms of intellectual activity as it is in kicking them downstairs' (ibid. p. 13). In short, in my terms, the rending apart procedure, as a distinctive manifestation of later medieval Western spirituality, has here begun. There is a new sense of option: will the closest possibility of relation to the divine fall on the side of affectivity (i.e., will), or on the side of intellect?

It is in this context that we must read probably the most celebrated of the remarks of *The Cloud* author (writing about 1370) on the nature of the self before God. He states (in chapter 4):

> Now all rational creatures, angels and men alike, have in them each one individually, one chief working power, which is called a knowing power, and another chief working power which is called a loving power; and of these two powers, God, who is the maker of them, is always incomprehensible to the first, the knowing power. But to the second, he is entirely comprehensible in each individually... (1981, p. 123)

In other words, central to *The Cloud*'s psychology of contemplation is precisely the driving of wedges into the self set up by Gallus: the choice of will over intellect as the faculty of divine interchange. For what 'contemplation' is in *The Cloud* is a 'naked' inclination of the will, a 'peeling back' to this *one* faculty with which the 'sharp darts of longing love' are launched at the darkness of the 'Cloud of Unknowing'.

It is, however, distinctly misleading to regard *The Cloud* as straightforwardly anti-intellectual. When, much later in his treatise (chapter 62 ff.), *The Cloud* author comes to spell out a more technical version of his view of the person, it is a broadly Augustinian package of distinct faculties with which we are presented, ranged under the inclusive rubric of 'mind', though it is a package modified by another Victorine, Richard of St Victor, which *The Cloud* takes over. The 'mind' here is said to 'contain' two principal powers – reason and will, and two secondary ones – imagination and sensuality. Reason (chapter 64) is the power of discrimination, which, since the Fall, is severely perverted. Will, on the other hand (and here we come to the more disjunct tones), is the faculty with which 'we love God, we desire God, and finally come to rest in God with full liking and full consent' (ibid. p. 245). Imagination and sensuality are lower animal faculties, working with the bodily senses.

What we have, then, in *The Cloud*, is a continuing polite bowing to the authority of traditional Augustinian sub-faculties of the mind (later to be rejected altogether by Descartes), but at the same time an entirely new sense of freedom of choice in stripping back to *one*, key mental faculty of divine apprehension, in this case the will. But other mystical authors of the period indicate how free, even bewilderingly free, was the sense of *choice* about the construction of the self at this period of intense mystical flowering. The 'peeling back' could be effected on either side of the will/intellect divide, or even beyond both. Eckhart, for instance, in some moods, chooses to assert intellect over will as the faculty capable of receiving the beatific vision; at other times, as in his treatise *On Detachment*, he speaks of an ascent beyond both knowing and loving (see McGinn, 1987, p. 17). The unifying and simplifying drive to one ultimate locus in the soul, however, is a characteristic trait; and it is no coincidence, I think, though a fascinating detail, that *The Cloud*'s seventeenth-century Benedictine interpreter Augustine Baker later chooses to describe this drive as a process of 'pure and total abstraction',[12] language not used by *The Cloud* author himself, but with distinctly Cartesian overtones.

Two other characteristics of *The Cloud* are also worth mentioning briefly for our purposes. The one is the distinctly problematic, though by no means totally divorced, relationship of soul and body. Fundamentally, in *The Cloud*, as in the later Descartes, the self *is* the soul, and not the body: 'Whenever you read the word "yourself" in a spiritual context, this means your soul and not your body' (chapter 62; ibid. p. 242). Thus 'Every kind of material thing is outside yourself' (ibid.). *The Cloud* does admit that contemplation will – indirectly and secondarily – have a beautifying effect on body as well as soul (chapter 54), and he thinks it is a good idea to look after oneself physically (chapter 41); but he is scornful of those – Richard Rolle is clearly in mind – who look for any kind of delicious bodily effects in contemplation (chapter 52). As an exercise contemplation is a matter for the naked will alone. Secondly, and significantly for our thesis too, *The Cloud* witnesses to another disjunction occurring in this same late medieval period of Western spirituality, and it appears in tandem with the split between intellect and will. This is the clear demarcation between 'meditation' and 'contemplation', and the reservation of the latter for an élite group of 'solitaries'. *The Cloud* is a striking witness to this development: the demanding nature of the 'work' of contemplation is to be attempted only by 'specials', he says (chapter 1), who may lead the 'life of the solitary'. This

[12]   McCann, 1924, p. 179.

disjunction between meditation and contemplation is a new departure in the West,[13] and not found in the same form in Eastern Christendom; and again, I suggest, it is not without interest in our search for prefigurements of 'individualist' traits in Cartesianism.

But now let me sum up what I have (and have not) claimed in this section in this rather strange and speculative parallelism, before turning to my last point of discussion, on Palamas.

I hope it will be clear that I am not claiming any direct linkage between fourteenth-century mystical theology and Descartes: that would be extremely hard, if not impossible, to sustain. In any case, the genres, aims, and contexts we are dealing with are utterly different: mystical treatises on the one hand and intellectual arguments against sceptical detractors (in a distinctly new climate of scientific objectivism) on the other. Moreover, Descartes' 'peeled-back' cognition seems the very inverse of the non-cognitional will of *The Cloud*. My thesis, to repeat, is a more modest, if relatively subtle one, viz. that the new tendencies evidenced in fourteenth-century spiritual treatises (against a wider background of an emerging sense of *choice* over against authoritative tradition) witness to a simplification and reduction of the Augustinian faculties to one, significant locus in the mind or 'soul'. With that goes the loss of the Thomistic integration of soul and body, such that a new and problematic dualism is reasserted; and at the same time the 'contemplative' becomes a professional solitary who recedes, introverts, 'abstracts', from normal practical reasoning for his own particular purposes in relation to God.

Is this not at least fertile ground for later (and in other ways I admit quite novel and different) Western intellectual developments? Certainly nothing quite like this package of assertions about the self emerged in the East, to which I now turn.

The Case of Gregory Palamas

I come here to my comparison with *The Cloud*'s slightly older near-contemporary (with whom of course he had no contact at all): the monk-bishop Gregory Palamas (1296–1359). My remarks here are necessarily brief and schematic, but I hope none the less suggestive in their comparative force.

Long before he became bishop of Thessalonica (in 1347) Gregory Palamas was a monk of Mount Athos, who spent long hours in 'hesychastic'

---

[13]   The development is charted in Tugwell, 1984, chs. 9–11.

prayer.[14] This was a type of monastic prayer which had evolved over a number of centuries in Eastern Christendom to incorporate the following characteristics: using a particular posture of the monk's body (resting his beard on his chest), and aligning his prayer with regular breathing, the monk constantly repeated the Jesus prayer ('Lord Jesus Christ, Son of God, have mercy on me a sinner', or some variation thereof). The claim of Athonite hesychasm, which was a large part of what Gregory later had to defend in it against detractors, was that this practice could in time result in the unspeakable joy of seeing the divine 'light' itself, as manifest in Christ's embodied transfiguration on Mount Tabor.

Even thus briefly and crudely described, it will be clear how different this form of prayer is from the 'contemplation' described in such Western treatises as *The Cloud*. Rather than being a prayer of naked stripping and simplification of the faculties, of disembodied yearning upwards into darkness, it has all the reverse features, both literally, and in the use of directional metaphor. That is, it involved a 'positive' use of the body, a pressing of the attention 'downwards' into the body, and a repeated christological emphasis, stressing the unity of body and mind. Note also that the Jesus prayer in the East slides across the West's divide between 'meditation' and 'contemplation': the Jesus prayer can start out as a 'meditational' prayer (in the Western sense, that is, reflection on the theological content of the phrases that are repeated), but can then spontaneously turn into what the West would call 'contemplation', the words becoming a sort of mantric background.

Gregory Palamas's sophisticated defence of this prayer arose because of a vehement assault on its theological assumptions by one Barlaam the Calabrian, a Greek significantly educated in the West, and steeped in the 'negative theology' of Pseudo-Dionysius.[15] Barlaam objected to hesychasm on two counts which naturally sprang from his Dionysian commitment. First, there was the hesychasts' claim to see God in 'uncreated light' in this life; and second, there was the positive use of the body in prayer. Palamas's complex response to the first charge (that is, the impossibility of seeing God in light in this life) involved a rather dubiously-coherent distinction between the 'essence' and 'energies' in God. Thus he attempted to marry and synthesize the darkness mysticism of Dionysius and the light mysticism of hesychastic claims, the essential unknowability of the divine and yet the radical

---

[14]   For a brief account of this tradition of prayer, see the sections by Kallistos Ware in Jones, Wainwright and Yarnold, 1986, pp. 175–84, 242–55.
[15]   An account is given of this debate in Meyendorff, 1964, ch. 3.

availability of God in mystical experience. This argument need not detain us here;[16] we are more interested in the other synthesizing move he made in order to justify the hesychasts on the second charge, that of bodily praying. However, we note that on both counts Palamas treats tradition in a significantly different way from that emerging in the West in this period: one cannot, on his view, pick and choose disjunctively. Spiritual practices have to be justified in terms of an existing rich tapestry of different strands of tradition.

On physical prayer, then, as intimated at the beginning of this chapter, Palamas wove *together* the intellectualist understanding of the self as immortal mind (*nous*), as found in the spiritual writings of Evagrius, with the more biblically-oriented psychology of the *Macarian Homilies*, where the self resides ultimately in the 'heart', a term used biblically to denote the psycho-somatic unity of the person. Palamas's core argument in the *The Triads* runs thus (and we note his shifts in terminology between 'soul', 'mind', 'heart' and 'body'):

> Our soul is a unique reality yet possessing multiple powers. It uses as an instrument the body, which by nature coexists with it. But as for that power of the soul we call mind, what instruments does that use in its operations? No one has ever supposed that the mind has its seat in the nails or the eyelids, the nostrils or the lips. Everyone is agreed in locating it within us, but there are differences of opinion as to which inner organ serves the mind as primary instrument. Some place the mind in the brain, as in a kind of acropolis; others hold that its vehicle is the very centre of the heart ... the great Macarius says ... 'The heart directs the entire organism, and when grace gains possession of the heart, it reigns over all the thoughts and all the members' ... Can you not see, then, how essential it is that those who have determined to pay attention to themselves in inner quiet should gather together the mind and enclose it in the body, and especially in that 'body' most interior to the body, which we call the heart. (1983, pp. 42–3)

Thus did Palamas justify, *ex post facto*, the so-called 'descent of the mind into the heart' in the long-term practice of hesychastic prayer. To assess the coherence of this psychology of the person and, not least, account for the precise evocations of 'soul', 'mind' and 'heart', and for the distinctly metaphorical character of the talk of the kenotic descent of the mind into the heart, would be a task going well beyond this present undertaking.

[16]   The theological and philosophical problems of this solution are discussed in Williams, 1977.

Nonetheless, my suggestion is that this would be a worthwhile task for philosophy of religion, and one that would hold up for critical scrutiny an integrative notion of 'soul' at least as sophisticated as that of Thomas Aquinas, and somewhat differently nuanced. But for our preliminary purposes here let us simply note some of the salient additional features of this view of the self. Not only is it clearly rooted in a particular individual prayer *practice*, but it is also integrated into a sacramental communality, and justified in terms of an incarnational principle. Thus, even though, in Palamas, the 'mind' is still seen as the most naturally divine element, the image of God in the person (that represents the Evagrian tradition), none the less the mind has to accept that it cannot save itself by its own powers. It 'needs grace and can find it nowhere but in the Body of Christ united to our bodies by Baptism and the Eucharist'.[17] Thus we note that this rationale acts as an immediate check against an individualistic understanding of the prayer practice. In this context, 'soul' (*psyche*) has the generalized evocation of the life-giving element in the whole person. Hence Palamas can sometimes talk of baptism as representing the 'little resurrection of the soul', by which he apparently means an earnest of the full future resurrection of the soul/body (Meyendorff, 1964, pp. 154–5). 'Deification' in Christ starts in this life, and thus the transformation of the person (body and soul) into the divine life is something that may be already manifest in 'light' now.

Conclusions

I have said enough here to indicate how starkly surprising are the contrasts between the newly disjunctive and individualizing trends of late medieval Western spirituality on the one hand, and what emerged as the triumphant Palamite synthesis in the Byzantine East on the other. Part of my plea here, as a theologian with interests in philosophy of religion, is that we should spend a good deal more time than we currently do in our debates on personal identity and theories of life after death analysing the rich *complexity* of spiritual traditions and accompanying theories of the self that Christianity contains; and above all, that we should attend to the way that prayer and sacramental practice (and all their implications) hold together in any implicit such theory of the self. Here I find myself thoroughly in tune with Fergus Kerr's sympathetic interpretation of Wittgenstein on the self (1986, pp. 148–9): how we carve up the self – and for that matter reassemble it – is

[17] See the exposition in Meyendorff, 1964, p. 154.

a matter of actual 'use', and is rooted in a whole complex of social arrangements, rituals, assumptions and ideology.

And that brings me to my final point, in a speculative chapter in which I have seriously taxed the reader's willingness to make leaps and bounds through time and space. I hinted earlier about the significant correlation in the late medieval West between societal and political change on the one hand, and changes in the conception of the self on the other: readjustments in power centres, the emergence of new classes and groups, the first flexing of nationalistic muscles; all these arguably find their counterparts in the new disjunct possibilities in theorizing about the self. But I have nowhere seen it remarked upon by Palamite scholars that a similar speculation could be made about Palamas's synthesizing *tour de force* of the body/mind. He wrote, we recall, as the Turks, the common enemy, were at the edges of the Byzantine Empire; but a dangerous civil war over imperial succession threatened its internal stability. Palamas, significantly, and in parallel with his treatment of the faculties of the self, was active in effecting reconciliation in the name of the unity of the Christian 'body'. He did this by urging the replacement of imperial and patriarchal powers in the *right place* in the body politic, and by using arguments strikingly parallel to his location of the 'mind' and 'heart' in the human individual (Meyendorff, 1964, p. 64). To draw a final lesson from these examples, then: whilst no suggestion of cultural *determinism* is intended, and whilst debates about identity and the nature of the self must of course continue to be conducted with the utmost philosophical rigour, it is none the less as well to be aware of the political and ideological undertow of our discussions in this area. If theologians seem currently almost united in their collective fury against Cartesian 'individualism', we may well ask what political and ideological agendas (as well as what theology) propel them in this direction. For as the anthropologist Mary Douglas is wont to remind us: 'the public idea of the self is part of a cultural commitment... Both self and community have to be examined together.'[18] At the very least, I hope this chapter will have provided some revealing examples of that principle, and with material that indicates the rich possibilities for further rapproachement amongst philosophy, spirituality and cultural analysis.[19]

---

[18]   I quote from an unpublished paper kindly shown me by the author; but much of Douglas's major published work is devoted to this theme.

[19]   I am grateful to John Clark, Andrew Louth, Tarjei Park, Jeffrey Richards and Patrick Sherry for conversations that have helped in the preparation of this chapter.

References

Buckley, M. J. 1987. *At the Origins of Modern Atheism* (New Haven: Yale University Press).

Bynum, C. W. 1984. *Jesus as Mother: Studies in the Spirituality of the High Middle Ages* (Berkeley: University of California Press).

Clark, S. A. L. 1992. 'Descartes' Debt to Augustine', in M. McGhee (ed.), *Philosophy, Religion and the Spiritual Life* (Cambridge: Cambridge University Press), pp. 73–88.

The Cloud of Unknowing (ed. with an intro. by J. Walsh). 1981. (London: SPCK).

Copleston, F. C. 1955. *Aquinas* (London: Penguin).

Gilson, E. 1979 (1913). *Index Scolastico-Cartésien* (Paris: J. Vrin).

Gregory Palamas. 1983. *The Trials*, selections trans. N. Gendle. (London: SPCK).

Gunton, C. 1985. *The One, the Three and the Many: An Inaugural Lecture in the Chair of Christian Doctrine* (London: King's College London).

Haldane, E. S. and Ross, G. R. T. (eds.) 1931. *The Philosophical Writings of Descartes*, vol. I. (Cambridge: Cambridge University Press).

Hick, J. 1976. *Death and Eternal Life* (London: Collins).

Jones, C., Wainwright, G., and Yarnold, E. (eds.) 1986. *The Study of Spirituality* (London: SPCK).

Kenny, A. 1968. *Descartes*. (New York: Random House).

Kerr, F. 1986. *Theology After Wittgenstein* (Oxford: Blackwell).

Lewis, H. D. 1973. *The Self and Immortality* (London: Macmillan).

Lloyd, G. 1984. *The Man of Reason: 'Male' and 'Female' in Western Philosophy* (Minneapolis: University of Minnesota Press).

Louth, A. 1976. 'Bernard and Affective Mysticism', in B. Ward (ed.), *The Influence of St. Bernard* (Oxford: SLG Press).

Lukes, S. 1973. *Individualism* (Oxford: Blackwell).

McCann, J. (ed.) 1924. *The Cloud of Unknowing and Other Treatises by an English Mystic of the Fourteenth Century with a Commentary on the Cloud by Father Augustine Baker, O. S. B.* (London: Burnes Oates and Washbourne).

McGinn, B. 1987. 'Love, Knowledge, and Mystical Union in Western Christianity: Twelfth to Sixteenth Centuries', *Church History* 56, pp. 7–24.

Meyendorff, J. 1964. *A Study of Gregory Palamas* (London: Faith Press).

Morris, C. 1987 (1972). *The Discovery of the Individual* (London: SPCK).

Penelhum, T. 1970. *Survival and Disembodied Existence* (London: Routledge and Kegan Paul).

Rorty, R. 1980. *Philosophy and the Mirror of Nature* (Oxford: Blackwell).

Swinburne, R. 1986. *The Evolution of the Soul* (Oxford: Clarendon Press).

Taylor, C. 1989. *Sources of the Self* (Cambridge: Cambridge University Press).

Thomson, J. 1983. 'Women and the High Priests of Reason', *Radical Philosophy* 34, pp. 10–14.

Tugwell, S. 1984. *Ways of Imperfection* (London: DLT).

Williams, R. D. 1977. 'The Philosophical Structures of Palamism', *Eastern Churches Review* 9, pp. 27–44.

Chapter 5

GENDER AND KNOWLEDGE IN MODERN WESTERN PHILOSOPHY: THE 'MAN OF REASON' AND THE 'FEMININE' 'OTHER' IN ENLIGHTENMENT AND ROMANTIC THOUGHT

In much recent Western theology,[1] and more especially in feminist philosophy and theology,[2] an anti-hero stalks: the Enlightenment 'Man of Reason'. Can we not all agree in despising him? This villain has a number of characteristics. Cogitating, lonely, individualist, despising the body, passions, women and indeed all sociality, he artificially abstracts from the very dependencies he takes for granted: the products of earth, the comforts of family and friends, and – not least – the miraculous appearance of regular meals.

But like many stereotypes, this 'Man of Reason' is himself an amalgam, a police identikit constructed from a variety of witnesses. In what follows I shall attempt to interrogate at least a few of the more influential amongst these Enlightenment witnesses, and to range their views alongside Romanticism's (ostensibly compensatory) quest for divine mediation through the 'eternal feminine'. My paradoxical conclusion, to anticipate, is that whilst the view of 'women' to emerge from these authors is on the whole depressingly unanimous in its stereotypes,[3] the various views of 'man' that they promulgate are not ones which modern feminists can afford to reject *simpliciter*. At the very least, or so I shall argue, they present us with

Originally published in E. Schüssler Fiorenza and A. Carr (eds.), *The Special Nature of Women: Concilium* 1991/6 (London, SCM Press, 1991), pp. 75–83. Reprinted with permission from SCM Press, with light revisions.

[1] See especially F. Kerr, *Theology after Wittgenstein*, Oxford 1986, ch. 1.

[2] See especially G. Lloyd, *Man of Reason*, London 1984; S. M. Okin, *Women in Western Political Thought*, London 1980; E. Kennedy and S. Mendus (eds.), *Women in Western Political Philosophy*, Brighton 1987; and consider the influence on feminist theology of C. Gilligan, *In a Different Voice*, Cambridge, Mass. 1982.

[3] See Kennedy and Mendus, *Women* (n.2), 16 ff., for a résumé of the pervasive stereotypes of emotionality and submissiveness.

remaining 'antinomies' with which feminism, and especially Christian feminism, is still struggling.

'Man of Reason'

Consider, first, the relation between 'man' and 'nature' as construed by Francis Bacon (1561–1626). Genevieve Lloyd rightly draws attention to the distinctively 'modern' tone of Bacon's argument: rejecting the classical Platonic quest for 'ideal forms' adumbrated in the natural world, Bacon construes matter as straightforwardly mechanistic; the task of the (male) scientific 'mind' is to attend to the mechanism, to experiment and test until predictive control is achieved. Notoriously, Bacon then identifies 'Nature' here as 'female', urging the scientist to enter a 'holy and legal wedlock', to 'bind [Nature] to your service and make her your slave'.[4] Despite Bacon's (touching?) request for 'chastity' and 'respect' in this 'marriage', the gender lines have been fatally drawn. And yet here is also our first enduring paradox for current feminism: for whereas some contemporary feminists (especially historians and anthropologists) are busy deconstructing, or relativizing, the view of 'nature' as a universal datum at all (let alone a datum identified with the 'female'),[5] other, 'radical', feminists rejoice in Bacon's very identification of 'nature' and 'women', urging instead a new release of the 'roaring inside her'.[6]

If we associate Bacon's witness with 'male' control of a 'female' Nature, René Descartes (1596–1650) is more commonly charged with creating a different, but arguably even more fatal, dualism between mind and body. In his famous *Second Meditation* Descartes conducts a thought-experiment of abstraction from the body until he arrives at a notion of identity distinct from it: 'At last I have discovered it – thought – this alone is inseparable from me.' But Descartes' views on the mind/body relation are more subtle and complex than he is commonly given credit for (and arguably the nature of their connection is never fully clarified).[7] But what Descartes strongly

---

[4]   Lloyd, *Man of Reason* (n.2), 12, citing Bacon's *The Masculine Birth of Time* (1653).

[5]   See e.g., C. P. MacCormack and M. Strathern (eds.), *Nature, Culture and Gender*, Cambridge 1980.

[6]   See S. Griffin, *Women and Nature: The Roaring Inside Her*, London 1984.

[7]   So A. Kenny, *Descartes*, New York 1968, 222–3. For a recent collection of feminist essays which reflect on the ambiguity of Descartes' heritage on the mind/body relation, see S. Bordo (ed.), *Feminist Interpretations of René Descartes*, University Park, PA 1999.

denies (in the *Sixth Meditation*) is any suggestion that his mind is in his body 'only as a pilot in a vessel'. And in his late work, *The Passions of the Soul*, he insists that 'the soul is united to all the portions of the body conjointly', speculating (curiously, as it now seems to us) that the bodily seat of the soul is not 'the whole of the brain' but the pineal gland.

It is as well to remember, too, the theistic moorings of Descartes' *cogito*, his underscoring of the significance of the radical *dependence* of the soul upon God, and his religious motivation in asserting its distinction from the body – its immortality. On a secular reading, Descartes' dualism may look crass and insupportable; but for Christians (including Christian feminists) it is hard to see how at least a *distinction* between soul and body – which is not the same as an ultimate separation – can be avoided. Again, then, we have remaining paradoxes here: we may well criticize the way Descartes has construed the soul/body relation, but it is hard to dispose of the problem altogether. Descartes' thinking was not explicitly sexist: in principle, the exercise of Reason was as open to women as to men, but, as emerges revealingly in his correspondence with the Princess Elizabeth, the arduous demands of his particular form of abstract reasoning were hard for a woman to sustain: 'Sometimes the interests of my household,' complains Elizabeth, 'sometimes conversations and civilities I cannot eschew...[do not] allow me enough free time to acquire a habit of meditation in accordance with your rules.'[8] From this perspective we may see the emergence of feminist epistemologies (such as Sara Ruddick's[9]) as a fit rejoinder to Descartes: the emphasis here is not so much on soul/body dualism as on the sheer complexity of maternal decision-making in the maelstrom of toddlers' demands and emotional blackmail. In this way we may turn Descartes (justly!) on his head, and defend the high sophistication of 'maternal thinking', the forging of peace and harmony and nurture out of the confused interstices of domestic existence.

If Descartes leaves a more complex intellectual inheritance for feminism than is often allowed, the legacy of Jean-Jacques Rousseau (1712–78) is even more bewildering, indeed riddled with self-contradictions.[10] Exponent of vegetarianism and maternal breast-feeding, he himself fathered five

---

[8] Lloyd, *Man of Reason* (n.2), 48–9, citing a letter of Princess Elizabeth to Descartes, 10/20 June 1643.

[9] S. Ruddick, *Maternal Thinking*, Boston 1989.

[10] There is now an extensive feminist literature on Rousseau. As well as Lloyd, *Man of Reason* (n.2); Okin, *Women in Western Political Thought* (n.2); Kennedy and Mendus, *Women in Western Political Philosophy* (n.2), see also J. B. Elshtain, *Meditations on Modern Political Thought*, New York 1986, and J. B. Elshtain (ed.), *The Family in Political Thought*, Brighton 1982.

illegitimate children who were left as foundlings; protected and sustained at crucial points in his career by rich and dedicated women, he himself recommended that the education of girls should merely attune them to lives of subordination ('Unable to judge for themselves, they should accept the judgment of father and husband . . .' *Émile*, Bk. V); devoting *The Social Contract* to an acute analysis of why 'man [*sic*] is born free' but yet 'everywhere . . . is in chains', he granted women no such ambitions to liberty and equality.

And yet Rousseau was an adulator of women, a positive defender of the importance of the family, the body, feeling and the imagination, as emerges especially from *Émile*, and from his novel *La Nouvelle Héloise*.[11] Here is no clear case, then, of our identikit 'Man of Reason'. Rather than rending thought and body apart, Rousseau constructed a rather different series of aligned dualities (male/female, reason/nature, reason/passion, public/private), based on a theory of sexual difference and 'complementarity'. Women are held up as close to Nature, as moral exemplars, as potentially dangerous in their capacity for passion, but as safely containable within the private, domestic enclave. (Julie, in *La Nouvelle Héloise*, manifests all these traits: she cultivates a little garden in which 'Nature has done everything'; she early falls prey to passion in the loss of her virginity to her tutor Saint-Preux, but places duty to her family before this passion, submitting to an appropriate marriage and domestic 'happiness', whilst yet finding real happiness elusive.[12]) On the other side of the sexual divide, 'male' Reason emerges dynamically from Nature ('The passage from the state of nature to the civil state produces a very remarkable change in man, by substituting justice for instinct . . .', *Social Contract* I, ch. VIII); yet there is also nostalgia for the 'natural' state, and a hope that the transformation of society might effect a new *rapprochement*. Reason, however, must hold sway in the public realm, lest passionate feelings conflict with the demands of state order.

It will be clear, perhaps, that Rousseau's theory of sexual 'complementarity' actually presents a 'difference' between the sexes by no means predicated on equality (and this point was not lost on Mary Wollstonecraft, Rousseau's spirited assailant on this issue in *The Vindication of the Rights of Women*, 1792). Thus, in *Émile* we are told that, 'A perfect man and a perfect woman should no more be alike in mind than in face . . . In the union of the sexes, each alike contributes to the common end, but in *different* ways.'

---

[11]   For discussion of these aspects of Rousseau's thought see especially Elshtain, *Meditations* (n.10), ch. 4.

[12]   See Okin, *Women* (n.2), ch. 8, for a treatment of this.

Reading on, the sting in the tail becomes apparent: 'From this diversity springs the first difference which may be observed between man and woman in their moral relations. The man should be strong and active; the woman should be weak and passive; the one must have both the power and the will; it is enough that the other should offer little resistance.'[13] No wonder, perhaps, that both Rousseau's famous heroines, Sophie in *Émile* (who loses her virtue decisively when she moves to a 'public', urban domain), and Julie in *La Nouvelle Héloise* (who maintains a listless virtue in marriage), have to be killed off at the end of their stories: their *subordinate* 'complementarity' leaves them little room for manoeuvre.

The remaining paradoxes of Rousseau's thought, then, are differently located from Descartes': the rhetoric of 'difference' still continues to fascinate (especially in contemporary French feminism), and indeed must do, if we are to avoid a straightforward aping of a 'masculinist' vision of humanity. Yet 'liberal feminism' (witness Mary Wollstonecraft herself) is understandably suspicious of any version of sexual 'complementarity' dreamed up by men; Enlightenment ideals of freedom, equality and autonomy might seem preferable in comparison. This gender tension is, interestingly, transferred and *internalized* in Rousseau in what Margaret Canovan has described as his 'longing for autonomy (to the point of solitude), on the one hand, and for integration (to the point of self-annihilation) on the other'.[14] Falling in love is a dangerous (albeit necessary) business in Rousseau's writings: *dependency* is, according to him, both an enticing requirement of sexual love and also its destructive pathology. Is there no way through this dilemma?[15]

The answer of Immanuel Kant (1724–1804), of course, was that autonomous reason should transcend any entanglements of dependency or 'heteronomy'. In this way he shuns Rousseau's fascination with sexual love and feeling. His essay 'What is Enlightenment?' (1784) is a charter document of independent critical judgment: '*Sapere aude*' (Dare to be wise) means the sloughing off of immature submission to mere authority; the individual must dare to take responsibility for entry into the public realm of universal principles of reason and morality. Significantly, Kant underscores that the 'entire fair sex' avoids this 'step to competence'. Yet ostensibly, the Kantian autonomous individual is sexless. Indeed in the *Groundwork for a Metaphysic*

[13] For discussion of this see C. W. Korsmeyer, 'Reason and Morals in the Early Feminist Movement: Mary Wollstonecraft', in C. G. Gould and M. W. Wartofsky (eds.), *Women and Philosophy*, New York 1976, 97–111, especially 99.
[14] In Kennedy and Mendus, *Women* (n.2), 79.
[15] See the discussion of this question in E. Rapaport, 'On the Future of Love: Rousseau and the Radical Feminists', in Gould and Wartofsky, *Women and Philosophy* (n.13), 185–205.

of Morals (1785), for instance, Kant insists that the moral principles enunciated there are not only applicable to all human beings, but to 'rational beings' *per se*. Sex seems irrelevant; especially when, in the *Critique of Pure Reason* (^{1}1781, ^{2}1787), the strange 'noumenal self' 'independent of, and free for all . . . necessity' is contrasted with the 'phenomenal self', known through actions in the empirical world. What, then, are we to make of the rampant sexisms of Kant's political writings, and especially his discussion 'Of the Nature of the Sexes' in the *Anthropology*? Here, as Susan Mendus puts it, 'Kant's mind, almost wholly uncluttered by any actual experience, is laid bare and the prejudice and bigotry are revealed.'[16] A married woman, for instance, is represented as promiscuous and unreliable, jealous and harsh ('In marriage the husband loves only his one wife, but the wife has an inclination for all men', etc.); no justification is given for these assertions, but the conclusion, notoriously, is that 'the woman should reign and the man should rule; because inclination reigns and reason rules'. The domestic power of women is ultimately superseded. No wonder, then, that in Kant's political philosophy women are only accorded the status of *passive* citizens; and in marriage woman is seen as relinquishing her equality in deference to 'the natural superiority of the husband over the wife'.

As Mendus concludes, 'It may well be that Kant is an honest but narrow-minded bourgeois, unable to see beyond the social conventions of his time.' But are his sexisms merely incidental? The more interesting question is whether his distinctive view of the autonomous, independent dispassionate *individual* 'cannot readily accommodate . . . social units such as the family, which transcend mere atomism',[17] and hence make the construction of this view of the self parasitic upon the submission of women (and indeed man-servants). It is, then, the paradox of 'autonomy' and 'heteronomy' that Kant's form of the 'Man of Reason' abidingly bequeathes to modern feminism. If women claim a Kantian form of autonomy, they risk all the traps of atomism; but if they compromise it, they fall back into subordination, or perhaps never fully emerge from the soup of undifferentiated relationship.

The 'Eternal Feminine' of Romanticism

Romanticism's answer to this problem was to compensate for the lonely male 'autonomy' by an adulation, indeed near deification, of the 'feminine'.

---

[16]   See Kennedy and Mendus, *Women* (n.2), 35.
[17]   Ibid., 40 f.

Once again, we are not dealing with a consensus of views; the earlier writings of Friedrich von Schlegel (1772–1829), in particular, could have a surprisingly 'modern' ring, viciously lampooning the emotive sex stereotyping of Schiller's lilting rhymes ('The Husband must enter/The hostile life/With struggle and strife.... [but] Within sits Another/the Chaste Housewife/The mild one, the mother – /Her home is her life').[18] Briefly, in the early Schlegel is an alternative vision (focused on the model of Antigone, but probably inspired by a real-life woman, Caroline Böhmer) of an independent woman achieving completion without the benefits of male love.[19] Much more characteristic of Romanticism, however, was an aspiration to 'androgyny' achieved through the love union; and to this view Schlegel himself later subscribed.

Sara Friedrichsmeyer[20] has illuminatingly traced the sources of the Romantics' *Androgyne* ideal. It goes back at least to Plato's *Symposium*, and Aristophanes' story there of the split selves who roam about in search of each other; but the Romantics' reassimilation of the theme was part of their fascination with esoteric literature – especially alchemy – and with their background in German pietist thought, itself influenced by the Protestant mystic Jakob Böhme. In all these sources the myth of the androgyne appears in some form; in Böhme (censored till 1682) there are daring justifications for sexual desire as a 'divine inclination', and Christ's last words on the cross (*consummatum est*) are taken to signify some final merging of the sexes.

In the Romantics, the myth can collect a number of different evocations. In Novalis's novels, 'romanticizing the world' means raising the 'lower self' to 'an elevated meaning... [of] an infinite lustre'; thus (male) consciousness is raised by contact with female inspiration, and the symbol of the androgyne represents their union. The working out of this theme, especially in Heinrich von Ofterdingen, is, as Marilyn Massey has demonstrated,[21] sexually and politically daring, even outrageous: it combines an unbridled eroticism, and (amongst other things) an adulation of unmarried goddess-mothers, and strange rites such as the drinking of the dissolved ashes of a mother so that she can be 'present in each'. The sexually arousing is (not unusually) combined with the fantasy world of the weird and wonderful. But it is revealing to know that Novalis's real-life experience

[18]   Ibid., 106–7.
[19]   See the discussion in S. Friedrichsmeyer, *The Androgyne in Early German Romanticism*, Bern 1983, ch. 5.
[20]   Ibid., chs. 1, 2.
[21]   M. Massey, *Feminine Soul: The Fate of an Ideal*, Boston 1985.

of androgynous union was the idealization of a twelve-year-old girl, Sophie, whom he met and fell in love with; she died three years later, but Novalis claimed to have some experience of mystic union with her (and with the world of spirit) at her graveside. Sophie's extreme youthfulness and her premature death are surely significant, and invite guesses both about the maturity of the androgynous relationship envisaged and about the extent of the woman's reciprocity in it. Is she ultimately dispensable?

The fate of Gretchen in Goethe's *Faust* is no less revealing of a double standard: for while Gretchen is responsible for the high task (as *das ewig Weibliche*) of leading Faust's soul to eternal salvation, she must herself nonetheless do penance for her own sexual transgression. 'Perhaps,' comment Susan Cocalis and Kay Goodman, 'it is this inequity that constitutes the real tragedy of Goethe's *Faust*.'[22] Likewise, it is hardly reassuring to be told (by Wilhelm von Humboldt) that women are 'closer' to the ideal human than men, when it turns out that any kind of active self-assertion or manifest talent is frowned upon in their case as 'unfeminine'.[23] The serious inequalities and sexisms of 'androgyny', balanced in favour of *male* development and integration, are manifest here, and notoriously repeat themselves in C. G. Jung's theory of the self some generations later, where the incorporation of a woman's *animus* is treated much more summarily (and indeed negatively) than the integration of a man's ('feminine') *anima*.

In Schlegel's novel *Lucinde*, in contrast, the lovers Julius and Lucinde exchange roles in their love-making (Julius exhibiting 'charming surrender', Lucinde 'considerate ardour'), and in this androgynous exchange Julius finds a 'wonderful . . . allegory of the development of male and female to full and complete humanity'. Despite the shift, then, from his earlier phase to the more obviously Romantic interpretation of the 'androgynous' idea, we see here in Schlegel a slightly more equitable interpretation of the theme. Arguably too, in Schleiermacher's 'Christmas Eve Dialogue' we have expressions of religious 'feeling' and the 'feminine soul' just as well represented by Josef (who chides the other men for their tedious speech-making and himself 'laughs and exults like a child') as by Sophie, the little girl who more obviously exhibits the spirit of Christmas and spontaneous religiosity.[24]

---

[22] S. L. Cocalis and K. Goodman (eds.), *Beyond the Eternal Feminine*, Stuttgart 1982.

[23] Kennedy and Mendus, *Women* (n.2), 110–11.

[24] So D. de Vries, 'Schleiermacher's *Christmas Eve Dialogue*: Bourgeois Ideology or Feminist Theology?', *Journal of Religion* 69, 1989, 169–83, taking issue with Massey's less positive interpretation in *Feminine Soul* (n.21), ch. 6.

We may well conclude: all Romantic 'androgynes' are 'equal', but some are decidedly more equal than others. But again, the paradoxes of this Romantic theme have far from been dispelled: the obsession with sexual 'difference' is still with us, and the idea (in radical feminists such as Adrienne Rich) that female nature, and motherhood, are capable of producing new and distinctive 'visions' of the world ironically echoes Romantic forebears. And when we recall that early Romanticism wished to loose men and women from fixed concepts of gender (whilst not retreating into an abstract sexless account of the person), we realize that that agenda is still with us too, however poorly it was served by individual Romantics' solutions. Moreover, for Christian feminism especially, the huge question still remains (poignantly begged by Romanticism) of the integration of sexual desire and the desire for God, and the extent to which such an integration might be constructed out of the resources of Christian history and spirituality. Is falling in love invariably nothing but a false delusion, a pathology of sexual dependence? Or is it in some way capable of alignment with a feminist account of human growth before God?

Conclusions

By a selective (and necessarily brief) account of Enlightenment and Romantic visions of the normative male self, and by reference to some of the burgeoning feminist literature on this topic, I have sought to avoid some of the more simplistic stereotypes of this 'Man of Reason' and to urge that many of the issues raised by the thinkers concerned are still – paradoxically – pressing ones for contemporary feminist thought. In short, our Enlightenment heritage is not easily dispelled; indeed without it, it is hard to imagine modern Western feminism having taken the form it has in the first place. And as the heady shift to postmodern relativism becomes an attractive philosophical option for increasing numbers of feminists, we may well question whether the Enlightenment demand for global principles in ethics (as opposed to *local* political agendas) can be lightly discarded when what we surely must still dream of is an 'abolition of the sex class system' *tout court*.[25]

---

[25]   For an important recent discussion of the heritage of the Enlightenment for feminism, see S. Lovibond, 'Feminism and Postmodernism', *New Left Review* 178, 1989, 5–28.

Chapter 6

ANALYTIC PHILOSOPHY OF RELIGION IN FEMINIST PERSPECTIVE: SOME QUESTIONS

Analytic philosophy of religion has to date shown a marked (if largely silent) resistance to feminist reflection of any sort. Its hostility to feminist *theology* (evidenced in a few scattered articles) is easily comprehensible, granted the initial genesis of that movement in the early 1970s from American "liberal" and "constructivist" theology (to which most analytic philosophers of religion are opposed on other grounds), the biblical and doctrinal conservatism that characterizes analytic philosophy of religion as a whole, and the relative lack of philosophical acuity displayed in much first-wave feminist theology. It will not, however, be the goal of this chapter to survey types of feminist theology. Rather the focus will be on philosophy of religion's more puzzling avoidance of the sophisticated work done in recent years in feminist *philosophy* (for useful surveys, see Grimshaw 1986, Rooney 1994). If taken seriously by philosophers of religion, this could have far-reaching implications for their fundamental assumptions and preoccupations; and it will be the task here to sketch out these implications in a preliminary form. It will be suggested that the central place accorded in much analytic philosophy of religion to what feminists call the "generic male" (i.e., the privileged male subject posing as a sexless individual of universal instantiation) results in the sidelining not only of issues important to feminism, but also – ironically – of rich spiritual options from the Christian tradition.

Originally published in Charles Taliaferro and Philip Quinn (eds.), *A Companion to Philosophy of Religion* (Oxford, Blackwell, 1997), pp. 601–6. Reprinted with permission from Blackwell, with light revisions.

The "Generic Male" and the Problem of Evil

There is a relative dearth of literature in analytic philosophy of religion on the concept of "self" in *all* its dimensions; attention is more commonly focused on specific issues such as the mind/body problem. The discussion of free will, however, is richly developed on account of the crucial theodicy questions raised by the problem of evil. Indeed one could argue that whatever solution the philosopher of religion proposes to this most pressing of contemporary religious questions, this will deeply affect the rest of the accompanying theological and philosophical system. The dominance of an "incompatibilist" view of freedom (in service of a "free will defense" on the problem of evil) is a striking feature of current analytic philosophy of religion – the more surprising, perhaps, when enunciated by those other-wise staunchly committed to the defense of Calvinism. The sovereign, *unconditioned* freedom of the individual to do evil (as well as good), and thereby to effect a temporary evasion even of divine conditioning, is deemed by many contemporary philosophers of religion to be the only acceptable first plank in a convincing solution to the problem of evil.

But it is here that feminist critiques of the "generic male" may be particularly telling, and provide important complements (strange as this may seem) to the theological objections to incompatibilism from the Thomist or Calvinist camps. Feminist philosophers point here, first, to the historical *specificity* of the visions of "autonomy" spawned by the Enlighten-ment, and the conditionings, relationships, and dependencies – not least those on wife and family – that go unmentioned in these accounts, whilst also being taken for granted in them (see Lloyd 1984). Thus in Enlighten-ment discussions, woman – the invisible "other" supposedly included under the "generic" autonomous male – turns out, in her occasional moments of explicit recognition, actually to be in need of lengthy education before she can enjoy the fruits of Enlightenment "freedom" (so Immanuel Kant); though she may meanwhile pursue a vocation as "cushion" for her husband against the slings and arrows of free (male) political exchange (so Thomas Carlyle).

One may ask whether these Enlightenment conceptions of "autonomy" continue to infect – albeit unconsciously – the incompatibilist vision of freedom promulgated by many philosophers of religion (including some distinguished women philosophers) in response to the problem of evil. What difference would it make if this were acknowledged? It would, for a start, make it impossible for the promulgators of the "free will defense" to proceed as if incompatibilism were unproblematic in either gender or class terms (quite apart from its more technical philosophical ramifications). When it is said that it is "good that an agent should have . . . power over the universe, the power to determine whether the morally good will prevail," and that "a creator has reason to allow him the opportunity to do so, to allow him through right choices to grow in freedom and morally relevant knowledge until he becomes as the angels" (Swinburne 1991, pp. 158–9), a feminist may appropriately inquire whether this presumes on the part of the (male) agent a particular level of education, political freedom, and financial independence. (And since women only occasionally appear in Richard Swinburne's narrative on the importance of "man's" free will, it is instructive to note what *they* are doing: as minimally necessary for the act of conception (p. 187), as hapless victims of other men's seductive purposes (p. 192), or as desire-inducing distractors from the monogamous path (p. 158).) Philosophers of religion are not accustomed to reading such "subtext"; one implication of an engagement with feminist philosophy would be to raise such gendered material to consciousness.

Furthermore, feminist philosophers of both Anglo-American and continental background have entered into revealing (and critical) debate with Sigmund Freud and his various intellectual descendants. In so doing they have inquired about the childhood development of "autonomous" behavior and its relation to maternal dependence. If this development is in some sense gender-specific (involving a more fundamental repudiation of the mother in the case of male children), then intriguing questions are raised about how philosophical notions of free will relate to this basic familial context, and whether they, too, are covertly "male." In the work of French feminism (strongly influenced by Jacques Lacan) a more radical suggestion is proposed: that even the child's entry into the linguistic realm constitutes a repression of a primal "feminine" creativity associated with the maternal identification of the breast-feeding phase (so Julia Kristeva). This may seem far removed from analytic philosophy of religion's concern with the free will defense: yet a confluence of these debates could have considerable import. If it could be argued that an incompatibilist vision of freedom is unconsciously motivated by rejection of the mother (and everything she symbolizes: dependency, relationship, affectivity, bodiliness, emergent sexuality), then it is hardly surprising that it can also be resistant, in a theological context, to a notion of God as matrix – as sustaining conditioner of all that we are and do (even of acts of compatibilist freedom). As Swinburne puts it in a related context (1991, p. 212), he would want to avoid a circumstance in which "God would be too close for [men] to work things out for themselves." It is left, then, to the staider defenders of Thomas Aquinas and John Calvin to propose a determinism less repudiating of God's "closeness."

The Concept of God and Feminist Critique

It is not so surprising, then, to note in analytic philosophy of religion a striking tendency to image God as a magnified version of the *human* "unmoved mover" (Roderick M. Chisholm) of incompatibilist freedom, an 'individual' of unrivaled power and autonomy who takes on the traditional attributes of classical theism, but more revealingly mirrors a (masculinist) vision of self specific to the Enlightenment. Such a predilection becomes evident when – according to some exponents – the traditional attributes have to be modified to accommodate the indeterminism of this privileged vision of human freedom; or the alternative view of divine–human relations (some form of determinism) is castigated as mere "puppetry" or "ventriloquism." To a feminist analysis, the dominance of such images of negative control in this debate bespeak a more fundamental failure to conceive of divine–human relations in anything other than competitive terms (where one "individual" either repressively dominates the other or else withdraws to make space for the other's autonomy). What is palpably missing is a sustained or positive reflection on the nurturing and all-encompassing dimensions of divine love – gendered metaphors that have well-known instantiations in the history of Christian theology and spirituality (e.g., Anselm, Julian of Norwich), but do not characteristically leap to the forefront of the analytic philosopher's imag- ination. In one striking recent counter-instance to this rule, Eleonore Stump (1994) can speak of a solution to the problem of evil in terms of the recognition of the "*mothering* guidance of God" (p. 242) superseding the ostensibly overwhelming presence of evil in the world. Stump does not, however, wish to acknowledge any connection with feminist thought in coming to this conclusion.

Other signs of "masculinist" visions of God in analytic philosophy of religion cracking under their own weight may be detected in recent discus- sions of the Trinity and the Incarnation. The lack of integration between analytic work on the arguments for the existence of God and more recent defenses of trinitarianism (on rational, not revelatory, grounds) witnesses to this. In the discussion about the arguments, little or nothing is said about the relational and internally complex nature of the Christian God; on the contrary, a great deal of play is made of the principle of simplicity (see again Swinburne 1991). That the divine "individual" established as existent by these arguments is then joined by two other "Gods" (so Swinburne, in more recent work) suggests a covert identification of the former with the "Father" (once again a decidedly non-Thomistic maneuver), and creates strain in dealing with the application of the simplicity principle. A feminist analysis of these developments would point to the failure to write divine *relationship* into the initial case for God's existence. Instead, a whiff of anti-trinitarian deism still tends to hang over the discussion of the arguments, such that the divine monad so established then needs to mount a new foray to the created world (according to one version of the Incarnation) in order to reestablish contact with the human family at all. Is this once more (in subtext) the disassociated 'Father' of post-Enlightenment individualism? It is revealing that enormous logical rigor has been applied by analytic philosophers of religion of late to decrying the possibility of a contemporary philosophical defense of Western, "Augustinian" trinitarianism (where priority is given to the unity-in-relationship of the divine triad). The so-called "Eastern," "Cappadocian" approach is preferred on account of its (purported) maintenance of "individual" identity for the "persons" and thus its greater coherence. In this, analytic philosophy of religion again displays a predilection for a certain vision of the self spawned long after the fourth century; and in general it reveals a "masculinist" lack of imagination to conceive of inner-trinitarian loving exchange in anything other than extrinsic or contractual terms. There is a notable failure in developing models of *trans*-"individual" identity. None the less, that "relationships" of (divine) "equals" are now on the agenda at all marks a minor advance in the discourse toward feminist ethical and theological concerns.

The 'masculinism' that infects discussions of the Incarnation in recent philosophy of religion is more subtly pervasive. It is once again the way that a particular *relationship* is construed that is significant here, in this case the vital "hypostatic" unity of the divinity and humanity of Christ. The favored model for their interaction (tellingly, since the force of the unconscious is so rarely acknowledged in analytic philosophy of religion) is the power of the unconscious over the conscious, as in the Freudian "divided mind." However, this is not a signal that a full range of Freudian themes on sexuality and the unconscious is now entering into the discussion (something that feminists would welcome, if not uncritically). On the contrary, one point of the analogy is to demonstrate how one may *maintain* a libertarian view of human freedom in Christ whilst simultaneously promoting a vision of total divine *control* – as if Christ had constraining electrodes implanted in his skull to prevent possible lapses from sinlessness (so Thomas V. Morris, utilizing a thought-experiment of Harry Frankfurt). Encoded here is a strange combination of semi-recognition of the potential importance of Freud for philosophical reflection on the divine and the human – the free and the un-free – and a stolid refusal to see in the narrative of Christ's life and death any *upsetting* of stereotypical (gendered) ideas about "power" and "weakness," "control" and "loss of control." Again, a feminist analysis of these Christological debates can reveal how certain favored (masculinist) "intuition pumps" restricted the range of theological options from the outset (see chapter 1 in this volume).

Feminism and Religious Epistemology

Arguably the most creative area of development in recent philosophy of religion has been that of epistemology, especially in its relation to "religious experience." But the last decade has also seen the emergence of sophisticated work in feminist epistemology (see, e.g., Code 1992, and the essays in Alcoff and Potter 1993) – a development wholly ignored in the debates of analytic philosophy of religion, despite the shared impact on both fields of the collapse of "classical foundationalism." Feminist epistemologists of different schools and philosophical persuasions have presented a range of alternatives, all of them stressing the political, racial, and gendered specificity of the privileged "knower" in mainstream epistemology. To ask "*who* knows" may, first, be the demand to *extend* an empiricist epistemology to include "knowers" previously excluded; as such, this option represents an advance in empirical "objectivity," not its demise. Alternatively, and second, it may involve a turn to "standpoint epistemology," stressing the socially constructed nature of the knowing subject and its partiality of vision (though not necessarily succumbing in all respect to postmodern relativism). Third, and rather differently, as in certain forms of French feminism, it may appeal to an *intrinsically* gendered form of "knowing" that is subversive of "male" rationality *tout court*.

If any of these feminist approaches were to be brought into critical play with analytic philosophy of religion's recent discussions of "religious experience," some interesting insights and new avenues of reflection might emerge. In the first place, it could be suggested that the current intensity of philosophical discussion in this area represents (albeit unconsciously) a heroic attempt to give *cognitive* and *justificatory* significance to an area which has traditionally been sidelined as "private" and "subjective," associated with intensified affectivity and expression in sexual metaphor, and in which women have "starred" as sites of divine intimacy. As such, the argument from religious experience represents a kind of "subjective" surd in the "cumulative case" for theism (see Swinburne 1991, ch. 13), and needs the crucial appeals to "testimony" and "credulity" to give it public cogency. A feminist critic might therefore ask whether this interest in "experiential" intimacy with God is not an intrinsically gendered matter – a move by masculinist philosophy of religion to appropriate the "feminine" power of "mystical" insight and simultaneously to adjust its form to meet the stand-ards of an already-assumed rationality. (Teresa of Ávila is the centerpiece of many recent philosophical analyses of "religious experience"; the fact that she was a *woman* mystic confronting male skepticism and disapproval in particular historical and political circumstances is noted by none of them.) Second, the crucial issue of "whose testimony, what credulity?" is a pressing one when once seen through a feminist lens (see Jantzen 1994 and 1998). If the veracity of appeals to 'religious experience' ultimately resides in some primary acceptance of Reidian "credulity," then it is pertinent to ask whether *anyone's* credulity (women's, children's, illiterates'?) will do. Bring-ing "religious experience" to the bar of rational "justification" may thus appear as the modern counterpart of the male confessor's hold over the medieval female saint's theological status and credibility. In both, the danger is ultimately one of reductive loss: in the case of contemporary philosophy of religion (for all its epistemological finesse) this loss resides in failing to accept the challenge to develop an *expanded* notion of the epistemic subject suggested by the literature of the great "mystics" – one in which affectivity is not subordinated, nor sexual metaphor derided as "smut," nor dark "unknowing" seen as a threat to rationality's stability. The acknowledgment that these latter issues are themselves "gendered" would be the first step in such an advance; the further explicating of the gendered "standpoints" concealed in the "doxastic practices" (William Alston) of Christian devotion would be another – and very complex – task.

What this shows is that there is still much work to be done – both critical and constructive – in future feminist philosophy of religion in the analytic mode. This chapter has been written with the conviction that the undeni-able clarity and apologetic strengths of the analytic tradition should not be *abandoned* by feminism (*contra* recent critical work by Jantzen, 1998, and Anderson, 1998, which rejects the analytic discourse wholesale), but rather undergo major adjustments to meet the feminist challenge. Crucial to these, as I have argued here, will be the clarification (in analytic terms) of the "free," but responsively dependent, relationship of the human to the divine, and its connections to the cultural complexities of gender.

References

Alcoff, L., and Potter, E. (eds): *Feminist Epistemologies* (London: Routledge, 1993).

Anderson, P. S.: *A Feminist Philosophy of Religion* (Oxford: Blackwell, 1998).

Coakley, S.: "*Kenōsis* and subversion: On the repression of 'vulnerability' in Christian feminist writing": chapter 1 in this volume.

Code, L.: "Feminist epistemology." In *A Companion to Epistemology*, ed. J. Dancy and E. Sosa (Oxford: Blackwell, 1992).

Grimshaw, J.: *Feminist Philosophers: Women's Perspectives on Philosophical Traditions* (London: Harvester Wheatsheaf, 1986).

Jantzen, G. M.: "Feminists, philosophers, and mystics," *Hypatia*, 9 (1994), pp. 186–206.

——: *Becoming Divine: Towards a Feminist Philosophy of Religion* (Manchester: Manchester University Press, 1998).

Lloyd, G.: *The Man of Reason: "Male" and "Female" in Western Philosophy* (Minneapolis: University of Minnesota Press, 1984).

Rooney, P.: "Recent work in feminist discussions of reason," *American Philosophical Quarterly*, 31 (1994), pp. 1–21.

Stump, E.: "The mirror of evil." In *God and the Philosophers*, ed. T. V. Morris (New York: Oxford University Press, 1994).

Swinburne, R.: *The Existence of God*, rev. edn (Oxford: Clarendon Press, 1991).

Part III

Doctrinal Implications

Chapter 7

'Persons' in the 'Social' Doctrine of the Trinity: Current Analytic Discussion and 'Cappadocian' Theology

In the first two parts of this book we have engaged in some novel interrogations of both spiritual and philosophical tradition in quest of a clarification of the gendered nature of classic representations of divine 'power' and human 'submission'. It was not for nothing that this undertaking began (chapter 1) with a *christological* focus; for in the doctrine of Christ, if anywhere, Christian theology has attempted to chart the nature and implications of that perfect intersection of the divine and human. As we have tried to show, classic Western discussions of topics as varied as 'contemplation', 'creaturehood', 'freedom', 'autonomy', and 'reason' all have strands of connection back to that archetypal Christian vision of perfected humanity. That insight in itself is not new; what has been neglected in earlier generations has been attention to the profound entanglement of questions of gender in this classic repertoire.

Now, in the final part of the book, we return again to specifically doctrinal themes. But this time the tables will be turned: not so much to examine the very *nature* of a 'contemplative' practice that might correctly construe the relation of divine power and (right) human submission; but instead to explore a strand of pre-modern tradition that has – as I shall argue – rich and creative possibilities for charting the implications of such practice for contemporary doctrinal exposition. The patristic figure who reappears in all three of these last essays is Gregory of Nyssa (*c*.330–*c*.395), the youngest of the so-called 'Cappadocians', and simultaneously the most elusive and compelling. As we shall attempt to show, his own combination

Originally published in Stephen T. Davis, Daniel Kendall, SJ and Gerald O'Collins, SJ (eds.), *The Trinity: An Interdisciplinary Symposium on the Doctrine of the Trinity* (Oxford, Oxford University Press, 1999), pp. 123–44. Reprinted with permission from Oxford University Press, with light revisions.

of contemplative practice, philosophical interlocution, and doctrinal expression is combined with extraordinarily searching reflections on what we would now term 'gender'; what we described in chapter 3 as an 'Eastern' tendency to covert hierarchalism in the Godhead and a 'spurious (and de-sexed) equality for female creatureliness' is here put to the test. Yet we 'moderns' have – I shall argue – misconstrued Gregory, reading him only selectively or with an eye to particular theological ends. By attempting to read his corpus in a more integrated way, I risk (admittedly) the charge of yet another hermeneutical manipulation by bringing his work into creative debate with contemporary analytic philosophy of religion (here in chapter 7), Wittgensteinian epistemology (chapter 8) and postmodern feminist theory (chapter 9). I make no attempt, note, to exonerate Nyssa from charges of inconsistency or time-boundedness: here is no plaster saint for our pedestalization. But here is a writer of astonishing spiritual insight, philosophical sharpness, and theological complexity, an ascetic guide to the exigencies of 'desire' who had no fear or horror of the sexual act, and whose musings on the goals of 'contemplation' are shot through with reflections on gender transformation and fluidity. It is his particular vision of how the *sui generis* 'submission' of contemplation infuses the theological task that we shall now explore, beginning with his most famous contribution – to the classic (so-called) 'Eastern' doctrine of the Trinity.

Introduction and Statement of Thesis

Let me begin this discussion by sketching out some intriguing features of the context in which the current trinitarian debate is taking place. In the remarkable recent outpouring of writing on the doctrine of the Trinity we may detect, I suggest, an interesting double paradox.

On the one hand, sophisticated logicians amongst the analytic philosophers of religion have devoted much energy to defending the so-called 'Social' (or 'Plurality') doctrine of the Trinity, whilst decrying the coherence of a 'Latin' (or 'Unity') model.[1] In so doing, however, they have – with only one or two important exceptions, to be examined below – paid relatively little attention to the *type* of entity that they are calling 'person' when they count 'three' of them in the Godhead. Indeed, when we probe a

---

[1] Brian Leftow's paper 'Anti Social Trinitarianism', in Stephen Davis, Daniel Kendall SJ and Gerald O'Collins SJ (eds.), *The Trinity* (Oxford: Oxford University Press, 1999), 203–49, provides a useful introduction to this issue and the literature concerned.

little with the tools of the hermeneutics of suspicion, we may detect distinct whiffs of influence from 'modern' perceptions of 'person' (or 'individual') smuggled into the debate and read back into the patristic texts which are being claimed as authoritative.

On the other hand, and simultaneously, systematic theologians have been at work debunking precisely those 'modern' notions of individualism that they perceive to have distorted Christian anthropology since the Enlightenment and to have undermined trinitarian conceptuality altogether.[2] For them, construing 'persons' *as* 'relations' (whatever this means exactly) has become a theological watchword. Unhappily, these two camps of scholarship, despite their shared commitment to the reinstatement of trinitarian theology, show little mutual regard for each other's work.

This paradox of intention and starting point recapitulates itself, in a rather curious way, in intra-feminist debates on the Trinity – a fact so far rarely commented upon; but this is why I speak of a 'double paradox'. On the one hand, we have the radical feminist spoof of trinitarianism (in Mary Daly's work) as the so-called 'Men's Association', a barely concealed symbolic endorsement, in Daly's view, of the all-male club, which on rare occasions admits a stereotypical 'feminine' principle into its magic circle as a token presence ('You're included under the Holy Spirit. He's feminine'[3]). Clearly what underlies Daly's deliberately 'absurd' accusation here is a deep – and not altogether unfounded – suspicion that modern patriarchal thinking has here found its projective trinitarian manifestation as an association of like-minded males. In contrast to Daly's dismissive rejection of trinitarianism, the patiently irenic work of Elizabeth Johnson on the Trinity attempts to reclaim its significance for feminism by concentrating on its celebration of 'mutuality' and 'relationship'.[4] So the divergence between analytic philosophers of religion and theologians on the Trinity is in some form replicated in the feminist camp: whilst Daly assumes a threefold 'individualism' in the doctrine (and rejects it), Johnson prefers to construe 'persons' *in terms of* 'relationships'.

It will be the central thesis of this chapter that *neither* side in either of these somewhat curiously parallel disjunctions has fully grasped the complexity and

---

[2]   I think here of recent work by British theologians such as Colin Gunton, Alistair McFadyen, or (rather differently) Elaine Graham. Harriet A. Harris's article, 'Should We Say that Personhood is Relational?', *Scottish Journal of Theology*, 51 (1998), 214–34, contains an astute account and criticism of this strand of thinking.

[3]   Mary Daly, *Gyn/Ecology* (Boston: Beacon Press, 1978), 38.

[4]   See Elizabeth A. Johnson, *She Who Is* (New York: Crossroad, 1992); see e.g. 'The ontological priority of relation in the idea of the triune God has a powerful affinity with women's ownership of relationality as a way of being in the world' (p. 205).

subtlety of late fourth-century trinitarianism at its best. Moreover, it will be suggested by the end that the modern contestants' predetermined commitments to (divergent) perceptions of 'personhood' may lead, in the end, to insoluble difficulties. In arguing thus I shall take Gregory of Nyssa as my focus and example, a figure whose trinitarian contribution is often too easily conflated with that of the other 'Cappadocians', but whose profoundly apophatic sensibilities make the assessment of the intended *status* of his trinitarian language a particularly subtle matter for reflection. One of the more surprising conclusions to which my argument will lead is that Gregory's approach to the Trinity is not 'social' in the sense often ascribed to that term today; it does not 'start' with three and proceed to the one. Nor does it attempt to 'nail' the meaning of divine *hypostasis* by particular reference to the analogy of three individual men: the analytic discussions here have been misled by an over-concentration on Gregory's *Ad Ablabium*, as well as by an insufficiently nuanced reading of that text. If we take a wider view of Gregory's corpus (and especially if we look at the rich range of imagery on the Trinity that he uses in contexts not restricted to the polemical or apologetic), a rather different perception of his trinitarian theology emerges, one which is in no doubt about the *unity* of the divine will in action, but which is highly diffident about probing the details of the nature of God in Godself beyond a certain, cautiously delimited point. Such diffidence may appear intrinsically unsatisfactory to the analytic school of philosophy of religion; but it raises questions about apophaticism that are, at the very least – or so I shall argue – worthy of greater analytic attention, and have implications for our understanding of the linguistic status of trinitarian claims.

If the gender interests of the feminist debates seem somewhat irrelevant to the analytic discussion as currently pursued, Gregory's example should also give pause for thought. The perplexing fluidity of gender reference which characterizes Gregory's trinitarian discussions as a whole gives the lie to attempts to sanitize the matter from any such 'taint;' as we shall attempt to show, Gregory's approach demonstrates how unwise it is to dislocate trinitarian debates from the matrix of human transformation that is that Trinity's very point of intersection with our lives. If Gregory is right, moreover, such transformation is unthinkable without profound, even alarming, shifts in our gender perceptions, shifts which have bearing as much on our thinking about God as on our understanding of ourselves.

In what follows, I shall first take a brief look at the analytic defence of the 'social' doctrine of the Trinity with an eye to the notions of 'person' that may be in play here. Then I shall turn to an explication of some suitably representative trinitarian texts in Gregory, and thereby suggest that those

from the analytic school who have sought to explicate his trinitarian intentions may have in large part missed the mark. (Current theology may be in
no better shape, however, from such a 'Nyssan' perspective, if it seeks to
reduce 'personhood' to 'relationality'.) I shall then suggest the implications of
my analysis of Gregory for the *status* of his trinitarian language – how it
stands on the literal/analogical/metaphorical spectrum now commonly
utilized in analytic philosophy of religion, and what difference Gregory's
profoundly apophatic perception of God makes to this account. Finally I
shall give a brief account of the gender-complexities of Gregory's understanding of the process of incorporation into the life of the trinitarian God,
and argue that such complexities are central, and not peripheral, to what
needs to be considered in any coherent defence of the notion of God as
Trinity. Whilst this short discussion cannot attempt a full philosophical
defence of the coherence of Gregory's viewpoint, it is intended as a first
(albeit mainly exegetical) step towards undertaking such a task more fully.

'Persons' in the Current Analytic Defence of the 'Social' Doctrine of the Trinity

Let us first take a brief sampling of some of the more sophisticated analytic
defences of the 'social' Trinity, so called, with an eye not only to how the
'social' view here is construed, but also to what notion of 'person' is in play,
whether explicitly or implicitly. Because they represent rather different
positions within this type, I take as my examples Peter van Inwagen,
Richard Swinburne, and David Brown.

Peter van Inwagen's seminal essay applying the notion of 'relative identity' to the Trinity explicitly states that 'it is Tritheism that I shall risk'.[5] He
gives the (not incontestable) following two reasons for such a move: first,
that the Creeds steer us away from Modalism anyway, but second, that
Modalism is nonetheless a 'far easier heresy than Tritheism to fall into in our
time'.[6] This announcement (asserted rather than argued) becomes the basis
for van Inwagen's willingness to risk a tritheistic reading. But everything
then depends on how the notion of divine 'person' is construed at the outset;
and although van Inwagen acknowledges this, he irritatedly deflects the
suggestion that the meaning of divine *hypostasis* might be significantly differ-

---

[5]   Peter van Inwagen, 'And Yet They Are Not Three Gods But One God', in Thomas V.
Morris (ed.), *Philosophy and the Christian Faith* (Notre Dame, Ind.: University of Notre Dame
Press, 1988), 247.
[6]   Ibid.

ent from the 'everyday' meaning of 'person'. Without providing a definition of the latter, van Inwagen presses on regardless, merely citing the view of Peter Geach that the 'normal' (*sic*) use of 'person' ultimately owes much to the technical patristic debates about Trinity and Incarnation.[7] The upshot of this (theologically unsatisfactory) section on the notion of 'person' is that van Inwagen never clearly tells us what sort of entities are at stake in his calculus; and since logic – however sophisticated – can only formalize pre-logical intuitions, we are left with a fundamental hiatus in the argument. The strong suspicion that it is three individual people that he has visually in mind (in the 'normal' sense of 'person'?) recurs when he returns in closing to the question of the danger of tritheism and addresses the problem of the potential 'clash' of divine wills.[8] In sum, as van Inwagen himself acknowledges, his appeal to 'relative identity' can, at most, only explicate how ' "is the same being as" does not dominate "is the same person as" '; it leaves the *explanation* of such a possibility, and the nature of the persons involved, quite untouched.[9] But the overwhelming impression of the article is that divine 'persons' are not intended to be thought of as significantly different from human 'persons'.

If van Inwagen's approach merely *suggests* the model of a closely meshed community of divine individuals, Swinburne's unashamedly embraces it. The embarrassingly tritheistic overtones of his early discussion of the matter ('Could There be More than One God?'[10]), is, to be sure, significantly modified in the more recent *The Christian God*,[11] but merits brief reflection nonetheless. It is doubtless significant that an (otherwise appreciative) footnote on van Inwagen's essay chides him for making the matter unduly 'mysterious'.[12] Swinburne's alternative makes no bones about its *unmysterious* vision of three 'Gods' (*sic*), each characterized in Cartesian terms as bodiless and self-conscious 'individuals' ('individual centres of consciousness and will'), though of course also possessing the necessary divine features of omniscience, omnipotence, and so on. The initial worry is that these three individuals might want to 'annihilate' each other (granted their assumed total freedom); but on reflection this power cannot be used for such a purpose, for it would be 'bad' to do so, and each depends on the others.[13]

[7]   Ibid. 248.
[8]   Ibid. 270–1.
[9]   Ibid. 271–2.
[10]   *Faith and Philosophy*, 5 (1988), 225–41.
[11]   (Oxford: Clarendon Press, 1994).
[12]   *Faith and Philosophy*, 5 (1988), 240 n. 19.
[13]   Ibid. 233.

In *The Christian God* this picture undergoes some considerable modification and clarification, but the fundamental image of three Cartesian 'individuals' endures, bound now by a more rigorously worked-out perception of their 'logical inseparability'.[14] Swinburne describes his position as a 'moderate form of social trinitarianism', and declares his sympathies to be more with Moltmann (and his 'three different consiousnesses') than with Barth's modalism.[15] It is noteworthy that Swinburne now cites Gregory of Nyssa's *Ad Ablabium* as his classic exemplar for the explication of inner-trinitarian differentiation in terms of causal relations;[16] but his understanding of 'person' is, as we shall shortly show, very far indeed from Gregory's intentions in that text. It is much more the inspiration of Richard of St Victor's argument (in his *De Trinitate*, III) for the necessity of three persons' cooperation in non-possessive love that propels Swinburne's 'social' doctrine than the intricacies of Gregory of Nyssa's explicit rejection of tritheism.[17] But Swinburne transmutes the Victorine view of self into a 'modern', Cartesian one, which continues to haunt the picture even after the sophisticated modifications of *The Christian God*.

So far we have suggested that both van Inwagen and Swinburne import notions of 'person' into their 'social' doctrines of the Trinity that are implicitly, or explicitly, beholden to modern forms of 'individualism',[18] and that lead their understandings of the doctrine to veer dangerously towards tritheism. The same charge can by no means be brought against David Brown, who above all such 'social' trinitarians has given the greatest amount of thought to the perils of importing anachronistic notions of 'person' into the patristic texts, and has attended to Gregory of Nyssa's

---

[14] *The Christian God*, 189. Swinburne's definition of 'person' in this book (see p. 31: having a 'mental life of at least the kind of richness and complexity which humans have'), still shelters a fundamentally 'Cartesian' set of presumptions in which one is 'constituted' by having a 'soul', which is then 'connected to a human body' (p. 26).

[15] Ibid. n. 26.

[16] Ibid. 184.

[17] See ibid, 190–1.

[18] At the 'Trinity Summit' Conference (New York, 1998) at which this paper was first presented, conversation focused on what qualifies as a 'modern' view of 'individualism'. Autonomy, privacy, individual rights, and reflective self-consciousness were all suggestions made by William Alston, who was the respondent to my paper. David Brown's discussion of the modern overtones of this term is useful here: see his 'Trinitarian Personhood and Individuality', in Ronald J. Feenstra and Cornelius Plantinga (eds.), *Trinity, Incarnation, and Atonement* (Notre Dame, Ind.: University of Notre Dame Press, 1989). Brown distinguishes 'individualism' (with the overtones of autonomy) from 'individuality' and 'individuation'. I do intend the definition of 'individualism' as given here.

work on the Trinity with especial care.[19] I wish here only to draw attention to two (to me puzzling) features of Brown's distinguished contribution to this debate. The first is, that despite previous disavowals of such a solution, Brown finally utilizes a 'modern' notion of 'person' (as 'self-conscious') in his construal of the Trinity, but shifts the locus of this self-consciousness to the Godhead as a whole, rather than to the three 'persons'.[20] Obviously this represents a considerable modification of the triplicated 'centres of consciousness' model, such as we saw in Swinburne, and it also marks a significant strengthening of Brown's own earlier position (in *The Divine Trinity*) that the 'persons' might be seen as unified merely in the way that some couples are unified in a 'successful marriage'.[21] But it raises the question why 'self-consciousness' *need* be the defining characteristic of divine 'personhood' at all, especially granted Brown's underscoring of the lack of attention to this criterion in the patristic period, and the complications Brown's 'solution' creates in splitting 'consciousness' and 'self-consciousness' apart in the Trinity.[22] Gregory of Nyssa, as we shall see, is more interested in underscoring the unity of divine *will* in the Trinity (and it remains unclear to me on Brown's analysis how many 'wills' are in play there).

The other point of exegetical contention raised by Brown's analysis is precisely the extent to which Gregory can be constrained into the category of 'social' trinitarianism *as Brown understands it*. Brown is himself admirably explicit about his understanding of (what he chooses to call) the 'Plurality Model' (PM); and it is clear that he sees Gregory as the prime historical instantiation of the type. For Brown, 'PM [is] the belief that what is fundamentally a trinitarian plurality is also ultimately a unity in the Godhead'; what is at stake then is whether one 'starts' with the 'threefoldness', as is the case with PM.[23] Put in experiential terms, PM implies that 'the experience of distinct Personhood antedates the realisation of a common identity'.[24] On Brown's reading, Gregory's utilization of the trinitarian analogy of individual men and the genus of humanity allows us to read him as a PM trinitarian in the sense described, and even also entitles us to find in him something close to a 'modern' concept of the person.

---

[19]   See ibid. and also *idem, The Divine Trinity* (London: Duckworth, 1985), and *idem*, 'Trinity' in Philip L. Quinn and Charles Taliaferro (eds.); *A Companion to Philosophy of Religion* (Oxford: Blackwell, 1997), 525–31.
[20]   'Trinitarian Personhood and Individuality', 69.
[21]   *The Divine Trinity*, 300.
[22]   See again 'Trinitarian Personhood and Individuality', 57ff.
[23]   See *The Divine Trinity*, 243.
[24]   Ibid. 287.

It is precisely these claims that I would now like to move to question. It will I trust have become clear from this section of the essay (as more fully in Brian Leftow's careful analysis[25]) that 'social' trinitarianism can come in more than one form, and – unsurprisingly, granted the intense contemporary philosophical debate on the defining characteristics of 'personhood'[26] – that the notion of 'person' in play is also capable of variation. What we have noted in each of the cases discussed, however, is the presumption that on a 'social' model one *starts* with the 'three' – whose individual identities are at least initially clearly and distinctively bounded – and that the task thereafter is to account for the unifying *community* which they share.

Is this then what Gregory of Nyssa is doing? I shall now argue that his trinitarianism subscribes to none of the features just described.

Why Gregory of Nyssa Is Not a 'Social' Trinitarian: Some Key Texts

What must first of all be openly admitted is that Gregory is not a wholly consistent or systematic thinker: it is not hard to find loopholes and terminological lapses in his work on the Trinity.[27] Once this is granted, however, it is

---

[25] See again Brian Leftow, 'Anti Social Trinitarianism' (n. 1, above).

[26] See e.g. the range of opinions expressed in Amélie Oksenberg Rorty (ed.), *The Identities of Persons* (Berkeley: University of California Press, 1976). At the Summit, William Alston noted the confusing plethora of definitions of 'personhood' currently in play, but nonetheless urged that there is a 'core concept of person' as a 'cognitive and conative subject' and that this could apply both to humans and to God. The trouble with this, as I see it, is that it begs precisely the question that Gregory is struggling with: *does* he intend 'persons' in the Godhead to have individualized wills, thoughts, and intentions, as human persons do?

[27] G. Christopher Stead is noted for his work exposing precisely such inconsistencies in Gregory: see, *inter alia*, his 'Ontologie und Terminologie bei Gregor von Nyssa', in Heinrich Dörrie, Margarete Altenbuger, and Uta Schramm (eds.), *Gregor von Nyssa und die Philosophie* (Leiden: Brill, 1976), 107–27. I am greatly indebted in what follows to the meticulously careful work of Lucian Turcescu, whose paper 'Gregory of Nyssa's Understanding of Divine Persons in *Ad Graecos* (*Ex Communibus Notionibus*)', given at the North American Patristics Society, 1997, discerns an important lapse in the consistency of Gregory's uses of the terms *hypostasis* and *prosōpon*. Despite these moments of inconsistency, it is my view that we can give a good account of Gregory's (generally consistent) intentions. In what follows it will be clear to the discerning reader that my interpretation differs in significant respects from that of Cornelius Plantinga in his important article, 'The Social Analogy of the Trinity', *The Thomist*, 50 (1986), 325–52. To anticipate: I interpret the import of the 'three men' 'analogy' differently from Plantinga, and this is partly because I take very seriously the *other* 'analogies' that Gregory holds up to us in *Ad Ablabium* and related texts.

possible, I suggest, to range a number of cumulative points together here to indicate how he has been misinterpreted as a 'social' trinitarian:

(1)   *Gregory does not 'start' from the three apologetically.* As Joseph Lienhard has shown in an excellent recent paper, the (somewhat messy political) context of Gregory's major apologetic writings on the Trinity does not present us with the opportunity for such a trimphant clarification of terms as the textbooks may lead us to expect.[28] The reality was not that neat: Gregory is countering both Sabellianism and Arianism at different points in his argument. But the anti-Eunomian writings, especially, are significant for their insistent stress on the divine *unity* as a counteraction to late Arianism. Persistently Gregory reminds us of the unified *will* and *power* of God; persistently he decries Eunomius' suggestion that there is a 'greater' and 'less' in the divine.[29] Apologetically, therefore, Gregory has every reason to give prime emphasis to the *unity* of the divine Nature.[30]

(2)   *The ordering of causality in the 'persons' gives a logical pre-eminence to the Father.* If any *logical* priority is at stake, it must surely be granted to the Father, rather than to three 'individuals'. In *this* sense Gregory 'starts' with this *one* 'person', as source and cause of the others: 'the Father [alone] is uncreate and ungenerate as well'.[31] But there is no sense of disjunction created thereby: 'there is one motion and disposition of the good will that is communicated from the Father through the Son to the Holy Spirit'.[32]

(3)   *The analogy of three men united by 'manhood' is also a significant disanalogy.* Here we come to the argument (especially as rehearsed in the *Ad Ablabium*) that has caused Brown (and others) to insist on Gregory's prioritizing of the 'three', and even to suggest a 'modernizing' or individualizing notion of the 'person' in play. But it should be underscored, first, that Gregory meets the initial objection of Ablabius thus: 'The argument that *you* state is something like this...', viz., that we freely call Peter, James, and John three men, even though we know them to be 'one nature'; so why not, asks Ablabius, call Father, Son, and Holy Spirit three Gods, even

---

[28]   Joseph T. Lienhard, SJ, '*Ousia* and *Hypostasis*: The Cappadocian Settlement and the Theology of "One *Hypostasis*"', in Davis, Kendall and O'Collins, *The Trinity*, pp. 99–121, esp. pp. 99–107.

[29]   See e.g. *Contra Eunomium*, I. 22; II. 3; III. 5, etc. (= NPNF, 2nd ser., v. 61, 103, 147).

[30]   Thus, in *Contra Eunomium* (NPNF, 2nd ser., v. 61 = *GNO* i. 101) Gregory discusses Eunomius' subordinationism and insists first and foremost on the nature of God as 'simple, uniform [and] incomposite'.

[31]   *Contra Eunomium*, I. 22; NPNF, 2nd series, v. 61 = *GNO* i. 102.

[32]   *Ad Ablabium*, NPNF, 2nd ser., v. 334 = *GNO* iii/1, 48–9.

though we know that they too have 'no difference of nature'?[33] The first point to note, therefore, is that it is Ablabius who 'starts with the three' here, not Gregory who recommends it. Gregory simply receives the gauntlet as it is thrown down. Second, Gregory goes on to assert *both* the radical unity effected by the analogy if it is taken seriously (since on the view of what Maurice Wiles has called Gregory's 'radical Platonism' the universal is *more real* than the particular[34]), *and* to question the analogy by stressing how profoundly different the divine case is from the human. For 'In the case of the Divine nature we do not [as in the case of men] learn that the Father does anything by Himself in which the Son does not work conjointly, or again that the Son has any special operation apart from the Holy Spirit.'[35] Thus we note that on both (somewhat problematically related) gambits, the emphasis is again thrown away from the 'threeness' to the unity.

(4)   *On an experiential (as opposed to logical) ordering, we might say Gregory 'starts' with the Holy Spirit, which then inexorably brings the other two 'persons' with it.* Since according to Gregory in the *Ad Ablabium* 'the same life is wrought in us by the Father, and prepared by the Son, and depends on the will of the Holy Spirit',[36] there is a sense in which the Spirit acts as the experiential point of entry into the divine flow from the 'spring' of the Father. But since the operations of the three are by definition inseparable, even this apparent experiential distinctness has an illusory quality to it: 'there is *one* motion . . .'.[37]

(5)   *There is no suggestion that three 'consciousnesses' are in play; 'hypostasis' does not denote consciousness or self-consciousness.* If we may ascribe to Gregory the *Letter* 38 previously contained in Basil's corpus,[38] then there we find Gregory providing a rare definition of *hypostasis*: it is, he says, 'the conception which, by means of the specific notes it indicates, restricts and circumscribes in a particular thing what is general and

---

[33]   NPNF, 2nd ser., v. 331 = *GNO* iii/1, 38.
[34]   Maurice Wiles, *The Making of Christian Doctrine* (Cambridge: Cambridge University Press, 1967), 133 ff.
[35]   Gregory, *Ad Graecos*, 24–25 = *GNO* iii/1, 47. G. Christopher Stead's article, 'Why Not Three Gods?', in Hubertus R. Drobner and Christophe Klock (eds.), *Studien zu Gregor von Nyssa und der christlichen Spätantike* (Leiden: Brill, 1990), 149–63, brings out well the double logic of Gregory's analogy *and* disanalogy in the argument here, though with less respect for the success of the argument than I have.
[36]   NPNF, 2nd ser., v. 334 = *GNO* iii/1, 48–9
[37]   Ibid.
[38]   This ascription is still debated, and may never find complete resolution. For the purposes of this essay I follow Cavallin, Hübner, and Fedwick (amongst others) in attributing this letter to Gregory.

uncircumscribed'.[39] We note that this 'definition' is peculiarly devoid of any overtones of 'personality', let alone of 'consciousness'. A *hypostasis* is simply a distinct enough entity to bear some 'particularizing marks' – in the case of the Trinity the distinctions of differing causal relations within the Godhead. As for the word *prosōpon*, more commonly used by Gregory, but arguably less technically, *prosōpon* in its human sense and evocations is nonetheless severely tempered when applied to God. As Gregory puts it in one intriguing passage in the *Ad Graecos*:

> All the persons belonging to Man [i.e. Humanity] do not directly pos-sess... their being from the same person, but some from this one and some from that one, so that with respect to the individuals caused there are also many and diverse causes. But with regard to the Holy Trinity, such is not the case, for there is one and the same Person, that of the Father, from whom the Son is begotten and the Holy Spirit proceeds.... For the Persons of the Divinity are not separated from one another either by time or place, not by will or by practice, not by activity or by passion, not by anything of this sort, such as is observed with regard to human beings.[40]

(6) *The talk is of 'communion'* (koinōnia) *between the 'persons', not of 'community'.* This distinction is significant, and crucial to the argument in *Letter 38*. Gregory is in this letter most certainly not enjoining the unifica-tion of separate 'individuals' into a 'community', as seems to be the model in the analytic discussion of 'PM'. On the contrary, he writes that 'there is apprehended among these three a certain ineffable and inconceivable com-munion (*koinōnia*) and at the same time distinction (*diakrisis*)' – which latter, however, does not 'disintegrate the continuity of their nature'.[41]

(7) *Number cannot strictly apply to God.* Although the *hypostaseis* have relational 'distinguishing marks', it is only in a Pickwickian sense that they are 'three', according to Gregory; as H. A. Wilson comments on the argument in *Ad Ablabium*, 'if [Gregory] has been willing to carry the use of numerical terms rather further than S. Basil was prepared to do, he yet is content in the last resort to say that number is not in strictness applicable to

---

[39]   *Ep.* 38, St Basil, *The Letters*, trans. Roy J. Deferrari, LCL, 4 vols. (Cambridge, Mass.: Harvard University Press, 1950), i. 200–1.

[40]   Gregory, *Ad Graecos*, 24–5 = GNO iii/I, 47; trans. in Daniel F. Stramara, 'Gregory of Nyssa, *Ad Graecos* . . .', *Greek Orthodox Theological Review*, 41 (1996), 385; see commentary on p. 379.

[41]   *Saint Basil: The Letters* I, trans. Roy J. Deferrari (Cambridge, Mass.: Harvard University Press, 1926), 210, 211.

the Divine *hypostaseis*, in that they cannot be contemplated *kat'idian perigraphen*, and therefore cannot be enumerated by way of addition'.[42] Such a perception may be deeply infuriating to contemporary analytic philosophers of religion; but it does indeed seem to be Gregory's view: we cannot 'add up' the numbers in the Trinity in the *same* way as we count heads at a gathering of humans.

(8)   *Gregory's favoured analogies for the Trinity stress the indivisibility of the 'persons' and even a certain fluidity in their boundaries.* If we can thus prevent ourselves being imaginatively dominated by the analogy of the three 'men' (which in any case we now see is treated by Gregory with great caution), we can allow some other (arguably more favoured) analogies to have their force. We have already mentioned the long-established analogy of a 'spring' from which water gushes forth in a continuous stream.[43] To this Gregory adds, in *Letter* 38, the idea of the inseparable links in a 'chain' ('just as he who grasps one end of a chain pulls along with it the other end also to himself, so he who draws the Spirit... through the Spirit draws both the Son and the Father along with It'[44]). Even more interesting, in this same letter, is the extended discussion of the analogy of the rainbow. Here, the 'light from light' of the Creeds is given the more colourful, and also directionally reflexive, imagery of the 'bow': 'When the sunbeam, intercepting obliquely the compact and opaque portion of the cloudy mass, then causes its own circle to impinge in a straight line upon a particular cloud, there occurs a sort of bending of the light and its return upon itself, for the sunlight returns in the opposite direction from what is moist and shiny.... when the rays of all the colours are seen together, they are both distinct and yet at the same time filch from our view the points of their juncture with one another...'.[45] This analogy, then, has the particular and additional merits of stressing the incorporative, reflexive flow of the divine 'persons', as well as the indeterminate boundaries, at least from our human perception, of the 'persons'' distinctness. Thus it is that Gregory can conclude this discussion by underscoring that pictorial 'analogies' such as this do better justice to the matter in hand than strict dogmatic definitions; for they appropriately draw attention to how we become 'dizzy' in the making of such distinctions, just as we become dizzy if we look into the sun.[46]

---

[42]   In the 'Prolegomena', NPNF, 2nd ser., v. 27.
[43]   *Ad Ablabium*, ibid. 334.
[44]   St Basil, *The Letters*, LCL, i. 210–11.
[45]   Ibid. 213–15.
[46]   Ibid. 216–17. 'We fall into a matter difficult to understand and become dizzy when we face the conflict of the different propositions.'

It is also worth reminding ourselves that Gregory can on occasion use a 'psychological' analogy for the Trinity (our 'word' and our 'breath' being distinct features of the self [47]), a ploy of course more commonly associated with Augustine and the West, but also giving the lie to the suggestion that Gregory is uniquely fixated on the image of 'three men'.

(9)   *A strongly apophatic sensibility attends any talk of the 'essence' of God.* This point is reiterated constantly even in the more philosophical and apologetic writings we have so far been covering. But if we turn now to the fascinating, and correlated, account of the effects of trinitarian incorporation in Gregory's *Commentary on the Song of Songs*, we find a wealth of discussions of the dark 'incomprehensibility' of the divine nature. It is as well to remember that the whole life-work of 'ascent' in Gregory culminates in noetic darkness, as did Moses' ascent of Mt Sinai, and we cannot afford to ignore this epistemological complication when considering Gregory's account of the Trinity. Again, it should give us pause when pronouncing on the effectiveness, or otherwise, of *particular* dominating models for the Trinity. In the *Song* it is the haunting image of the 'hand of the bridegroom', reaching out to draw us into darkness, that reminds us of the deep impossibility of circumscribing the divine 'essence' in intellectual terms: ' "My beloved has put his hand through the hole of the door." Human nature is not able to contain the infinite, unbounded divine nature.'[48]

(10)   *Freer, and more instrumental, imagery for the divine 'persons' is thus also used evocatively by Gregory in his exegetical work, without any apparent concern for philosophical precision.* With this apophaticism constantly underlined, Gregory is thereby freed up to allow a plethora of other (less philosophically precise) images for the process of trinitarian 'incorporation' into the divine, and these should also be borne in mind when assessing the full texture of his trinitarianism. I draw gratefully here on a (as yet unpublished) paper by my pupil Francis Yip ('The Trinity and Christian Life in the Dogmatic and Spiritual Writings of Gregory of Nyssa'). Yip fascinatingly supplements the material usually surveyed by dogmaticians and philosophers in assessing Gregory's trinitarianism by drawing attention to a number of creative – even bizarre – trinitarian images in the *Song*: the 'arrow' of the Word which wounds the soul and the tip of the arrow that is the Spirit,[49] for instance, or the wind of

---

[47]   See 'The Great Catechism', ch. II, in NPNF, 2nd ser., v. 477 = ed. J. H. Srawley, *The Catechetical Oration of Gregory of Nyssa* (Cambridge: Cambridge University Press, 1903), 13–14.
[48]   *In Cant.* 11; ET *Commentary on the Song of Songs*, trans. Casimir McCambley (Brookline, Mass.: Hellenic College Press, 1987), 208 = *GNO* vi. 336.
[49]   *Cant.* 4; ibid. 103 = *GNO* vi. 127–8.

the Spirit blown against the ship of the church of which Christ is the pilot.[50] Often these images mutually bombard one another in a flood of inter-corrective ideas. Such, it seems, is precisely Gregory's intention, since he wishes us not to fixate on one set of images, but to allow all of them to be permeated by the profoundly apophatic sensibility that propels us from one to the other.

To sum up this section of the argument: what, then, have we learnt from these ten cumulative points? It has been my concern above all to divert the analytic discussion from the mesmeric hold that the 'three men' argument has appeared to have on it, and to suggest that even when Gregory uses that analogy he is deeply concerned to underscore its limitations. Nor is there any suggestion, on my reading, of a 'modern' sense of 'individual' in play (with, for instance, a focus on 'self-consciousness', or 'autonomy') even when this analogy is to the fore. Rather, what we are presented with is the idea of a unified *flow* of divine will and love, catching us up reflexively towards the light of the 'Father', and allowing to the 'persons' only the minimally distinctive features of their different internal causal relations. Such, I suggest, is very far from the tritheistic-tending accounts of the analytic material discussed in our previous section; and equally far (though this point cannot be spelled out in detail here) from the well-meaning, but arguably finally incoherent, accounts of human 'personhood *as* relation' (only?) which have become popular in recent theological writing, often on the basis of trinitarian appeals.[51] Gregory is quite clear about the *difference* between human and divine 'persons', as I trust has now been established. And he does not, whether apologetically, logically, or experientially, 'start' with 'three'. This is not a 'community' of 'individuals'; nor, incidentally, does it – on my reading – *prioritize* 'person' over 'substance' (a matter that has become polemical in the thought of John Zizioulas[52]). A final irony, in the terms of our 'Summit' discussion, is that my account of Gregory's trinitarianism can I think rather more easily shelter under what Brian Leftow defines as 'Western' 'LT' than under his (and other analytic philosophers') account of 'Eastern' 'ST'(see n.1, above) .

---

[50] *Cant.* 12; ibid. 213 = *GNO* vi. 341–2.

[51] Harriet A. Harris (see n. 2) points out the oddity of this kind of appeal: 'We cannot jump from recognising the relationality involved in being a person to affirming that persons are relational entities. Persons are ontologically prior to relations'.

[52] See John D. Zizioulas, *Being as Communion* (Crestwood, NY: St Vladimir's Seminary Press, 1985). The interpretation I have offered here, in which Gregory's 'radical Platonism' is stressed, gives logical priority to the divine *ousia*.

What, then, is the precise linguistic status of the various components of Gregory's trinitarian terminology? To this somewhat tricky question we shall now devote an exploratory short section, before turning, finally, to the (related) complications of gender.

What Sort of Language Is Trinitarian Language for Gregory of Nyssa?

This question is a doubly complicated one if we choose to apply contemporary philosophical distinctions to patristic texts that do not utilize these particular distinctions, and which are in themselves already complex and disputed. Nonetheless a brief exploration will be attempted here. In what follows I am assuming (not uncontentiously!) that neither 'metaphorical' nor 'analogical' language for God is incompatible with 'literal' claims. (I use 'literal' speech here to mean making a statement in which 'one is attributing to the subject the property with which the predicate is associated by its semantic status in the language', rather than merely meaning 'univocal with common usage', as in some discussions.[53]) If I am right, then a profound apophatic sensibility about the divine 'essence', such as Gregory exemplifies, does not necessarily lead to a 'pan-metaphoricism', nor even to the claim that metaphors are irreducible.

If we allow that 'metaphorical' language, first, involves (at least in its inception) a *surprising* conjunction of terms whose meaning is disclosed by context, there is no need to assume, as many do, that no purchase on reality is thereby attempted or achieved;[54] on the contrary, there may be realms of linguistic endeavour (many theological statements included) where such artful conjunction *best* suits the attempt to make serious metaphysical claims. Moreover, metaphors of this creative sort can, on reflection, often be seen to *encode* 'literal' meanings.[55] If I say, for instance, that 'Christ is a rock', I clearly do not mean this 'literally' (it is a metaphor); but I do mean ('literally') that Christ is reliable, unchanging, etc.

How one construes what a theological 'analogy' is, in contrast, may differ according to one's prior metaphysical and theological commitments

---

[53] See Richard Swinburne, *Revelation* (Oxford: Clarendon Press, 1992), ch. 1, for the 'univocal' meaning; compare William P. Alston, *Divine Nature and Human Language* (Ithaca, NY: Cornell University Press, 1989), chs. 1 and 2, esp. p. 25, for the meaning I am using.

[54] For the contextual understanding of metaphor, see Swinburne, *Revelation*, ch. 3.

[55] See Alston, *Divine Nature*, ch. 1.

(whether, for instance, one accepts on authority, revelation or reasoned argument that 'pure perfection' terms such as 'love' belong supremely to God and therefore only secondarily, and by analogical extension, to humans). A good rule-of-thumb definition of an 'analogy' is that it involves 'stretch[ing] [a term] to fit new applications, . . . *without generating for the native speaker any imaginative strain*'[56] (with which we contrast the imaginative *frisson* of the newly coined metaphor). But of course we need to know in any given case *which* way we are 'stretching'; that is (to continue the example above), it matters whether we know – on one of the grounds already mentioned – that God supremely embodies love and humans embody it only derivatively, or whether the 'analogy' here is merely a settled (or 'dead') metaphor, that speaks of God as love as imaginatively 'obvious' simply because we have had several centuries to get used to a conjunctive idea that was originally coined as a metaphor. If it is the latter case, then, as Swinburne has recently argued, the lines between 'metaphorical' and 'analogical' language for God are often transitionally and diachronically blurred.[57]

If we take this much as read, what sort of language *is* trinitarian language for Gregory? The answer, I suggest, is different depending on what term or terms we are discussing, and how fluid their own 'common' meanings are. *Hypostasis*, for instance, can mean a bewildering number of things in the patristic era; but in the technical sense explicitly delimited by Gregory (that which 'restricts and circumscribes in a particular thing what is general and uncircumscribed'), I see no reason to deny its 'literal' status as applied to Father, Son, and Holy Spirit in the Godhead. *Prosopon*, however (also translated 'person' in English, but having a more obviously 'relational' or 'psychological' meaning as visage or personal presentation[58]), is utilized more commonly than *hypostasis* by Gregory, but with a more profound sense of its disjunction from its usage as applied to humans, as we have already noted above: 'For the Persons [*prosopa*] of the Divinity are not separated from one another either by time or place, not by will or by practice, not by activity or by passion, not by anything of this sort, such as is observed with regard to human beings.'[59] On these grounds it would seem that the language of *prosopon* used for the divine entities in the Trinity

[56] Janet Martin Soskice, *Metaphor and Religious Language* (Oxford: Clarendon Press, 1985), 64.
[57] See again Swinburne, *Revelation*, ch. 3.
[58] See the discussion in Stramara, 'Gregory of Nyssa', 379.
[59] Ibid.

is best seen as analogical (and perhaps even metaphorical in its original coinage).

The case of 'Father' language in the Trinity, however, is more subtle and difficult again. It might be tempting to judge it metaphorical, granted the great lengths that Gregory goes to to *distinguish* human fatherhood from divine fatherhood in the late Arian debates; but the picture is complicated by a strain of thought in Gregory that sees the language of God as 'Father', 'Son' and 'Holy Spirit' as authoritatively *given* in revelation. In *Contra Eunomium* 2[60] there is an interesting passage where Gregory insists: 'Once for all, from the Lord . . . we have learned this, that is the Father and the Son and the Holy Spirit. We say that it is a terrible and soul-destroying thing to misinterpret these Divine utterances and to devise in their stead assertions to subvert them, – assertions pretending to correct God the Word, Who appointed that we should maintain these statements as part of our faith.' This non-negotiable and revelatory appeal is perhaps reminiscent of a notable passage in Athanasius, where Athanasius avers that the *proper* meanings of 'Father' and 'Son' (which logically imply one another) reside in the divine prototype rather than being applied from the creaturely realm of passion and bodies.[61] It is not entirely clear to me that Gregory is making a parallel move here; but if he is, then human 'father' language would become an analogical derivative from the divine, rather than divine 'Father' language being either metaphorical or analogical language on the basis of human prototypes.

In the case of the visual trinitarian images such as 'chain', 'rainbow', 'spring', or 'humanity' (as are in play in *Ep.* 38 and the *Ad Ablabium*, and argued above to be vital to understanding Gregory's position on the Trinity), we have what Gregory *calls* 'analogies', but would seem to be more appropriately described as 'metaphors' in terms of the modern distinctions we have rehearsed. Each of these also bears with it a strong accompanying sense of the finally inexpressible nature of the divine; as such, the metaphorical status of the language does not detract from the realistic seriousness of the claim, but merely draws our attention to the limitations of what we can 'nail down' linguistically where God is concerned.

Such, it seems, is the unavoidable complexity of attending to the linguistic status of the various strands of Gregory's trinitarian argument.

---

[60] NPNF, 2nd ser., v. 101–2 = GNO ii. 298.

[61] See Athanasius, *Contra Arianos*, I. 21; there is an illuminating discussion of this point in Catherine Osborne, 'Literal or Metaphorical? Some Issues of Language in the Arian Controversy', in Lionel R. Wickham and Caroline P. Bammel (eds.), *Christian Faith and Greek Philosophy* (Leiden: Brill, 1993), 148–70.

But there is yet one further complication to add: that of the 'gender fluidity' that Gregory sees both in God-in-Godself, and in the human seeking of that (trinitarian) God. If I am right, then any account of Gregory's trinitarian theology that fails to explore his own literature of spiritual assimilation into the divine has given only an excerpted version of the whole.

The Trinity and Gender According to Gregory

I made the claim at the beginning of this chapter that it is deeply unwise to divorce Gregory's more apologetic or expository works on the Trinity from his trinitarian spirituality of human transformation. Especially in his late work the *Commentary on the Song of Songs*, Gregory charts in highly imagistic and eroticized language the ascent of the soul into intimacy with the life of the Trinity. Two features are especially striking about this process, as recent work by Verna Harrison on gender in Gregory has fascinatingly demonstrated.[62]

First, the stages of ascent to God that Gregory maps out in this work and elsewhere (most notably in the *Life of Moses*), involve a progressive and final *darkening* of the mind; at the height of the ascent on the mountain, Moses, the 'type' of the Christian soul, finds his mind no longer able to absorb what God is giving him: 'When, therefore, Moses grew in knowledge, he declared that he had seen God in darkness, that is, that he had then come to know that what is divine is beyond all knowledge and comprehension . . .'.[63] When this theme of noetic darkness is discussed in the erotic language of the *Commentary on the Song of Songs*, it becomes clear that another set of faculties (the 'spiritual senses') take over from the *nous* (intellect) in this heightened state of intimacy with the divine. What has occurred is a profound transformation of the physical senses (sight, however, is significantly omitted) into a deep receptive sensitivity. At the same time, Gregory charts a symbolic gender reversal: what has up to now been the spiritual quest of an ardent 'youth' going courting for Sophia, becomes here conversely the 'more mature character of the bride who actively seeks, yet is still more open to receive, the divine bridegroom'.[64]

---

[62] See Verna E. F. Harrison, 'Gender, Generation, and Virginity in Cappadocian Theology', *Journal of Theological Studies* 47 (1996), 38–68; and *eadem*, 'Male and Female in Cappadocian Theology', *Journal of Theological Studies* 41 (1990), 441–71.

[63] Gregory of Nyssa, *The Life of Moses*, trans. Abraham J. Malherbe and Everett Ferguson (New York: Paulist Press, 1978), 95 = *GNO* vii/1, 87.

[64] Harrison, 'Gender, Generation, and Virginity', 61.

The gender fluidity that Gregory charts at the *human* level of transformation finds also its metaphysical counterpart, secondly, in God. Whilst Sophia (Christ) is being actively courted by the soul, she is described as a 'manly woman'; but when the soul adopts the darkened epistemological state of active receptivity, Christ becomes the bridegroom seeking *her*. A further complication arises when we add the fully trinitarian picture of incorporation that tends to emerge in fits and starts in the *Commentary on the Song of Songs*. In the seventh Homily[65] the bridegroom's *mother* is aligned with God the Father: Gregory explains that the names 'father' and 'mother' are effectively the same in meaning, granted that we know that there is really 'neither male nor female' (see Gal. 3: 28) in God. In the fifteenth Homily[66] the Holy Spirit is perceived as a dove who is also the mother of the bride. In all these transferences and reversals, the message Gregory evidently wishes to convey is that gender stereotypes must be reversed, undermined, and transcended if the soul is to advance to supreme intimacy with the trinitarian God; and that the language of sexuality and gender, far from being an optional aside or mere rhetorical flourish in the process, is somehow necessary and intrinsic to the epistemological deepening that Gregory seeks to describe.[67]

What then are the implications of this discussion for the question of trinitarian conceptuality with which we started this chapter? The answer as I see it is twofold: on the one hand, the *Commentary* material is vital further evidence that the 'three men' analogy of the *Ad Ablabium* is a highly partial one in Gregory's view for expressing the spiritual complexity and richness involved in the ascent and incorporation into the realm of the Trinity.[68] (In this sense Mary Daly's spoof is vindicated, although in a way more subtle and positive for an alternative trinitarian picture than Daly would ever acknowledge.) Second, it is clear from Gregory's *Commentary*

---

[65]   *Commentary*, trans. McCambley, 145 = *GNO* vi. 212–14.

[66]   *Commentary*, 468–9 = *GNO* vi. 468–9.

[67]   It is important to note that this gender-play bespeaks shifts in human epistemological *capacity* which cannot be gained except through painstaking spiritual growth. If Gregory is right about this, then there may be different (more or less spiritually mature) ways of discussing the Trinity, depending on the spiritual growth of the discussants. This is a complication, we note, that is as yet completely ignored in analytic discussions of the matter.

[68]   In a discussion at the 'Trinity Summit' conference, Michel Barnes posited the *genesis* of the reading of Gregory I am here questioning, and attributed it to de Régnon's influence. See the illuminating section on Gregory and de Régnon's interpretation of him in Michel René Barnes, 'Augustine in Contemporary Trinitarian Theology', *Theological Studies* 56 (1995), 245–6.

material that a *reduction* of 'persons' to 'relationality' is not what he intends. To be sure, we are forced back to his expository doctrinal texts for a more precise account of how the *hypostaseis* actually distinguish themselves without separation (as we have sketched); but what the overlapping and bombarding images of the *Song* commentary remind us is that the 'persons' of the Trinity are always being reconfigured and reconstrued as the soul advances to more dizzying intimacy with the divine. And in this progress the engagement of the self with deep levels of erotic as well as epistemological re-evaluation are unavoidably predictable. Hence, whatever 'analogy' (in Gregory's meaning) seems most adequate to express the doctrine of the Trinity convincingly in doctrinal or philosophical terms, the less we should become permanently fixated upon it, and the more the profusion of available biblical and allegorical allusions should draw us on beyond complacency.

Conclusions

The material I have covered in this chapter has taken us in a number of different directions. My chief goal has been to call into question a tendency to read Gregory's trinitarianism solely in terms of the 'three men' analogy, especially with the overtones of psychological self-consciousness or 'individualism'. Along the road I have gathered some other pieces out of Gregory's trinitarian armoury which are, I have argued, insufficiently attended to in the current philosophical debate. Gregory's expository and apologetic works on the Trinity should at all costs be read in tandem with his 'spiritual' writings and his intriguing (if disturbing) views about gender and epistemological transformation. Without these *addenda*, I want to suggest, we do not appreciate the subtlety, spiritual depth, and striking contemporary challenge of his trinitarian alternative. The explication of these complexities thus remains an important future task for the analytic school of philosophy of religion.

Chapter 8

THE RESURRECTION AND THE 'SPIRITUAL SENSES': ON WITTGENSTEIN, EPISTEMOLOGY AND THE RISEN CHRIST

My interest in this chapter is in what we may call the *epistemic conditions* for 'seeing' the risen Christ, an interest that will cause me to bring into play some seemingly unlikely conversation partners: the patristic authors Origen and Gregory of Nyssa on the one hand, and the philosopher Ludwig Wittgenstein on the other. The resultant confluence of ideas will admittedly be novel and speculative; and I shall leave it a deliberately open question whether my argument would have met with Wittgenstein's favour – a matter, I suspect, of some exegetical sublety. But I take these risks in order to try and explicate how a form of *deepened* spiritual perception – 'not with the eye only', in the words of the poet R. S. Thomas[1] – has to be in play if we are to account for seeing the risen Christ today, a possibility that much modern Western theology has either despaired of completely, or reductively demythologized.

Peter Carnley has recently written:

> I . . . think the task of providing an epistemology that can account for the Christian claim to identify the presence of the raised Christ as a religious object in present experience, rather than just engage in what I think is a somewhat futile quest for the historical resurrected Jesus, is the most important challenge facing resurrection theology today. . . . It is understandable that it is the area that most theologians of the resurrection put into the too-hard basket.[2]

What follows, then, is my attempt to respond to this challenge, to delve into this 'too-hard basket'.

To be published in D. Z. Phillips et al. (eds.), *Biblical Concepts and Our World* (London, St Martin's Press, forthcoming). Reprinted with permission from St Martin's Press, with light revisions.

[1]   From R. S. Thomas, 'Suddenly', *Laboratories of the Spirit* (London, 1975), 32, quoted in full later in this chapter.

[2]   Eds. S. T. Davis, S. Kendall SJ and G. O'Collins, SJ, *The Resurrection* (Oxford, 1997), 40.

What I hope to illuminate by my speculation is the epistemic *reason* for the believer seeing the world in a different way from the non-believer, in being able to give meaning, that is, to the language of 'encounter with the risen Christ'. My suggestion is that this difference between the believer and the non-believer, whilst certainly hinging on what Wittgenstein called the 'grammar' of religious belief (and involving thereby a consideration of the life-forms and 'practice' that necessarily attend the language of resurrection faith), nonetheless cannot finally be explained except by an account of a transformation of the believer's actual epistemic *apparatus*.[3] We are in the realm here of what some patristic and medieval writers called 'the spiritual senses': the transformed epistemic sensibilities of those being progressively reborn in the likeness of the Son. As far as I know, Wittgenstein never reflected explicitly on this subject matter, this possibility of senses-beyond-senses; nor would he have been at ease, I admit, with the reifying language of epistemic 'apparatus'. But we shall have reason to conclude, as we go along, that he had at least some intimations of this possible line of thought.

My argument will proceed thus. I start on familiar territory, with a crude sketch of two approaches to the resurrection which have dominated the theological scene in the modern period – let us call them the 'Lockean' and the 'Barthian' approaches, as a convenient shorthand. At first sight they look like extreme competitors, mutually exclusive alternatives; but on closer inspection they are revealed more as two sides of the modernistic coin. Moreover, while each has apologetic strengths, each too has rather notable theological weaknesses; and neither can give a convincing account of certain subtle features of the New Testament appearance narratives which seem epistemologically determinative. In order to escape through the horns of this dilemma, we are in search of a third (putatively 'Wittgensteinian'?) alternative, which does justice to the narratives, practices and 'forms of life' that sustain a spiritually mature response to the 'resurrected' life. It is here that the tradition of 'spiritual senses', reaching back to Origen in the third century, may help us fill out this picture: according to this view, it is not just *referring* that may differ in differing contexts, but even *perceiving* (here I shall extend an argument of Hilary Putnam's in relation to a 'realist' reading of

---

[3] I have been greatly helped here by Ingolf U. Dalferth's brief, but penetrating, account of the evocations of 'grammar' in Wittgenstein, and its ontological significance, in his paper, 'Wittgenstein: The Theological Reception' (circulated at the Claremont Wittgenstein conference, 2000), esp. 23–9; see also idem, *Jenseits von Mythos* (Freiburg, 1993), ch. 6. The *novum* of what I am going to suggest here lies not in ascribing ontological import to Wittgenstein's views on religion in general, but in my hypothesis about a malleability in the faculties' capacity to respond to certain kinds of divine reality.

the later Wittgenstein and its significance for religious claims[4]). In short, the reception of religious truth does not occur *on a flat plane*: even within the ranks of 'believers' the understanding or perception of the 'risen Christ' will have variations of depth. We have focused too much in the era of 'secularism', I shall argue, on the great gulf apparently fixed between the 'believer' and the 'non-believer' (and even some of Wittgenstein's conversations seem to get stuck here[5]); yet epistemic and religious transformation surely does not stop with conversion or baptism, and we need to be able to give an account of this.

Finally, I shall deliver a last speculative aside about the relation of these arguments to question of *gender*, and draw some lines of connection with suggestive themes from current feminist epistemology, as well as from other pre-modern theological material. This is not – I should underscore with some emphasis – an 'essentialist' suggestion: not, that is, an argument that women (*qua* physically or genitally female) have responded more sensitively to the 'risen Christ' than have men. Rather, I am drawing attention to the way that theological and philosophical traditions in Christendom and the modern West have from time to time valued some forms of epistemic response over others; and how, more or less unconsciously, the forms of response needed to access the 'risen Christ' have on occasions been associated normatively with women or with stereotypical 'femininity'. That this line of argument is no mere aside or afterthought will, I trust, emerge in the course of my exploration.

So much by way of preliminary overview. I now turn to the more detailed exposition of my thesis.

Two Sides of the Modern Coin: The Resurrection as 'Historical' or 'Ahistorical' Event?

As has often been remarked, two characteristic ploys for explicating the status of the resurrection as 'event' have dominated in the modern period,

[4]   See Putnam, *Renewing Philosophy* (Cambridge, MA, 1992), chs. 7–8.
[5]   See the discussion of the Last Judgement in L. Wittgenstein, *Lectures and Conversations on Aesthetics, Psychology, and Religious Belief* (Berkeley, CA, 1966), 53–9; and also – taken by itself – the section on the resurrection in *Culture and Value* (Chicago, 1980), 32e–33e. (For an extended discussion of the meaning of this passage in context, see intra.) D. Z. Phillips's treatment of the problem of the apparent mutual incomprehension between believers and unbelievers, which starts from Wittgenstein, concludes – rightly in my view – that 'there is no sharp line between belief and unbelief' (*Religion Without Explanation* (Oxford, 1976), 187). A facile reading of Wittgenstein, however, might easily come to the opposite conclusion.

and still continue as major competitors in the field.[6] The first is the approach that attempts to rein in resurrection faith to the standards of Lockean 'probabilism': the rational basis for such a belief is adumbrated, the evidence carefully surveyed, and the degree of appropriate firmness of belief on the basis of that evidence calculated. When the Humean *dicta* about the miraculous are added to this (and interpreted in a non-reductive mode), we have the principle that 'the wise man [*sic*] proportions his belief to the evidence', conjoined with the concession that a 'miracle' (in the new, modernistic sense of a non-repeatable violation of a 'natural law') may be appropriately believed if and only if the disbelieving of it would prove 'more miraculous' than the believing of it.[7] These are, by any accounts, tough criteria of adjudication to bring to the inconsistent, fragmentary and elusive testimony of the New Testament texts: the situation might seem desperate from the outset. Yet those contemporary writers such as Wolfhart Pannenberg and Richard Swinburne who (from rather different starting points) continue to attempt an historically demonstrated case for the resurrection in this mode are propelled by a fundamentally *apologetic* conviction: that the resurrection of Jesus, if it is to be rationally believable, must be subject to the *same* level of critical scrutiny that we would accord to any (secular) 'historical' event.[8]

Whether this conception of the apologetic task is a strength or a weakness may here remain a moot point; more important for our immediate purposes in this chapter is to reflect on the features of the New Testament texts that make this Lockean/Humean modernistic rereading distinctly *odd* from the

[6] This is evident in the recent compendium volume on the resurrection, eds. Davis, Kendall and O'Collins, *The Resurrection* (see n. 2). Here some contributors remain firmly fixed within the framework of 'historical' discussion of Jesus' *post mortem* existence, whilst Barth's alternative perspective is also aired (see ch. 12). Peter Carnley sets the tone for a third alternative, as already mentioned.

[7] D. Hume, 'Of Miracles', from *An Enquiry Concerning Human Understanding*, section X, reprinted in R. Wollheim (ed.), *Hume on Religion* (London, 1963); see pp. 206, 211.

[8] The (now classic) treatment of this theme by Pannenberg is to be found in his *Jesus – God and Man* (London, 1968). Richard Swinburne, from the rather different perspective of British analytic philosophy of religion, shares Pannenberg's concern to subject the resurrection events to the scrutiny of secular historiographical method, even though – in his more recent work – he admits the importance of a prior commitment to theism in the assessment of the evidence: see his *The Concept of Miracle* (London, 1970); *The Existence of God* (Oxford, 1979), esp. ch 12; *Revelation* (Oxford, 1991), esp. ch. 7; and 'Evidence for the Resurrection', in Davis, Kendall and O'Collins, *The Resurrection*, ch. 8. I subject the views of Pannenberg and Swinburne to critical scrutiny in my 'Is the Resurrection a "Historical" Event? Some Muddles and Mysteries', in P. Avis (ed.), *The Resurrection of Jesus Christ* (London, 1993), ch. 6, arguing that whilst it does seem an initial apologetic duty to assess the resurrection narratives from the standpoint of critical historiography, the conclusion can only be that of an alluring question mark.

perspective of achieved resurrection faith in biblical style. Even Thomas the Doubter, the one potential 'British empiricist' of the New Testament scene one might feel, drops his preannounced conditions for belief instantly on encountering the risen Christ face to face (John 20:24–9). (John's text, be it noted, gives no hint that Thomas actually put his hands in the wounds: it is the patristic tradition from Ignatius of Antioch on, and the more haunting visual realism of the already modern Caravaggio that mislead us here.) Thus it is that both Pannenberg and Swinburne, in their different ways, have trouble doing justice to the more alluring and mysterious features of the 'appearance' traditions: the priority given to women witnesses, the suggestion that they were not at first believed, the uncertainty about the events at the grave itself and whether fear, awe and confusion dominated, the difficulties in even recognizing the risen Christ.[9] To turn these features to *good* account on a Lockean reading is a *tour de force*;[10] whether one would even *want* to do so is of course the pointed question precisely raised by the 'Barthian' objector.

In the famous words of Barth's *The Epistle to the Romans*, 'If the Resurrection be brought within the context of history, it must share in its obscurity and error and essential questionableness.'[11] The 'Barthian', in other words, is no less in search of foundational *certainty* than the 'Lockean' approach which he rejects; he merely choses not to risk letting it reside in philosophical ratiocination or historical evidences. His 'foundation' is the risen Christ himself, encountered in the unspeakable *Krisis* of judgement, so elusive that his revelatory presence intersects history only as a tangent touches a circle.[12] By appealing to the pure paradoxes of Kierkegaardian thinking, the early Barth protects the resurrection from the probings of secular historiography (an apologetic gain, seemingly); but at the same time he wraps it in total epistemological obscurity (an apologetic loss, one might

---

[9]   I provide a more detailed examination of these characteristics of the New Testament 'appearance' narratives below, intra. For a useful analysis of how these features of the narratives have been treated by recent New Testmament scholars, see G. O'Collins, SJ, 'The Resurrection: The State of the Questions', in Davis, Kendall and O'Collins, *The Reurrection*, ch. 2, esp. pp. 13–17.

[10]   Pannenberg's is surely the most sophisticated and tenacious attempt so to do: see my account of his attempt in *Jesus – God and Man* in 'Is the Resurrection a "Historical" Event?' (see n. 8).

[11]   K. Barth, *The Epistle to the Romans* (London, 1933), 204, commenting on Romans 6: 8–11. There is a sensitive recent re-evaluation of the role of 'history' in Barth's *Romans* in B. L. McCormack's *Karl Barth's Critically Realistic Dialectical Theology* (Oxford, 1995), ch. 3.

[12]   Ibid., 30: 'In the Resurrection the new world of the Holy Spirit touches the old world of the flesh, but touches it as a tangent touches a circle, that is, without touching it.'

counter). If one is not already one of the elect, the *cognoscenti*, it is unclear how one could do anything about it (and indeed even to try would be to convict oneself of works-righteousness); the leap into the void ('Genuine faith is a void...'[13]) is on this view more truly like lurching beyond Kant's boundary into the *noumenal* realm than being progressively lured by the 'dazzling darkness' of the pre-modern apophatic tradition. I am not of course the first to read Barth as the reverse side of Kantian epistemology.[14] But it remains ironic that Barth – as we have seen – accuses those who approach the resurrection as a 'historical' event of falling into 'obscurity'; for nothing, it seems, could be more epistemologically obscure than the early Barth's own 'ahistorical' alternative.

Strangely too, or so I would argue, it is some of the same features of the New Testament appearance texts that cause trouble for this 'Barthian' approach as they did for the 'Lockean'. It is especially the narratives that chart a *change* of epistemological response that are noteworthy here, or else indicate the possibility of simultaneous and different responses to the same event (such that some vital shift is again required for recognition of the risen Christ to take place). Significantly, these features arise in more than one strand of the 'appearance' traditions: the interaction between Mary and the 'gardener' in John (where Mary has to 'turn' several times before she recognizes Jesus [John 20:11–18]); the lovely story of the walk to Emmaus in Luke (in which it was possible to walk all that distance without recognizing the risen Jesus, until he broke bread [Luke 24:13–35]); the strange possibility of simultaneous recognition and 'doubting' in Matthew (Matthew 28:17); the obscurity and fear as apparent preconditions for resurrection belief in Mark (Mark 16:1–8); the only gradual recognition of Jesus by the lakeside after the miraculous catch of fish (John 21:1–14): not all of these intriguing features, surely, can be explained away as merely redactional or apologetic embroidery? And if not, what do they tell us about the epistemological conditions under which the risen Christ *comes to be* apprehended – a matter on which the 'Lockean' answers inadequately and the 'Barthian' seems not to answer at all? To this – rather subtle – question we now turn with a speculative suggestion. Thereafter we shall consider whether Wittgenstein could possibly have approved of it.

---

[13]   Ibid., 88.

[14]   This is a persistent theme, for instance, in the work of David Tracy: see, e.g., *Blessed Rage for Order* (New York, 1975), 27–31. B. L. McCormack (n. 11) also explores Barth's indebtedness to Kant.

The Resurrection and the Spiritual Senses: A Suggestion

The doctrine of the spiritual senses has its Christian inception in the work of Origen (*c.*185–254), although Origen builds the theory entirely from his creative scriptural interpretation.[15] The promotion of the idea that there is a realm of 'spiritual' sense, different from, and superior to, the gross physical senses, is seemingly motivated not merely by a Platonic distaste for the material world (although this is undeniably a strand in Origen's thinking), but at least as much by the desire to explain the progressive *transformation* of the self's response to the divine through a lifetime of practice, purgation and prayer. In other words, our perception of God, and thus too our grasp of doctrinal verities, does not occur on a flat, or procrustean, bed, but is appropriately open to its object only to the extent that the faculties have been progressively purified.

According to Origen this process involves three stages, all engendered and sustained by ever-deepening meditation on Scripture: *ethikē* (being appropriately formed in the moral life), *physikē* (learning to see the world from the perspective of the 'forms'), and *enoptikē* (contemplation of the divine itself).[16] The climax of the 'enoptic' stage is a deep communion with the eternal Word;[17] and, following the rabbis, it is Origen's insistence that the ultimately indispensable metaphor for this union is an erotic, 'sensual' one – the language of the *Song of Songs*, on which Origen wrote a notable

---

[15] Karl Rahner traced some important aspects of the history of the spiritual senses tradition in his first major theological publications. See his 'The "Spiritual Senses" According to Origen' (originally in a longer version in French in *Revue Ascétique et Mystique* 13 (1932), 113–45), and 'The Doctrine of the "Spiritual Senses" in the Middle Ages' (also originally in *RAM* 14 (1933), 263–99), both now in *Theological Inverstigations*, vol. 16 (London, 1979), chs. 6 and 7. In the first essay Rahner gives a well-documented account of the scriptural passages Origen draws on to support his position (see ibid., 82–9, esp. 83 n. 12). Also compare the important treatment of the spiritual senses in vol. 1 of H. U. von Balthasar's *Herrlichkeit* (orig. Einsiedeln, 1961): Eng. tr., *The Glory of the Lord I: Seeing the Form* (Edinburgh, 1982), 259–308.

[16] Origen assigns these three stages to scriptural meditation on Proverbs, Ecclesiastes and the Song of Songs respectively. For a detailed account of Origen's three-stage theory of ascent see A. Louth, *The Origins of the Christian Mystical Tradition: From Plato to Denys* (Oxford, 1981), ch. 4.

[17] As Louth's account (see n. 16) well illustrates, this undertaking is for Origen conceived in essentially Platonic vein, as an escape from the material: 'So the mind, purified and passing beyond everything material, so that it perfects its contemplation of God, is made divine in what it contemplates' (*Commentary on John*, XXXII. xxvii; cited in Louth, *Origins*, 73).

(and notably beautiful) commentary.[18] It is this pressure – itself Platonic – to unite the noetic and the erotic that gives Origen's Christianized Platonism its special flavour: sometimes Origen will talk of the spiritual senses as the 'faculties of the heart',[19] for with them love – properly purged – finds its integration with mind and its final resting place in the Logos (Christ): 'after realising the beauty of the divine Word, we can allow ourselves to be set on fire with saving love, so that the Word itself deigns to love the soul in which it has encountered longing for it'.[20]

Although Origen did not specifically devise this theory to answer the problem of the recognition of the *resurrected* body, it is noteworthy that in his debate with his famous interlocutor Celsus, Celsus explicitly chides Christianity for a reliance on material sense knowledge because of its belief in a resurrection of the body.[21] And it is precisely in answering this charge that Origen sketches out his doctrine of the spiritual senses. Yes, he responds, the resurrected body is indeed described via sense knowledge, as Scripture shows us; but this is *transformed* sense knowledge, the sense knowledge of the 'inner' self, which uses the language of the physical senses only figuratively.[22]

Origen himself, then, draws a sharp disjunction between the 'inner' and the 'outer' senses:[23] there is no *clear* sense in which the latter gives meaning to the former, except by an exceedingly paradoxical use of metaphor. Nonetheless, the metaphor remains hallowed and indispensable; the *language* of 'divine sensuality' is irreplaceable in charting the ascent to union with the resurrected Christ, even if Origen remains notoriously squeamish about the final redeemability of physical matter itself. Here, indeed, there is an interesting contrast with Origen's important fourth-century follower in the 'spiritual senses' tradition, Gregory of Nyssa (*c.*330–*c.*395); for Nyssa's subtly adjusted views seem to allow for some significant point of *continuity* or

---

[18] Available in English translation, along with two *Homilies* by Origen also devoted to the subject of the *Song*: ed. R. P. Lawson, *Origen: The Song of Songs – Commentary and Homilies, ACW* 26 (New York, 1956).

[19] *De Principiis* 1, II; discussed in Rahner, 'The "Spiritual Senses" According to Origen', 85.

[20] From the *Prologue* to the *Commentary on the Song*, as translated in Rahner, 'The "Spiritual Senses" According to Origen', 95.

[21] See *Contra Celsum* 1. VII.

[22] Ibid. The subtle question of how this 'figure' conveys the passion of the physical whilst also (purportedly) abstracting completely from it is well discussed in Louth, *Origins*, 67–70.

[23] See the *Song Prologue* (tr. Lawson, 29): 'if anyone still bears the image of the earthly according to the outer man, then he is moved by earthly desire and love; but the desire and love of him who bears the image of the heavenly according to the inner man are heavenly'.

development from the physical to the spiritual in the spectrum of purgation of the senses. Thus it is that Gregory can write in the 'Prologue' to his own commentary on the Song of Songs (in other respects deeply dependent on Origen's): 'I hope that my commentary will be a guide *for the more fleshly-minded*, since the wisdom hidden [in the Song of Songs] *leads to* a spiritual state of soul.'[24] Doubtless this modification reflects the autobiographical difference between Origen's stern vision of celibacy (possibly involving actual castration) and Gregory's own later move from married to monastic life.[25] Whatever the explanation we might prefer, the difference is non-trivial epistemologically, since on Nyssa's view the toehold for spiritual perception is precisely *in* the physical, a possibility that is rendered problematic by Origen's sterner disjunction. Nyssa's strongly apophatic sensibilities also make the treatment of spiritual 'sight' quite differently nuanced from Origen: the hegemony of clear visual perception is completely toppled, for him, in the dark intimacy of the embrace by Christ. Either way, however, we should note that the gender implication of the privileged use of the allegory of the Song of Songs is that the 'Bride' (feminine), when suitably prepared for the nuptial embrace of the Bridegroom, becomes the supreme knower and recognizer of Christ – a point to which we shall shortly return.[26]

Origen's and Gregory's teaching on the spiritual senses was a strand of thought curiously neglected in the West until the medieval period (when it was richly recast by Bonaventure and others);[27] it then took another turn in Spanish Counter-Reformation spirituality, where Ignatius of Loyola's rules for the 'discernment of spirits' became more a *spiritual* means for making

---

[24] Gregory of Nyssa, *Commentary on the Song of Songs*, tr. Casimir McCambley (Brookline, MA, 1987), 35, my emphasis. (Oddly, Gregory's crucial contribution to the spiritual senses tradition is not singled out for discussion in Rahner's seminal study.)

[25] On the subtlety of Nyssa's views about virginity and celibacy (granted his early marriage), see the important and suggestive article of M. D. Hart, 'Reconciliation of Body and Soul: Gregory of Nyssa's Deeper Theology of Marriage', *Theological Studies* 51 (1990), 450–78.

[26] This theme has been importantly explored by Verna Harrison, 'Male and Female in Cappadocian Theology', *JTS* 41 (1990), 441–71. Harrison's view of gender, however, owes much to a Jungian theory of 'complementarity', which arguably Nyssa himself does not espouse: compare my 'The Eschatological Body: Gender, Transformation and God', chapter 9, below.

[27] This development in the medieval West is covered by Rahner in 'The Doctrine of the "Spiritual Senses" in the Middle Ages' (see n. 15); and also by H. U. von Balthasar, *The Glory of the Lord*, vol. 1 (Edinburgh, 1982), 284–308.

well-considered vocational decisions in response to Christ than a complete lifetime's *epistemological* programme.[28] (Already we see the seeds of the modern divide between 'spirituality' – now fixed as a noun – and emergent secular epistemology.) In Calvin and the Protestant divines, however, the spiritual senses tradition transmuted into a discussion of the (generalized) *senses divinitatis*, the inbuilt capacity for human response to God which has become tragically besmirsched by sin and has to be refurbished by the graces of the Holy Spirit.[29] What we note in this shift into the early modern period, then, is a an apparent loss of the subtle *multi-levelled* aspect of the pre-modern spiritual senses tradition. For Origen, as we have seen, there are distinct and different levels of perception, depending on one's spiritual maturity and (concomitant) epistemological capacity; for Calvin, this necessarily elitist and progressivist model is replaced by a theory of double predestination. It is not that some people get only so far in their perception of the divine and others a little further; rather, some people receive intellectual revelation and the affective graces of the Holy Spirit, and others do *not*. It is a significant difference, and one which I now wish to explore. For whilst the Protestant strand of this story has recently received important philosophical attention from 'Reformed' epistemology,[30] the earlier, Origenist (or, better, Nyssan) reading of the spiritual senses has seemingly yet to be evaluated as a serious current epistemological option.[31] Let me here make a few preliminary, if somewhat speculative, suggestions.

How might this tradition of the spiritual senses throw light on our initial discussion of the epistemological problem of the resurrection narratives? My suggested response to this is threefold. First, we note how this tradition is capable of explaining a range of *different* responses to the risen Christ, even amongst the faithful. Not all responses are equally deep; and the closest recognition (involving dark 'ecstasy' in Nyssa or actual mingling with the Word in Origen) will often – in the era of the church – involve long years of moral and spiritual preparation, prolonged *practice* in 'sensing' the presence of Christ. Second, then, this approach also indicates how seeking and recognizing the resurrected Christ require a *process* of change, one only

---

[28]   Illuminatingly discussed by von Balthasar, *The Glory of the Lord*, 297–8 (though he does not explicitly draw the distinction between 'spiritual' and 'epistemological' that I essay here).

[29]   See J. Calvin, *Institutes of the Christian Religion*, orig. 1559, tr. F. L. Battles (Philadelphia, 1960), III, ii. 7, etc.

[30]   See the discussion by A. Plantinga in *Warranted Christian Belief* (Oxford, 2000), chs. 8 and 9.

[31]   I made a first attempt to adumbrate this approach in my 'Response' to W. P. Alston in Davis, Kendall and O'Collins, *The Resurrection*, 184–90.

rarely achieved at speed;[32] it will involve an initial 'turning-around' morally, then practice in seeing the world differently, then only finally the full intimacy of 'spiritual/sensual' knowledge of Christ. What happens in this process is a transformation of one's actual epistemic capacities through their 'purgation' (understood somewhat differently, I have argued, in Origen's and Gregory's case). Thirdly, this approach stresses the absolutely crucial significance of the integration of the affective and the erotic in any adequate understanding or 'knowledge' of the risen Christ (although this is differently the case in Origen and Gregory, Origen being notoriously ambivalent about the final significance of the material body). Yet in neither author are the affective/erotic and the noetic set off *against* each other as disjunct alternatives, or even as a complementary duality.

If we now apply these insights to the intriguing features of the New Testament resurrection narratives to which we have already drawn attention, it must be readily acknowledged that the links, suggestive as they are, involve significant disanalogy as well as analogy: the New Testament appearance stories seem to involve 'epistemic transformations' much more instantaneous than those described in Origen's schema. This granted, the points of connection are still striking. The first feature just delineated indicates how doubt and faith could strangely coexist in response to an 'appearance' of the risen Christ (Matthew 28:16–17); or how it might be difficult, *initially*, and prior to some change in one's normal demands for perceptual evidences, to recognize the risen body (John 20:24–8). The second feature, correlatively, underscores how some 'turning' in one's posture or attitude, some difference of perspective or visual angle, or transformation of the nature of physical 'touch', might be required in order so to grasp the resurrected reality (John 20:11–18). And the third feature, finally, would suggest that a narrowly noetic investigation would take one *nowhere* in this quest; that the evidences of the 'heart', and of orienting and worshipful practices of the body, could not be neglected if Christ-as-risen were to be apprehended (Luke 24:28–35). Such are the suggested (if speculative) points of connection.[33] If I am right, then the

---

[32]   That is not to say that the full *consciousness* of recognition may not come 'suddenly': for this theme in Plato and Origen, see Louth, *Origins*, 70–1. Also compare the R. S. Thomas poem, 'Suddenly' quoted at the end of this chapter.

[33]   A very original and suggestive reading of the resurrection narratives by a New Testament scholar, along somewhat similar lines to mine, is to be found in M. Sawicki, *Seeing the Lord* (Minneapolis, 1994). Sawicki draws on Bourdieu's notion of 'practice' (rather than appealing to Wittgenstein's epistemology) in order to give content to the *conditions* of 'practice' under which the early Christian communities could come to know the risen Christ.

'spiritual senses' tradition represents one powerful way in which reflection on seeking and finding Christ remained cogent in an era after the end of the 'apostolic' appearances were over (see 1 Cor. 15: 5–8), even as it recapitulated and extended some central features of those appearances.

Now let us ask whether Wittgenstein might possibly have intuited some of these same points; and – further – what we might conceivably make of this line of approach as a *contemporary* religious epistemological option, especially in relation to the subtle question of recognizing the risen Christ.

Wittgenstein and Resurrection Epistemology

In this (necessarily brief) section, I wish to focus primarily on some characteristically dense and rich remarks made by Wittgenstein in the year 1937, and enshrined – in English – in the volume *Culture and Value* (hereafter *CV*).[34] Not only does Wittgenstein here make his only direct remarks about the resurrection (*CV* 33e); but the surrounding *obiter dicta* are, from the perspective of the particular epistemological questions I have so far opened up in this chapter, extraordinarily apposite. Indeed the speculative novelty of my undertaking here is a hermeneutical one: I suggest that we read the remarks on the resurrection *in the light* of the surrounding aphorisms. It will be worth quoting an excerpted number of phrases and sentences before drawing out their apparent (combined) significance:

> The *edifice of your pride* has to be dismantled. And that is terribly hard work. (*CV* 26e)
> The way to solve the problem you see in life is to live in a way that will make what is problematic disappear. (*CV* 26e)
> Christianity is not a doctrine, not, I mean, a theory about what has happened and what will happen to the human soul, but a description of something that actually takes place in a human life. (*CV* 28e)
> ...a man who is not used to searching in the forest for flowers... will not find any because his eyes are not trained to to see them.... – And this is no wonder for someone who knows how long even the man with practice, who realizes there is a difficulty, will have to search before he finds it. When something is well hidden it is hard to find. (*CV* 29e)
> Religion says: *Do this! – Think like that!* – but it cannot justify this and once it even tries to, it becomes repellent;... It is more convincing to say: 'Think like this! however strange it may strike you.' Or: 'Won't you do this? –

---

[34]   L. Wittgenstein, *Culture and Value* (Chicago, 1980).

however repugnant you find it.' (*CV* 29e)

Everything that comes my way becomes a picture for me of what I am thinking about at the time. (Is there something feminine about this way of thinking?) (*CV* 31e)

Kierkegaard writes: If Christianity were so easy and coy, why should God in his Scriptures have set Heaven and Earth in motion and threatened *eternal* punishments? . . . what you are supposed to see cannot be communicated even by the best and most accurate historian . . . . (*CV* 31e)

In religion every level of devoutness must have its appropriate form of expression which has no sense at a lower level. This doctrine, which means something at a higher level, is null and void for someone who is still at the lower level; he *can* only understand it *wrongly* and so these words are *not* valid for such a person. (*CV* 32e)

Christianity is not based on a historical truth; rather, it offers us a (historical) narrative and says: now believe! But not, believe this narrative with the belief appropriate to a historical narrative, rather, believe through thick and thin, which you can only do as the result of a life. (*CV* 32e)

Queer as it sounds: The historical accounts in the Gospels might, historically speaking, be demonstrably false and yet belief would lose nothing by this . . . . This message (the Gospels) is seized on by men believingly (i.e., lovingly). (*CV* 32e)

. . . I cannot utter the word 'Lord' with meaning. *Because I do not believe* that he will come to judge me; because *that* says nothing to me. And it could say something to me, only if I lived *completely* differently. (*CV* 33e)

What inclines even me to believe in Christ's Resurrection? It is though I play with the thought. – If he did not rise from the dead, then he decomposed in the grave like any other man. . . . But if I am to be REALLY saved, – what I need is *certainty* – not wisdom, dreams or speculation – and this certainty is faith. And faith is faith in what is needed by my *heart*, my *soul*, not my speculative intelligence. For it is my soul with its passions, as it were with its flesh and blood, that has to be saved, not my abstract mind. Perhaps we can say: Only *love* can believe the Resurrection. Or: It is *love* that believes the Resurrection. . . . What combats doubt is, as it were, *redemption*. . . . So this can come about only if you no longer rest your weight on the earth but suspend yourself from heaven. Then *everything* will be different and it will be 'no wonder' if you can do things that you cannot do now. (*CV* 33e)

The immediate feature that strikes us, first, in considering this collocation of remarks, is the forceful rejection of what I earlier termed the Lockean/Humean approach to religious belief in general, and the resurrection in particular; and this, as is well known, is even more forcibly stressed in the *Lectures and Conversations on Aesthetics, Psychology and Religious*

Belief.[35] Religious beliefs and doctrines are not to be demonstrated by 'evidences'. Embracing them is more like the adopting of a whole new way of life, or 'picturing' differently, or making a particular narrative central to one's existence, than coolly adjudicating on their likelihood with the 'speculative intelligence'.

The most obvious alternative, then, is the Kierkegaardian (and 'Barthian') lurch to another sort of 'certainty', the certainty of 'faith'. And since Wittgenstein here, and indeed elsewhere,[36] makes no bones about his attraction to both these thinkers, it is natural enough to box him up as a consistent devotee of this line of thinking. Here is the 'normative' side of his view of religion that he is nonetheless loath to own up to:[37] faith has its certainties which are *given*, not 'justified' (*CV* 29e); the move to faith is obscure and better not probed (it cannot in any case be brought about by 'works' (*CV* 32e)); it has nothing to do with ordinary 'events' or secular 'history' (*CV* 31e, 32e); its occasion cannot be wilfully or mentally triggered: 'love' and the speculative intellect find themselves in problematic disjunction (*CV* 33e); 'faith' involves, *in se*, unshakeable 'certainty' (*CV* 33e). None of these sentiments would seem compatible with the spiritual senses tradition we have just outlined.

Yet the suggestive remarks that *surround* these more obviously 'Kierke- gaardian' purple passages are worthy of further probing; for a number of them do not seem so easily compatible with what we earlier termed the early 'Barthian' perspective on resurrection belief. Some, indeed – if I am right – show distinct marks of coincidence with the pre-modern spiritual senses tradition (especially when backed by cognate remarks in the same volume and elsewhere from the same period), and stand thereby in at least a problematic relation to this 'Kierkegaardian'/'Barthian' alternative. Let me expatiate briefly. I shall comment on four such 'marks', the first being the most significant and thus here treated at some greater length than the others.

This first clue comes in the noteworthy passage on *CV* 32e: 'In religion every *level of devoutness* must have its appropriate form of expression...', etc. (my emphasis). Here Wittgenstein explicitly addresses – and embraces – the

---

[35] See n. 5, above, for the *Lectures*; and ibid., 57–9, for Wittgenstein's rejection of Fr. O'Hara's appeal to 'scientific' evidences for religious belief.

[36] On Wittgenstein's attraction to Kierkegaard, see Putnam, *Renewing Philosophy*, 144–50. On the rather more ambiguous evidence about Barth, see the discussion in F. Kerr, *Theology After Wittgenstein* (Oxford, 1986), 152.

[37] I. U. Dalferth makes a telling point about Wittgenstein's unwillingness to *own* the normative side of his views about religion in 'Wittgenstein: The Theological Reception' (see n. 3), 32–3.

possibility that people at different levels of spiritual maturity, understanding or practice (the German is *Religiosität*) might construe the force of religious language differently. Indeed, for one at a lower level, some language could actually have little or no such force ('these words are *not* valid for such a person'). We can readily see how this might apply to someone seeking 'meaning' in the somewhat elusive doctrine of the resurrected body of Christ. Yet this idea of a sliding scale of 'levels' of 'devoutness' is surely hard to square with the disjunctive Kierkegaardian *Either/Or*, or with dramatic 'leaps' into 'faith'. (Even if, as Kierkegaard avows, the 'certainty' of faith may paradoxically continue to be attended by nagging doubt, his model is hardly compatible with the idea of structured epistemic *levels*).[38] Rather, the sliding-scale approach suggests, in the spirit of the pre-modern tradition we have been considering, a subtle range of *differing* possibilities of religious and epistemic responses to the divine, even within the ranks of the faithful. And it is here that a link with Putnam's recent 'realist' rereading of the later Wittgenstein's thought on religion may be significant and inviting. Let me give a brief résumé of Putnam's argument in order to extend it.

Putnam argues first – and to my mind convincingly – against the view that Wittgenstein's appeal to 'picturing' in religious language somehow suggests a non-cognitive view of such language.[39] On the contrary (and this will shortly be significant for our assessment of the subliminally gendered dimension of resurrection belief), Wittgenstein begins to aver strongly in lectures during the 1930s that 'pictures' are intrinsic to much of our thinking, and no less to religious thinking; but nothing is implied thereby about such thinking being non-cognitive or merely 'emotive'.[40] More ingeniously, Putnam then goes on to argue (via a subtle interpretation of the *Lectures on Religion*[41]) that even the concept of 'referring' in the later Wittgenstein is a 'family resemblance' notion: what 'referring' is is mastering the technique of the appropriate use of a word, but such use (appropriately) *differs* in differing realms of discourse. Thus 'there isn't some one thing which can be called referring', even though there may be 'overlapping similarities' between one sort and

[38] On the possibility of the co-incidence of certainty and doubt in Kierkegaard, see Putnam, *Renewing Philosophy*, 145; and ibid., on the closeness of some of Wittgenstein's views to Kierkegaard's *Concluding Unscienctific Postscript* (Princeton, NJ, 1941), esp. 25–48. The drama of doubt and certainty is, however, a paradox not easily subsumed into a graded theory of 'ascent'.

[39] Putnam, *Renewing Philosophy*, 154–7.

[40] See ibid., 158–61.

[41] Ibid., 160, citing Wittgenstein's *Lectures*, 67.

another.[42] So the suggestion that Wittgenstein's notion of religious language involves complete 'incommensurability' with other forms of language also fails to convince. It is not that Wittgenstein thinks that, when the religious person and the non-religious person 'talk past' one another, one is being non-realist and the other (incommensurably) realist, or one failing to 'refer' and the other succeeding. On the contrary, concludes Putnam, no 'language game' (or, better, in the case of religion, *set* of language games[43]) is in worse shape than another, epistemologically speaking, because of its failure to provide a 'transcendental guarantee'; for at the base of any such language game is an appeal to 'trust' which is as unavoidable as it is challenging.[44]

Putnam leaves us thus suspended; yet although he has – to my mind – convincingly routed the 'non-realist' interpretation of Wittgenstein's religious views, he has not said as much as he might about the problem of apparent incomprehension between religious and non-religious folk (a matter from which he starts, and which is pointedly raised in the *Lectures*[45]). Nor, we note, has he explicated the intriguing words in *CV* 32e about 'levels of devoutness' and their relation to 'meaning'. It is not just religious and non-religious people who 'talk past' each other, it seems, but even different parties of those within the churches; and of this Wittgenstein seems willing to give some account in *CV* 32e. My suggestion, then, is that we read this important passage as a further epistemological counterpart of the fluid theory of 'referring' explicated by Putnam. Just as 'referring' has no *one* ('essential') meaning from a 'family resemblance' perspective, so too 'perceiving' seemingly has no *one* meaning either. We 'perceive' at different 'levels', according to the development of our 'devoutness'. If this is indeed Wittgenstein's meaning (and it does seem to be the 'plain sense' of the text), then we are extraordinarily close to the central insight of the spiritual senses tradition.[46] The closest

[42] Ibid., 167.

[43] Putnam occasionally falls into the trap of referring to a whole religion as 'a language game' (e.g. ibid., 173); compare the excellent discussion in P. Sherry, *Religion, Truth and Language-Games* (London, 1977), ch. 2, which reminds us that Wittgenstein himself did not use the terms 'language-game' or 'form of life' for anything as large as a whole religious system, but rather for much smaller elements within such.

[44] See Putnam, *Renewing Philosophy*, 177.

[45] See again Wittgenstein, *Lectures*, 53–9.

[46] I am abstracting here from the attendant Platonism of Origen's version of the theory, with – as we have seen – its notorious disjunction between *nous* and *soma*, a disjunction that Wittgenstein's philosophy of mind of course stringently questions. It is this feature of Origen, not the rather subtle aspects of his spiritual senses doctrine, which causes Fergus Kerr to point to Origen as the ultimate progenitor of the Cartesian tradition fundamentally brought into question by Wittgenstein: see Kerr, *Theology After Wittgenstein*, 168.

contemporary counterpart in today's epistemological scene might be found in the analysis of so-called 'proper functioning';[47] yet in Wittgenstein's case, if I read him aright, this is a 'layered' understanding of types of functioning, one which involves not only the removal of sin for its full effect, but some actual change in the perceptual capacities.

There are other hints, too, of such an alliance with the spiritual senses tradition: further features of this section of *Culture and Value* fit uneasily with the Kierkegaardian perspectives that are otherwise explicit. For when Wittgenstein talks, secondly, of the necessity to 'dismantle one's pride' (stressing that it is 'hard work'), or to lead a life of a *'completely* different' sort as a precondition of belief, or to train one's eye to look 'with practice' for the right things, one is struck by the *progressive* nature of the epistemological undertaking and its accompanying preparatory moral seriousness. (And, as I am suggesting, may we not read these comments in *relation to* the surrounding remarks on religious matters?) Here, it seems, is no sudden lurch into 'certainty', sweeping aside all human cooperation or preparedness, but more truly a progressive unfolding of insights based in patient moral transformation. The picture is akin to what we now term a 'virtue epistemology'.

Further, and thirdly (and relatedly), the insights about living a 'picture',[48] or relating, unshakeably, to a particular narrative (*CV* 32e), are worth comparing with an important passage a little later in *Culture and Value* (from the year 1946), which we must certainly acknowledge as self-consciously 'Kierkegaardian':

> I believe that one of the things Christianity says is that sound doctrines are all useless. That you have to change your life. (Or the *direction* of your life). (*CV* 53e)
> The point is that a sound doctrine need not *take hold* of you; you can follow it as you would a doctor's prescription. – But here you need something to move you and turn you in a new direction.... Once you have been tunred round, you must *stay* turned round. Wisdom is passionless. But faith by contrast is what Kierkegaard calls a *passion*. (*CV* 53e)

The pressing question that here confronts us is whether Wittgenstein himself, having located the significance of 'turning' (the reminiscence of

---

[47] See esp. the treatment of an 'Extended Aquinas/Calvin Model' along these lines of 'proper functioning' in Plantinga, *Warranted Christian Belief*, Part III.
[48] Wittgenstein acknowledges (*CV* 32e) that 'pictures' too can have different valences at different times, depending on one's spiritual state: 'at my level the Pauline doctrine of predestination is ugly nonsense . . .'.

Mary Magdalene's 'turning' at the graveside is not insignificant: it involves the possibility of seeing differently), and then having used Kierkegaardian *rhetoric* to describe it, could himself ever satisfactorily account – either personally or theoretically – for the possibility of such an unexpected event. Again, his casting around for antecedent preparations for such an eventuality – moral transformation, focus on a 'life' or a 'narrative', or (elsewhere, late in *Culture and Value*) the preparations of 'suffering'[49] – seem to give the lie to a *consistently* 'Kierkegaardian' or 'Barthian' account of faith. We have at least here a hermenuetical *aporia*: a Protestant rhetoric of pure and unmerited grace vies with intimations of a more ancient 'Catholic' spirituality of progression into holiness.

Fourthly, and finally – and again paradoxically – it is perplexing, in the light of the Kierkegaardian disjunction set up between 'love' and 'speculative intelligence' in relation to the resurrection specifically (*CV* 33e), and between 'wisdom' and 'passion' in relation to doctrine generally (*CV* 53e), to find Wittgenstein also insisting that redemption can only occur 'if you no longer rest your weight on the earth but suspend yourself from heaven' (*CV* 33e).[50] For what can this mean, if the 'passions', and 'flesh and blood' (ibid.) are precisely what is at stake (*not*, as Wittgenstein insists, a disembodied mind)? Does this not imply some *transformation* of the passions, of 'flesh and blood', in order that their natural earthiness be precisely 'suspended from heaven'? Wittgenstein does not tell us; but the question mark remains in the air, and intriguingly resummons the notion of 'levels' of different forms of response.

To sum up the results of this necessarily dense section: I have been arguing that the epistemological remarks that surround Wittgenstein's analysis of resurrection belief in *Culture and Value* are worth reading in relation to it; and that if we do this, we find a certain tension between the (occasionally explicit) avowals of 'Kierkegaardianism' and strands of thought more compatible with a 'spiritual senses' approach such as outlined above. Whilst there is nothing in Wittgenstein's text, of course, to suggest the Platonizing overtones of Origen's particular reading of the spiritual senses, other points of continuity are striking, and give the lie – or so I have argued – to a *consistently* 'Kierkegaardian' or 'Barthian' understanding

---

[49]   *CV* 86e (from 1950).

[50]   Note that the Kierkegaardian disjunction between 'passion' and 'intelligence' is not the same as the Origenistic dualism between 'mind' and 'body'. Here Wittgenstein seems to be embracing the former, yet simltaneously reaching out for a non-dualistic understanding of the transformative capacities of the enfleshed self – a possibility that reminds us more of some aspects of Gregory of Nyssa's rendition of the spiritual senses tradition than of Origen's.

of faith.[51] (Indeed, we may perhaps speculate whether this tension may have been a contributing factor in Wittgenstein's notable inability to embrace faith in any robust sense for himself.[52]) Yet here, as we have seen, is a view of faith profoundly sensitive to its differing 'levels' of intensity, perceptual/ tactile response, and spiritual and moral maturity. Here is a view of faith rooted in 'practice', involving *particular* forms of vision and a 'layered' understanding of doctrine's possible 'meanings'. Here is a view of faith that involves 'turning around' and coming to perceive ('picture') *differently*.

Why then, finally, does Wittgenstein speak of such 'picturing' as 'feminine'? (*CV* 31e)? It is to the neglected question of the 'gendered' nature of the 'grammar' of resurrection belief that we turn, finally.

'Femininity' and the Resurrection

Wittgenstein's aside is elusive as it stands, and there is no intrinsic reason – we must admit – to connect the supposed 'femininity' of 'picturing' with the resurrection specifically. Nonetheless, there are reasons why such a gendered connection could be illuminating. Let me mention four such reasons.

First, there is the obvious New Testament evidence for the primacy of women's testimony in witnessing to the resurrection, and the apparent scepticism or delay involved in some of the male disciples' responses. It is a commonplace of New Testament scholarship to acknowledge the apparently apologetic massaging of the Lukan and Johannine traditions to allow for an earlier response from Peter and John.[53] More likely is it, however,

---

[51]   See again my remarks and citations in n. 46. It goes beyond the scope of this chapter to chart *all* the twists and turns of the spiritual senses tradition as aspects of it were recast in scholastic (and much later, neo-scholastic) religious epistemology. The inheritance with which Wittgenstein may have been somewhat familiar, from his upbringing and continuing interaction with Catholicism, is the type of neo-scholastic reflection on levels of 'rational' and 'super-rational' knowledge found in (e.g.) J. Maritain, *The Degrees of Knowledge* (New York, 1938). It is not part of the thesis of this paper that Wittgenstein was directly cognizant of the patristic form of the spiritual senses doctrine.

[52]   On this see Ray Monk's pertinent remark: 'Still there is a persistent and nagging doubt about how Wittgenstein expected, or hoped, . . . redemption to come about – whether, so to speak, it was in his hands or God's' (R. Monk, *Ludwig Wittgenstein: The Duty of Genius* (London, 1990), 412).

[53]   See Luke 24:11 (expressing strong initial disbelief of the women by the male disciples), compared with the added variant text at this point, which has Peter immediately coming to verify the women's tale; and John 20:2–10, which (unconvincingly?) interrupts the story of Mary Magdalene's first encounter with the risen Jesus by insisting that both Peter and John also came early to the tomb.

that the women (and especially Mary Magdalene) were the initial recipients of 'appearances' (whether of angels or of Jesus himself) and their witness at first treated with some scepticism: it was, after all, fragmentary, awestruck and somewhat incoherent, and apparently attended by strong elements of 'fear'.[54] Further, a woman's witness was, in Jewish law, regarded as less convincing and reliable than that of a man. Yet it was in all probability women who were first enabled to 'see' the risen Christ.[55]

In the hands of later tradition, however, 'femininity' and the resurrection are treated as correlative for another reason, which seems to build, gender stereotypically, upon this memory. As Thomas Aquinas puts it in a notable but neglected passage in the third part of the *Summa* (ST 3a, 55, 1 ad 3), it is women's supposedly greater capacity for 'love' (shown in their fidelity to Jesus at the crucifixion and their early presence on Easter morning) that will guarantee them a quicker share than men in the beatific vision. It is here that we are reminded not only of Wittgenstein's insistence that 'love' rather than dispassionate intellectual curiosity is what responds to the resurrection, but also of the rich exegesis in the spiritual senses tradition of the *Song of Songs*, where, as we explicated earlier, it is also only the 'feminized' soul that can fully respond to the embraces of the Bridegroom, the exalted and heavenly Christ.

A third suggestive point of connection is raised by Wittgenstein's acknowledgement that his 'picturing' epistemology is not quite *normative* in the epistemological terms of his day; that it smacks of a form of 'feminized' subversion of normal ways of thinking about reference and meaning. A creative link may be made here with recent developments in feminist epistemology,[56] which has incisively challenged the hegemony of the 'recognition-of-hard-objects-at-five-paces' model for normative epistemological discussion, a challenge that draws attention instead to the *contextual* significance of any 'S-knowing-p', and to the varieties of types of possible

[54] This is especially emphasized in the Markan account: see the famous last sentence of Mark (16:8).

[55] For a contemporary feminist account of the significance of this likelihood, see E. Schüssler Fiorenza, In *Memory of Her* (New York, 1983), ch. 4, esp. 138–40. For an incisive recent account of the probable primacy of Mary Magdalene's witness to the resurrection, see G. Theissen and A. Merz, *The Historical Jesus: A Comprehensive Guide* (Minneapolis, 1998), 496–9.

[56] See, e.g., L. Alcoff and E. Potter (eds.), *Feminist Epistemologies* (New York, 1993), and esp. Lorraine Code, 'Taking Subjectivity into Account' (ibid., ch. 2), for the critique of epistemology which fails to acknowledge the primary significance of 'knowing' other *people* as a condition for reidentifying objects.

'knowing', personal as well as cognitive. Unsurprisingly, these feminist writers find themselves drawing on occasions on Wittgenstein.[57] 'Knowing' can take many forms in 'the stream of life';[58] and if a culture dubs some of the more subtle forms 'feminine', it may well be more a sign of the lesser significance it grants to them (as personal, affective, hard to grasp) than necessarily connected with a spuriously 'essential' nature of 'woman'.

Fourthly, and finally, we do well to connect here with the insights of contemporary French feminism (especially with the work of Julia Kristeva and Luce Irigaray), which – utilizing the distinctions of Jacques Lacan's linguistic theory – dubs 'semiotic' that style of speech that subverts or destabilizes the ordered 'symbolic' language of normative 'masculinist' culture.[59] 'Mystic speech', from this perspective, is unsurprisingly often a mode of subversive 'female' utterance;[60] and 'woman's' association with the fearful events of death and birth also links her with the 'semiotic' – with what is repressed in the efforts at stabilizing cultural order.[61] From this (gendered) viewpoint, is it surprising that the 'grammar' of 'raised' has proved so elusive to the *modernistic* bias in philosophy, with its demand for stiff foundational universals? Or that alternative visions of epistemology might fall – as we have seen Wittgenstein suggested – under the suspicious rubric of 'feminine'? Or again, and finally, that poets – ever in the vanguard of the 'semiotic' – should have proved in this period so much more successful in evoking the subtle responses of resurrection belief than their theologian counterparts?

One cannot do better, surely, than the late lamented R. S. Thomas, whose poem 'Suddenly'[62] remarkably encapsulates what I have tried to

---

[57] See ibid., 9, 17, 23, 163–5; and compare the account of Wittgenstein's objection to viewing 'the self as a detached spectator' in F. Kerr, *Theology After Wittgenstein*, 134. Kerr does not himself make a connection to feminism, but his points are exactly parallel to the ones wielded by Lorraine Code (n. 56) in explicitly feminist mode.

[58] See Wittgenstein's *Remarks on the Philosophy of Psychology*, vol. II (Oxford, 1980), 687: 'Words have meaning only in the stream of life.'

[59] For a succinct account of this theory of language and of Kristeva's and Irigaray's versions of it, see C. Weedon, *Feminist Practice and Post-Structuralist Theory* (Oxford, 1987).

[60] See Luce Irigaray's justly famous essay, '*La Mystérique*', in *Speculum of the Other Woman* (Ithaca, NY, 1985), 191–202.

[61] See Julia Kristeva's equally renowned article, 'Stabat Mater', in T. Moi (ed.), *The Kristeva Reader* (Oxford, 1986), 160–86.

[62] R. S. Thomas, *Laboratories of the Spirit*, 32 (see n. 1). Worth comparing with Thomas's 'semiotic' evocation of the spiritual senses is the equally remarkable poem on a similar theme, 'The Transfiguration' by Edwin Muir: *Edwin Muir: Collected Poems* (Oxford, 1960), 198–200. It starts:

express in this paper about the complexity and subtlety of 'seeing' the risen Christ:

> As I had always known
> he would come, unannounced,
> remarkable merely for the absence
> of clamour. So truth must appear
> to the thinker; so, at a stage
> of the experiment, the answer
> must clearly emerge. I looked
> at him, not with the eye
> only, but with the whole
> of my being, overflowing with
> him as a chalice would
> with the sea. Yet was he
> no more there than before,
> his area occupied
> by the unhaloed presences.
> You could put your hand
> in him without consciousness
> of his wounds. The gamblers
> at the foot of the unnoticed
> cross went on with
> their dicing; yet the invisible
> garment for which they played
> was no longer at stake, but worn
> by him in this risen existence.

Conclusions

I have in the course of this chapter presented a number of intertwined theses. In the first place, I have suggested that the apparently disjunctive modern choice between an approach to the resurrection in the spirit of

---

So from the ground we felt that virtue branch
Through all our veins till we were whole, our wrists
As fresh and pure as water from a well,
Our hands made new to handle holy things,
The source of all our seeing rinsed and cleansed
Till earth and light and water entering there
Gave back to us the clear unfallen world.

Locke and Hume (on the one hand), or Kierkegaard and the early Barth (on the other), is a false one, which does not in any case do justice to some of the more alluring and subtle features of the New Testament narratives. Secondly, my brief exploration of the 'spiritual senses' tradition – rooted in Origen's thought but finding a less harshly dualistic reading in the writing of Gregory of Nyssa – attempted to sketch out a third alternative in which *transformation* of normal sense perception becomes the requisite of resurrection belief. Turning thirdly to the work of Wittgenstein I have tried, admittedly more speculatively, to indicate a strand in his thinking that is redolent of this 'spiritual senses' tradition, and which I believe stands in some tension with his acknowledged – though sometimes baffled – attraction to the thought of Kierkegaard and Barth. Finally, in feminist vein, I have suggested a number of ways in which the elusiveness of 'seeing the Lord' has at times been associated with 'woman', 'femininity', or the 'semiotic'; and how this gendered dimension of the 'grammar' of resurrection faith is seemingly intrinsic to our continuing difficulties in expressing the reality of a risen Christ who cannot finally be *grasped*, but rather 'seen' – 'not with the eye only'.[63]

[63]   I am grateful to Ludger Viefhues, SJ and Heinrich Watzka, SJ for some stimulating conversations on Wittgenstein whilst I was writing this chapter; and to Ingolf Dalferth and Anthony Baxter for critical comments on an earlier version of it.

Chapter 9

THE ESCHATOLOGICAL BODY: GENDER, TRANSFORMATION AND GOD

Introduction: Bodily Obsessions

In this final essay I shall attempt to substantiate what may appear to be an initially implausible thesis. I shall be arguing that the obsessive interest in the "body" which has been such a marked feature of late twentieth-century Western culture hides a profound eschatological longing; only a *theological* vision of a particular sort, I shall suggest, can satisfy it. More specifically, I shall test this contention by reference to the work of one leading post-modern secular feminist, Judith Butler, whose work on gender,[1] and the subversion of "gender binaries", is fast achieving the status of dogma in some American women's studies and religious studies circles. Butler, perhaps, we may see as the high priestess of anti-essentialist feminism, presiding (by means of suitably liturgical *performative* utterance) over the sacrificial death of gender stability. Yet Butler's ingenious attempts to escape the repressive net of sexual stereotypes are – I shall suggest – ironic, if ultimately depressing, secularized counterparts of an *ascetical* programme of gender fluidity into the divine that Christian tradition may hold out to us, especially as we find it in the work of Gregory of Nyssa; and Nyssa's programme works with a necessarily eschatological *telos*. This unlikely pair of interlocutors, then, will form the focus of my analysis: in introducing Judith Butler to Gregory of Nyssa, I shall not merely be inviting a comparison of a post-modern perspective on "body"

Originally published in *Modern Theology* 16 (2000), pp. 61–73. Reprinted with permission from Blackwell Publishers, with light revisions.

[1] Butler's four influential books on gender to date are: *Gender Trouble: Feminism and the Subversion of Identity* (New York, NY: Routledge, 1990); *Bodies that Matter: On the Discursive Limits of "Sex"* (New York, NY: Routledge, 1993); *The Psychic Life of Power: Theories in Subjection* (Stanford, CA: Stanford University Press, 1997); and *Excitable Speech: A Politics of the Performative* (New York, NY: Routledge, 1997).

and "self" with a pre-modern one (such comparisons have all the dangers of anachronism, but can nonetheless prove theologically instructive[2]); rather, my goal is to educe a theological answer to a latent – if repressed – eschatological question in our millennial cultural milieu.

But first we need to ask: why do "bodies" "matter" so much? No one can have failed to notice the obsession with the "body" that has gripped the late-twentieth-century popular imagination; yet this very phenomenon bears all the marks of our current deepest *aporias*, fears and longings.[3] The notable explosion of thought and literature on the subject of the "body" in recent decades[4] has, for a start, begged a question of definition which is not so easily grasped, let alone answered. It is as if we are clear about an agreed cultural obsession, but far from assured about its referent. As Judith Butler herself has put it, "I tried to discipline myself to stay on the subject, but found I could not fix bodies as objects of thought ... Inevitably, I began to consider that this resistance was essential to the matter in hand."[5] Or, as put from a rather different methodological perspective, by Mary Douglas: "Just as it is true that everything symbolizes the body, so it is equally true that the body symbolizes *everything else*."[6] It seems that "bodies" are as elusive as they are ubiquitous – curiously hard to get our "hands" around, even as we constantly refer to them as the locus of potential meaning.

The question that seems to press in a post-modern age is this: if we[7] can no longer count on any universal "grand narrative" to bear the burden of religious and philosophical needs for meaning-making, is it perhaps only

---

[2] Caroline Bynum warns against the dangers of such anachronistic comparisons in her article "Why All the Fuss about the Body? A Medievalist's Perspective", in *Critical Inquiry* 22, 1995, pp. 1–33; see pp. 29–30 for Bynum's remarks about Origen and Judith Butler. I wish to acknowledge my indebtedness to Bynum for her inspiration and friendship; in this matter, however, I have chosen to risk her opprobrium for nonetheless comparing two authors from such widely differing contexts.

[3] I repeat here some of the material discussed in the introduction to my edited volume, *Religion and the Body* (Cambridge: Cambridge University Press, 1997), pp. 1–12.

[4] Extensive bibliographies of this inter-disciplinary literature can be found in (e.g.), M. Feher (with R. Naddaff and N. Tazi), *Fragments for a History of the Body* (New York, NY: Zone Books, 1989); M. McGuire, "Religion and the Body: Rematerializing the Human Body in the Social Sciences of Religion", *Journal of the Scientific Study of Religion* 29, 1990, pp. 283–96; T. J. Csordas, "Embodiment as a Paradigm for Anthropology", *Ethos* 18, 1990, pp. 5–47; and ed. S. Coakley, *Religion and the Body* (see n. 3).

[5] J. Butler, *Bodies that Matter*, p. ix.

[6] M. Douglas, *Purity and Danger: An Analysis of Concepts of Pollution and Taboo* (London: Routledge & Kegan Paul, 1966), p. 122, my emphasis.

[7] I use "we" here, in these next two paragraphs, in a general (secularized) cultural sense.

resistant fleshliness that we can look to as an Archimedean point of stability – a seemingly unambiguous focus for longings, myths and quasi-religious hopes? Yet on closer reflection this too – the post-modern "body" – becomes subject to infinitely variable social constructions. The "body" thus comes to bear huge, and paradoxical, pressure in post-modern thought: just as its Enlightenment partner, the "mind/soul" of Cartesianism, is seen off with almost unexamined vehemence,[8] so, simultaneously, what is left (the "body") becomes infinitely problematized and elusive. It is all that we have, but we seemingly cannot grasp it; nor, more frighteningly, are we sure that we can control the political forces that seek to regiment it. Devoid now of religious meaning or of the capacity for any fluidity into the divine, shorn of any expectation of new life beyond the grave, it has shrunk to the limits of individual fleshliness; hence our only hope seems to reside in keeping it alive, youthful, consuming, sexually active, and jogging on (literally), for as long as possible.

Yet even as we do this (in America, at any rate, with an unexamined neo-ascetical self-righteousness, what from a Christian standpoint we may deem a *sweaty* Pelagianism), the anxious question presses: what is this "body" that I "have"? From what other site of control am "I" pummeling it into submission, beauty or longevity? Herein lie what Daniel Bell has, in another context, called our "cultural contradictions".[9] For in the late-twentieth-century affluent West, the "body", to be sure, is sexually affirmed, but also puritanically punished in matters of diet or exercise; continuously stuffed with consumerist goods, but guiltily denied particular foods in aid of the "salvation" of a longer life; taught that there is nothing *but* it (the 'body'), and yet asked to discipline it with an "I" that still refuses complete materialistic reduction. Despite the legion cries for *greater* "embodiment", for a notion of self as body,[10] the spectres of religious and philosophical dualism die hard;[11] somewhere the last smile on a Cartesian Cheshire cat still lurks, or is it even a more ancient manifestation of "soul"?

---

[8]   See chapter 4, above: "Visions of the Self in Late Medieval Christianity", where I have tried to analyse the political and theological reasons for this unexpected vehemence towards the Cartesian heritage.

[9]   See D. Bell, *The Cultural Contradictions of Capitalism* (New York: Basic Books, 1976).

[10]   See, *inter alia*, Csordas (n. 4), for a discussion of the need for a more "embodied" vision of the self in anthropology, an account that draws on the philosophy of Merleau-Ponty and the anthropology of Bourdieu.

[11]   This "cultural contradiction" is well addressed in S. Bordo, *Unbearable Weight: Feminism, Western Culture and the Body* (Berkeley, CA: University of California Press, 1993).

It is, I suggest, precisely these contradictions that should alert us to a latent cultural yearning in the matter of "bodies" – not towards the immediate sexual fulfillment that appears as the ubiquitous cultural palliative (if only in fantasy), but an equally erotic yearning towards a more elusive eschatological goal. From this perspective the bodily obsessions just described – the quest for longevity, beauty, health, sexual performance – bespeak a prevailing denial of death.[12] But as Caroline Bynum remarks, in a penetrating little essay entitled "Why All the Fuss about the Body? A Medievalist's Perspective",[13] it is also in contemporary "popular" cultural products, such as the film *Truly, Madly, Deeply*, that we encounter an incipient countervailing *acknowledgment* of the facts of death, of a longing for a body beyond death, and of confusion in the face of the changed features of the ghostly body (which, interestingly, will not return without bringing a host of other new "dead" friends with it; the body beyond death, it seems, is intrinsically communal, much to the disgust of the grieving widow in this entrancing and evocative film).

Is, then, the post-modern *intellectual* obsession with "body" as it relates to the theorizing of sexuality and gender an equally subtle subterfuge, another evasive ploy? Is it perhaps fuelling, as well as feeding off, more "popular" manifestations of death-denial, and screening us from political and social horrors that we otherwise cannot face? That, at any rate, is the view of Terry Eagleton, in his pounding assault on the *Illusions of Postmodernism*;[14] and it is a thesis not without point. For Eagleton shows how post-modern loss of faith in "teleology" (what Eagleton terms "holophobia") has undermined the political commitment to classic socialist goals and diverted us from the grinding poverty of the world's dispossessed; yet meanwhile the "power of capital" (a new "grand narrative" if ever there was one) has sneaked up and taken us over whilst we have been comforting ourselves with the more sensuous and narcissistic "new somatics": "The body . . . is currently en route to becoming the greatest fetish of all", Eagleton charges, and in this he tars "feminism" undifferentiatedly with the same brush, for he sees much of it as all-too-comfortably compatible with the new global capitalism.[15] Bynum's contention is not dissimilar. For her, "modern treatments of person and body have recently concentrated rather too much on issues of

---

[12] For a now-classic account of this phenomenon, see E. Becker, *The Denial of Death* (New York, NY: Free Press, 1973).

[13] See n. 2. The discussion of *Truly, Madly, Deeply* is on pp. 10–12.

[14] T. Eagleton, *The Illusions of Postmodernism* (Oxford: Blackwell Publishers, 1996).

[15] Ibid., p. 25.

gender and sexuality to the detriment of our awareness of other things" (and here she enumerates death, work, and – elsewhere – "fecundity").[16]

But it is here that I shall beg to differ from Bynum's (and Eagleton's) otherwise perceptive and illuminating analyses. By focusing on the feminist theory of Judith Butler, I shall attempt to demonstrate that her radical theory of gender "performativity" leads us inexorably to the questions of eschatological longing that Bynum seeks to retrieve, and thereby – albeit unintentionally – to the horizon of a *divine* "grand narrative". Whilst Butler's own prescriptions relate only to a secular realm and are tinged with a deep pessimism about radical social change, her thematizations of desire, of gender fluidity, and of subversive personal agency all echo older, theistically-oriented traditions of personal transformation within and beyond the "body" of this mortal life. Butler has been accused of "dissolving" the body into "discourse"; I shall argue, on the contrary (and doubtless to Butler's own dismay!), that her theory has the remaining marks of a body longing for transformation into the divine. Like Gregory of Nyssa, with whom I shall compare her, Butler sees the point of "practices" of transformation that start now but have their final goal in the future: they create the future by enacting its possibilities. As Jürgen Moltmann has well said of a falsely-futuristic eschatology, "The person who presses forward to the end of life *misses life itself.*"[17] Both Judith Butler and Gregory of Nyssa, as I shall now attempt to demonstrate, know the meaning of that aphorism and present us with visions of bodily (and gendered) transformations that press forward from the present.

Judith Butler on Gender Performativity

Butler's impenetrably opaque prose obfuscates as much as it reveals: this is arguably all part of her strategy of linguistic subversion. (It is certainly a challenge to the analytically-trained mind.[18]) At once speculative theorist and practical reformer, Butler invites her reader into a dizzying engagement

[16]   Bynum, "Why all the Fuss". (see n. 2), p. 33. Also see her *Holy Feast and Holy Fast: The Religious Significance of Food to Medieval Women* (Berkeley, CA: University of California Press, 1987) for an extended exploration of the theme of repressed "fecundity".

[17]   J. Moltmann, *The Coming of God: Christian Eschatology* (London: SCM Press, 1996), p. xi, my emphasis.

[18]   Butler has recently won first prize in the annual "Bad Writing Contest" sponsored by the journal *Philosophy and Literature*; the equivalent "honor" in the UK might be appearing in "Pseuds' Corner" in *Private Eye*.

with (strangely masculinist) forebears as diverse as Nietzsche, Freud, Althusser, Austin, Foucault and Kripke. Not all of these are invoked immediately in her earliest work; but previous feminist theorists of whom she is critical from the start include de Beauvoir, Irigaray, Kristeva and Wittig – all figures whom she regards as veering too closely to gender essentialism. Out of this strange concoction of heroes, detractors and resources, she constructs in *Gender Trouble* (1990) her central theory about the persistent oppressiveness of compulsory heterosexuality. "Gender" is not "natural" but repetitively "performed": "The univocity of sex, the internal coherence of gender, and the binary framework for both sex and gender are . . . regulatory fictions that consolidate and naturalize the convergent power regimes of masculine and heterosexist oppression."[19] Thus the "body" is no "ready surface awaiting signification, but . . . a set of boundaries, individual and social, politically signified and maintained".[20] Sex is "[n]o longer believable as an interior 'truth' of dispositions and identity", but is rather a "performatively enacted signification . . . , one that, released from its naturalized interiority and surface, can occasion the parodic proliferation and subversive play of gendered meanings."[21] Hence Butler, as a lesbian theorist, is out to make "gender trouble", "not through the strategies that figure a *utopian* beyond, but through the mobilization, subversive confusion, and proliferation of precisely those constitutive categories that seek to keep gender in its place by posturing as the foundational illusions of identity".[22]

Butler's theory, we note, assumes both a fluidity of gender and its (re)creation through repeated practice. There is nothing "natural" about it; indeed "de-naturalization" of gender is the point of the whole project.[23] But this is not to say (as Butler is often misunderstood) that gender can be constituted at will, or by mere verbal fiat; that would be to underestimate the "established" nature of the gender binaries that Butler seeks to destabilize: "To enter into the repetitive practices of this terrain is not a choice, for the 'I' that might enter is always already inside: there is no possibility of agency or reality outside of the discursive practices that give those terms the intelligibility that they have."[24] Thus: "The task is not whether to repeat, but how to repeat or, indeed, to repeat and, through a radical proliferation of gender, *to displace* the very gender norms that enable the repetition

---

[19] *Gender Trouble*, p. 33.
[20] Ibid.
[21] Ibid.
[22] Ibid., p. 34, my emphasis.
[23] See ibid., pp. 147–9.
[24] Ibid., p. 148.

itself."[25] The "performance" of gender is, on this view, *both* a repeated (if unconscious) act in favour of "compulsory heterosexuality" *and* a potentially subversive act of homosexual or lesbian defiance; but the former undeniably has the cultural upper hand, and provides the resistant backing to the latter. Nonetheless, to some undisclosed extent we can at least spoof the social forces of gender that so exercise us.

The spiritual significance of Butler's analysis should at this point give us pause. The "denaturalization" of sex and gender is, as we shall shortly see, a theme shared with an older tradition of ascetical transformation. The possibilities for labile, fluid transformation towards a goal of liberation and personal authenticity is what Butler's vision has in common with this more ancient wisdom. Moreover, it is the yoking of "practice" (Butler's "performance") and theory that also strikes a note of spiritual reminiscence: change cannot occur by mere thought, but is precisely the product of arduous exercise – an exercise *against* the grain of the predominant cultural assumption, the assumption, that is, of heterosexual "marriage and giving in marriage". To the extent that this vision of transformation hangs over Butler's theorizing, then, it begs a question about the possibilities of "grace"; whereas a more cynical reading would suggest that Butler's theory of resistance is merely reinstantiating the conditions of sexual oppression against which she chafes.

Martha Nussbaum, in an intemperate recent review of Butler's corpus,[26] takes the latter interpretative perspective. If "performing" resistance represents the heart of Butler's thesis, she argues, then does it not signal the *necessity* of the remaining conditions of sexual oppression? "For Butler", she charges, "the act of subversion is so riveting, so sexy, that it is a bad dream to think that the world will actually get better. What a bore equality is! No bondage, no delight. In this way [Butler's] pessimistic erotic anthropology offers support to an amoral anarchistic politics."[27] Such a critique has its point (since Butler does not explicitly promise us that the world will ever become less "compulsorily heterosexist"); but it fails to engage with the profounder levels of spiritual yearning that I detect in Butler's text.

In other ways, too, Butler's theory of "body" is capable of serious distortion. Bynum is not the only one to charge her with dissolving bodily matter into "discourse". (Were this so, it would be an ironic triumph for

---

[25] Ibid.

[26] Martha C. Nussbaum, "The Professor of Parody", *The New Republic*, February 22, 1999, pp. 37–45.

[27] Ibid., p. 44.

feminism, so to elevate the final power of the "word" over body.) But Butler's second major book on gender theory, *Bodies that Matter* (1993), explicitly addresses this question, and wards off the suggestion of the reduction of physical bodiliness to mere forms of verbal instantiation. "Performance", to be sure, as becomes clearer in Butler's new usage here of Austin's *How to Do Things with Words* (1962), effects what it proclaims verbally. But it is gender that is performed, not the material bodies themselves. Language cannot *create* bodies (that would be an odd claim indeed); rather, Butler is insisting that there is no access to bodies that is not already a gendered access: "there is no reference to a pure body which is not at the same time a further formation of that body . . . In philosophical terms, the constative claim is always to some degree performative."[28] Here we see clearly, then, the distinction in Butler between bodiliness and subjectivity; the one cannot simply be reduced to the other. As one perceptive commentator (Amy Hollywood) has put it, "Butler's most important work in *Bodies That Matter* . . . lies in its assertion that sites of resistance to dominant discourses can be articulated without relying on a concept of materiality that lies untouched by that discourse. Rather than arguing for a transcending idealism of a transcendent materiality, Butler demonstrates the . . . possibilities for transcendence that emerge in and through complex bodily experiences."[29] It is the nature of that "transcendence" with which we are especially concerned – an excess of possibility that refuses to limit "desire" to its physical locus of pleasure. "Desire" for Butler always signals a form of "loss", an obscured yearning, an exclusion of possibilities that "compulsory heterosexuality" rules out. Again, we shall have reason to compare this with a more explicitly Christian perception of unending desire (for God) that informs Gregory's "erotic" spirituality.

In Butler's more recent work, it is a post-Foucaultian analysis of "power" that comes to the fore in her analysis, and at points suggests comparison with the "Yahweh" of her Jewish heritage who still lurks at the corners of her discussion.[30] "Power", as one critic has acutely noted, is now the "God-term" in Butler's text; no wonder, then, that this "power" is inescapable, the only modality in and through which "agency" even becomes possible: "there is no formation of the subject without a passionate attachment to

[28] *Bodies that Matter*, pp. 10–11.
[29] Amy Hollywood, "Transcending Bodies", *Religious Studies Review* 25, 1999, p. 14.
[30] See, for instance, the discussion of Freud, Žižek and the "unnameable Yahweh" in "Arguing with the Real", *Bodies that Matter*, ch. 7, esp. p. 200. The exploration of Hegel's master/slave parable in *The Psychic Life of Power*, ch. 1, also cannot help but resummon, if only veiledly, the question of divine power.

subjection".[31] Yet out of this learned subjection, even out of degradation, come the possibilities of hope and resistance. (Somewhere the myth of cross and resurrection lurks, mediated no doubt through the Hegel who forms the focus of Butler's meditations in *The Psychic Life of Power*.) Less clear now than before is the *optimistic* call to fluid gendered transformation; more clear is her insistence that speech can effect occasional punctures in existing power relations.[32]

Why does Butler's vision exercise such "power" itself? Despite Nussbaum's derisive critique of Butler's "hip defeatism", Butler's work continues to exercise an uncanny degree of influence. Somehow it is the allure of gender liberation (not now sexual liberation, note) that has fascinated the late-twentieth-century mind, the prospect of an escape from stereotype, the hope of an elusive personal transformation beyond normal human expectations and restrictions. But to what (eschatological) end? That is a question not answered by Butler herself, although surely her argument begs it. The comparison with an equally fluid Christian spirituality of gender now becomes pressing.

Gregory of Nyssa (c.330–c.395) and the Transformations of Gender

Nyssa is, as in many other matters, notoriously inconsistent in his theorizing about the resurrection body and our own eschatological end;[33] sure it is, however, that his fascinating suggestions in this area should not be considered in abstraction from his equally subtle understandings of gender, which are deeply entangled with them. Bynum, in her recent magisterial

---

[31] See the illuminating analysis of Butler's recent work by Michael Levenson, "The Performances of Judith Butler", in *Lingua Franca* 8, September 1998, pp. 61–7, cf. p. 62.

[32] Levenson (see n. 31) sees a disjunction here between Butler's two most recent books, *The Psychic Life of Power* and *Excitable Speech* (see n. 1): the former seems less optimistic than her earlier works about opportunities for genuine change in gender expectations; the latter, however, rehearses again the political possibilities for performative utterance.

[33] See the classic article by Jean Daniélou, "La Résurrection des Morts chez Grégoire de Nysse", *Vigiliae Christianae* 7, 1953, pp. 154–70. Bynum re-surveys this material in her *The Resurrection of the Body in Western Christianity, 200–1336* (New York, NY: Columbia University Press, 1995), pp. 81–6. A more nuanced account of the changes in Gregory's views on the nature of the resurrected body over the course of his career, and his eventual careful distancing of himself from Origenism, is provided in Morwenna Ludlow, *Universal Salvation: Eschatology in the thought of Gregory of Nyssa and Karl Rahner* (Oxford, Oxford University Press, 2000), ch. 2. I am grateful to Morwenna Ludlow for letting me see her MS in preparation.

volume *The Resurrection of the Body* (1995), gives an illuminating account of Gregory's eschatology but says relatively little about the place of gender in it. We are indebted to Verna Harrison for a first careful consideration of Nyssa's theory of gender, and I draw most gratefully on her pioneering work.[34] However there are points in Nyssa's consideration of gender stereotype (what Butler would call the oppressive "gender binaries") which need deeper consideration than I think has yet been given: Gregory's gender theory, like Butler's, does not claim to *obliterate* the binaries that remain culturally normative, but seeks – also like Butler – to find a transformative way through them. Whereas in Butler, however, this escape is effected by punctiliar subversive acts of "performativity", in Gregory it represents a life-long ascetical programme, a purification and redirection of *eros* towards the divine, a final withdrawal from the whirligig of marriage, child-rearing, the quest for social status and financial security.[35] In Gregory's case this is especially poignant, since we know that he was married as a younger man and he writes of the tragic death of children with enormous insight and grief; but nowhere – and how interestingly contrastive is this with Augustine – does he agonize with guilt or fear about the sexual act itself. Indeed, one might argue on the contrary that his spirituality of progressive ascent and increasing loss of noetic control (as set out in *The Life of Moses*) is figured precisely by analogy with the procreative act; Gregory says as much in the introduction to his *Commentary on the Song of Songs* – that the passage from the physical to the spiritual is not effected by repression of the memory of physical love: "I hope that my commentary will be a guide for the more fleshly-minded, since the wisdom hidden [in the Song of Songs] *leads* to a spiritual state of the soul."[36]

As Bynum shows with exemplary clarity, Gregory's eschatological body is an ever-changing one; like Origen, the Syriac writers Ephrem and Aphra-

---

[34] See Verna Harrison, "Male and Female in Cappadocian Theology", *Journal of Theological Studies* 41, 1990, pp. 441–71; and *eadem*, "Gender, Generation and Virginity", *Journal of Theological Studies* 47, 1996, pp. 38–68.

[35] This theme is illuminatingly discussed in relation to the Cappadocians in Peter Brown, *The Body and Society: Men, Women, and Sexual Renunciation in Early Christianity* (New York, NY: Columbia University Press, 1988), ch. 14. Mark D. Hart's "Reconciliation of Body and Soul: Gregory of Nyssa's Deeper Theology of Marriage", *Theological Studies* 51, 1990, pp. 450–78, however, gives a brilliant new reading of Gregory's *de Virginitate* (utilizing the interpretative tool of irony), and argues that Gregory saw marriage, as well as celibacy, as a potential school of "non-attachment".

[36] Gregory of Nyssa, *Commentary on the Song of Songs*, trans. Casimir McCambley (Brookline, MA: Hellenic College Press, 1987), p. 35 (my emphasis). For the Greek text, see ed. Werner Jaeger, *Gregorii Nysseni Opera* (Leiden: E. J. Brill, 1960-), (hereafter *GNO*), VI, 4.

hat, and Cyril of Jerusalem before him, he takes Paul's "seed" metaphor in 1 Cor. 15 to heart: the body is labile and changing in this life and is on its way to continuing change into incorruptibility in the next. (This is *unlike* a rival tradition forged in reaction to Origen, which sees the resurrection body as the reassemblage of "bits", or as what Bynum finds in Augustine as a final freezing of "flux".[37]) For Gregory, however, change does not necessarily signal decay, but can on the contrary mark the endless transformations "from glory to glory". Famously re-defining "perfection" as "never arriving" – a daring move for a Platonist – he similarly understands the partaking of Eucharist in this life as an already-anticipated reception of heavenly food. We are on a continuum, then, from this "body" to our "angelic" future "bodies", and death need not be a *dramatic* shift in the case of a holy ascetical body, as we shall see.

Where, then, does gender fit into this picture? As is well known, and Verna Harrison has explicated with especial care, Gregory holds (on the basis of a particular reading of Gen. 1:27, in conjunction with Gal. 3:28) that the original creation was of non-sexed (that is, non-genitalized) beings; his text *On the Making of Man* suggests that it was only *en route*, so to speak, to the Fall, that "man" was distinguished from "woman".[38] So too, at the end of times, as he expounds in *On Those who have Fallen Asleep*, we shall expect to be de-genitalized again, and so receive that angelic status that was our lot originally (the contrast with the Augustine of *The City of God* is of course instructive: Augustine becomes sure that we shall be able to recognize each other as men and women in heaven).[39] It is a mistake, however, as Harrison helps illuminate, to read Gregory here as divorcing our development from the exigencies of *gender*, even if our genitalia are finally irrelevant to our "bodily" condition before God, that does not mean that we are released from what Butler would (rather differently) term the "performances" of gender. On the contrary, the whole point of a life of virginity (as Gregory argues in his early work *De Virginitate*, bemusingly enough written at a time when he was probably married), is to become spiritually "fecund".[40] And the continual purgative transformations of the ascetical life involve forms of

---

[37] See the discussion in Bynum, *The Resurrection of the Body*, p. 102.
[38] See *De opificio hominis*, 16–17, discussed by Harrison (n. 34) in *Journal of Theological Studies* 41, 1990, p. 468.
[39] See the discussion of *On Those who have Fallen Asleep* in ibid., p. 469. (For the Greek, see *GNO* IX, 28–68, esp. 63.) A comparison with Augustine, *The City of God* XXII, ch. 17, is instructive.
[40] See Harrison, *Journal of Theological Studies* 41, 1990, p. 469, citing Gregory's *De Virginitate* (*GNO* VIII, 1, p. 305).

gender fluidity and reversal (as we shall show) that undercut and subvert what could be expected of someone living according to the late-antique norms of married gender roles.

Three themes in Gregory's eschatologically-oriented theory of gender strike us now as suggestive points of comparison with Butler's more pessimistic secular alternative. First, we must not overlook (as it is tempting to do) the undeniable examples of Gregory's rehearsal of "gender binaries". A particularly revealing example of this phenomenon occurs at the beginning of Book II of *The Life of Moses* (1–8).[41] There Gregory discusses the exegetical meaning to be attached to the fact that "Moses was born at the time Pharaoh issued the decree for *male* offspring to be destroyed": how are we now to "imitate" this, he asks? Surely coming to birth (as a "male") is not something in our power to imitate? However Gregory immediately rehearses here *both* a binary gender stereotype *and* an insistence that gender is fluid and volitional: "For the material and passionate disposition to which human nature is carried when it falls is the female form of life ... The austerity and intensity of virtue is the male birth ... (2). [But] ... In mutable nature nothing can be observed which is always the same ... We are in some manner our own parents [literally, 'fathers'], giving birth to ourselves by our own free choice in accordance with whatever we wish to be, whether male or female, moulding ourselves to the teaching of virtue or vice" (3). Is then the stereotype of "female" passion or vice left intact by Gregory? It is a nice point, just as it is a nice point whether Butler's subversive "performativity" of gender needs the gender binaries it seeks to upend. But Gregory adds a further complexification − not found in Butler − when he earlier suggests that such disjunctive gender binaries apply as points of reference primarily for "those who wander outside virtue" (Book I, 11), that is, for mere beginners on the slope of Moses's mystical ascent. Abraham and Sarah (12) are set before such as exemplars, "the men to Abraham and the women to Sarah"; but then, of course, it turns out that they do not represent the "virtue = male" and "passion = female" binary previously named; indeed, with their example we are already well on the way to a set of reversals of such expectation.

Herein lies what I have termed the "eschatologically-oriented" feature of Gregory's complex theory of personal (and gendered) transformation into the divine life, and thus herein too lies our second revealing point of

---

[41]   In what follows, I am using the *CWS* translation, *The Life of Moses*, trans. A. H. Malherbe and E. Ferguson (New York, NY: Paulist Press, 1978), see pp. 55–7 (Bk. II), and pp. 31–2 (Bk. I). For the Greek, see *GNO* VII, 1, 34–7 and 4–6 respectively.

comparison with Butler. As Harrison has tellingly expounded, it is not that either "body" or gender are disposed of in this progressive transformation to a neo-angelic status. Rather, as advances are made in the stages of virtue and contemplation, *eros* finds its truer meaning in God, and gender switches and reversals attend the stages of ascent: the increasingly close relation to Christ marks, in the *Commentary on the Song of Songs*, a shift from active courting of Christ as "Sophia" to passive reception of embraces of Christ as the bride-groom.[42] Does this not, then, at some deeper level merely reinscribe normative gender binaries? This is by no means clear. At this (higher) stage of ascent, one can no longer assume – Jungian importations are distractions here – that the woman ascetic is "primarily" enacting the pole of gender associated at the outset with the "female" and then "adding" "male" virtues to the amalgam. On the contrary, the fascinating banter between Gregory and his older sister Macrina in *On the Soul and the Resurrection* give the lie to such a suggestion. Here, as in the related *Life of Macrina*, Gregory takes the part of the passions and Macrina manifests the stern rational asceticism in which Gregory manifestly fails.[43] As Rowan Williams has put it in a deft analysis of this interaction, its implications for "soul", "body" and gender are subtle ones: "For Gregory . . . we could say, there is no such *thing* as the soul in itself; it is always implicated in contingent matter, and even its final liberation for pilgrimage into God . . . depends . . . upon the deployment and integration of bodiliness and animality . . . the ungenderedness of the soul is never the actual state of a real subject."[44] Part, at least, of this could be applauded by Butler too, we could now suggest. But what she cannot assert unambiguously is that divine referent that forms the final point of meaning in Gregory, what Williams thematizes as "that fundamental *eros* for the endless God that binds the polyphony of our intentionality into some sort of unity".[45]

---

[42] See Verna Harrison's exposition of this material from the *First Homily on the Song of Songs* in *Journal of Theological Studies* 47, 1996, pp. 58–62. For the Greek of the first homily, see *GNO* VI, 14–42.

[43] See *On the Soul and the Resurrection*, trans. Catherine P. Roth (Crestwood, NY: Saint Vladimir's Seminary Press, 1993), esp. chs. 3–7. For the Greek, see ed. J. G. Krabinger, *S. Gregorii Episcopi Nysseni De Anima et Resurrectionecum sorore sua Macrina dialogus: Graece et Latine* (Leipzig: In Libraria Gustavi Wuttigii, 1837), pp. 3–102.

[44] Rowan Williams "Macrina's Deathbed Revisited: Gregory of Nyssa on Mind and Passion", in eds. Lionel Wickham and Caroline P. Bammel, *Christian Faith and Greek Philosophy in Late Antiquity* (Leiden: E. J. Brill, 1993), p. 244.

[45] Ibid.

Our third instructive point of comparison with Butler leads on from here. Butler speaks little of death; yet death, as Gregory well sees, is the most incisive test of a person's life. (Or, as Stanley Hauerwas has put it recently, "Perfection is the art of dying",[46] an aphorism that fits interestingly in Gregory's case with his assurance that "Perfection is never arriving".) As we have already hinted, death for Gregory is merely a passage into further "bodily" – albeit de-genitalized – life; for his sister Macrina, already so holy that she becomes a "relic" anticipatorily on her death-bed, the continuum between this life and the next is almost complete. Even the little scar on her breast from a miraculous earlier cure of cancer remains, however; as with Christ's scarred risen body, nothing is lost that represents suffering confronted and overcome: "a memorial of the divine intervention, the result and the occasion of perpetual turning toward God through the action of grace".[47] Bynum writes of this touching passage that it is really always Macrina that Gregory has in mind when he tries to speak of the eschatological body: "The resurrected body is both the ascetic who becomes a relic while still alive and the relic that continues after death the changelessness acquired through asceticism."[48] Do we not perhaps detect a yearning for such completion in Butler's remorselessly sophisticated and tortured maneuvers?

Conclusions: Gender, Transformation and God

I have been suggesting in this essay that Judith Butler's profound desire to shift or subvert the weight of "gender binaries" does not grip our late-twentieth-century imaginations for no reason. Much is at stake here; and it is more – frankly – than a debate about politics, speech and homophobia, important though that is. Rather what seems to be being enacted is the gesturing to an eschatological horizon which will give mortal flesh final significance, a horizon in which the restless, fluid post-modern "body" can find some sense of completion without losing its mystery, without succumbing again to "appropriate" or restrictive gender roles. In introducing Judith Butler to Gregory of Nyssa I have courted the dangerous charge of

---

[46] Stanley Hauerwas, "The Sanctified Body: Why Perfection Does Not Require a 'Self'", in *Sanctify Them in the Truth: Holiness Exemplified* (Nashville, TN: Abingdon Press, 1999), p. 89.
[47] From the *Life of Macrina*, cited in Bynum, *The Resurrection of the Body*, p. 86. For the relevant passage in the Greek edition, see ed. Pierre Maraval, *Grégoire de Nysse: Vie de Sainte Macrine*, Sources Chrétiennes 178 (Paris: Éditions du Cerf, 1971), pp. 242–7.
[48] Bynum, *The Resurrection of the Body*, p. 86.

anachronism for the sake of a spiritual challenge of some severity: for it is not, note, the goal of Gregory's vision to enjoy various forms of previously-banned sexual pleasure; or to escape or sneer at a supposedly "repressive" pornography law. Rather, *Gregory's* vision of final "erotic" fulfillment demands an asceticism costing not less than everything; and to a culture fed on bowdlerized Freud and equally bowdlerized Foucault[49] – in which erotic "purification" can seemingly only signal "repression" – this is hardly likely to have instant appeal. That Gregory's insights may provide us with the clues to some of our profoundest cultural riddles about the "body" it has nonetheless been the burden of this final essay to suggest; the "submission" to which Gregory gives his body is a submission of "desire" in which gender binaries are curiously upended, and the self at its deepest level transformed and empowered by the divine.[50]

[49] I use the term "bowdlerized" ironically, of course, since Dr. Bowdler himself would presumably have had some difficulty trying to work out what to do with either Freud or Foucault! I mean that most popularized readings of Freud and Foucault 'expurgate' not so much the sexual content of their writings but their subtler points of analysis.

[50] This final chapter was originally presented to the annual conference of the *British Society for the Study of Theology*, Edinburgh, April 12–15, 1999. I am most grateful for the comments received there. I must also acknowledge my gratitude to my Harvard colleagues Nicholas Constas and Gary Anderson for an interesting recent cooperative Greek reading-group on the gender theory of Gregory of Nyssa.

INDEX

Printed in the United States
100994LV00003B/258/A